The Cheyenne

The Peoples of America

General Editors
Alan Kolata and Dean Snow

This series is about the native peoples and civilizations of the Americas, from their origins in ancient times to the present day. Drawing on archaeological, historical and anthropological evidence, each volume presents a fresh and absorbing account of a group's culture, society, and history.

Accessible and scholarly, and well illustrated with maps and photographs, the volumes of *The Peoples of America* will together provide a comprehensive and vivid picture of the character and variety of the societies of the American past.

Already published

The Moche
Garth Bawden

The Tiwanaku:
A Portrait of an Andean Civilization
Alan Kolata

The Timucua
Jerald T. Milanich

The Cheyenne
John H. Moore

The Aztecs
Michael E. Smith

The Iroquois
Dean R. Snow

In preparation

The Nascas
*D. M. Brown and
Helaine Silverman*

The Incas
Terence N. D'Altroy

The Navajo
Alan Downer

The Sioux
Guy Gibbon

The Cherokee
Gerald F. Schroedl

The Mayas
Don S. Rice

THE CHEYENNE

John H. Moore

BLACKWELL
Publishers

First published 1996

2 4 6 8 10 9 7 5 3 1

Blackwell Publishers Inc
238 Main Street
Cambridge, Massachusetts 02142
USA

Blackwell Publishers Ltd
108 Cowley Road
Oxford OX4 1JF
UK

Library of Congress Cataloging-in-Publication Data

Moore, John H., 1939–
The Cheyenne/John H. Moore.
p. cm. – (The peoples of America)
Includes bibliographical references and index.
ISBN 1-55786-484-5
1. Cheyenne Indians – History.   2. Cheyenne Indians – Antiquities.
3. Cheyenne Indians – Social life and customs.   4. Great Plains – History.
5. Great Plains – Antiquities.   I. Series.
E99.C53M95   1996
978'.004973 – dc20   96-12798
                                      CIP

ISBN 1-55786-484-5

British Library Cataloguing in Publication Data

A CIP catalogue record for this book is available from the British Library.

Typeset in 11 on 12½ pt Sabon
by CentraCet Ltd, Cambridge
Printed in Great Britain by
Hartnolls Limited, Bodmin, Cornwall

This book is printed on acid-free paper

Contents

Preface

I have already published a scholarly and somewhat technical book on the Cheyennes entitled *The Cheyenne Nation*. After reading that book, several reviewers faulted me for not sharing with them in print the details of my "obviously intimate" relationships with Cheyenne people and Cheyenne culture. The present book will help to satisfy those critics and to repay a tremendous debt I owe to the generation of Cheyenne elders who have just departed.

In 1970, I arrived at the Cheyenne Sun Dance in Oklahoma in my old, beat-up Volkswagen van, with a sleeping bag and rented umbrella tent, a credit card for gas and about $100 in my pocket. Looking at my miserable condition, the Cheyennes essentially took me in, as if I were a hungry, affectionate stray dog who needed some food and attention. I had little to offer them, but for two weeks at the ceremonial site I put up tents and tipis, hauled water and ice, ferried people around the countryside, and ran errands. At the end of that time, hearing that I wanted to know about Cheyenne religious symbolism to complete my "schoolwork," Roy Nightwalker, with the approval of the priests and elders, took me aside and told me everything I needed to know to finish my doctoral dissertation, in one night. Driving back to New York City after the ceremonies, I reflected on how odd it was, and how unfair, that Roy could tell me everything I needed to know to become "Doctor Moore" in one night, but could not do the same for himself.

I returned again and again to the Cheyenne reservations in Oklahoma and Montana in the next several years, staying with Cheyenne families and eating their food, still the impoverished graduate student. I received a doctorate in 1974. One of the high points of my life was when Henry and Irene Tall Bull visited me at my first job at Albion College in Michigan where Henry gave a series of lectures.

Over the next several decades, especially after I moved to Oklahoma in 1977, I was able to repay the Cheyennes in material terms, somewhat, for all they had done for me. Having a good job, I was able to help support the ceremonies, and I received money from grants which I used to hire, for health research, many of the same elders who had helped me, and other members of their families as well. I also helped the Cheyennes by conducting historical research concerning several political and cultural issues mentioned in this book. But I have nowhere yet described in print the good and bad times I experienced living with Cheyennes, the respect I have for their dignity and resilience in the face of unsolvable problems, and especially the love I feel for those kind, hospitable people who had no good reason to be nice to a white person in 1970, but who nevertheless took me in, took care of me, and helped me become a professor. In my own fashion, I am trying to honor them with this book about their history and culture.

The first few chapters of the book present the highlights of my research into Cheyenne prehistory and history, drawn from my published book and several other articles published since. In these chapters I try to blend together the picture of the Cheyenne as seen by scholars, and the way they see themselves, as presented in their oral traditions. As the book progresses into more recent periods, there is less citation of scholarly works by non-Indian scholars, and more of my personal observation and the narratives of Cheyenne people.

Before 1977, I worked equally at the Northern Cheyenne Reservation in Montana, and the Southern Reservation in Oklahoma. But after I moved to Oklahoma, I traveled to Montana very seldom, although I heard a lot of news and gossip from people who had married a Northern Cheyenne, or who visited there from Oklahoma. My most intensive period of fieldwork was between 1979 and 1981, when my expenses were paid by grants from the National Science Foundation and the National Institute of Health.

Let me mention here the names of some Cheyennes who were my special friends, most of them now gone. Although I have come to know hundreds of Cheyenne people over the years, these are the people to whom I owe a special debt, because of their many kindnesses in introducing me to their friends and families, and to Cheyenne culture. And here are some things I remember about them.

Jim Medicine Elk – the former Keeper of the Sacred Arrows who calmed me down when we had to use the back door and sit in the "Indian booth" in a restaurant in Canton, Oklahoma. Henry Tall Bull – who showed me how to move a drunk quietly away from the bar at Jimtown so that we could sit on the bar stools and have a beer. Alex Brady – who taught me not to stare. Edward Red Hat – who succeeded Medicine Elk as Arrow Keeper, and was the wisest, kindest, most thoughtful person I ever knew. Irene Tall Bull – who demonstrated how to live a good life though afflicted with incessant physical pain. Minnie Red Hat – who told me when I moved to Florida that she would never forget me, and I'll never forget her. Ted Rising Sun – who taught me that Indian Christians were not collaborators. John Greany – who took my son into the Arrow Tipi. Kathryn Bull Coming – who gave me a purple vest and took my son into the Sun Dance arbor. Laird Cometsevah – who taught me that it was good for men to cry. Eugene Black Bear – who scared the ghosts from my new house. Eddie Burns, Jr. – who taught me how to maintain your temper and your conscience in a difficult situation. Lucy Cometsevah – who made me a pair of moccasins. Roy Nightwalker – who tolerated me when I used to think his name was Roy Netwalker. Willie Fletcher – who always gave me good advice. Terry Wilson – a loyal friend who doesn't want me to say what he did for me. Agnes Hamilton – who helped me find Walter's medicine pipe even though she had to pretend she didn't know where it was.

I especially want to thank Dean Snow for his advice and encouragement in the writing of this book, and John Davey, who kindly extended my book deadline when I moved to Florida. I also thank Greg Campbell, Fred Hoxie, and the copy editor, Jane Hammond Foster, for their helpful comments. I appreciate the patience and help of my wife, Shelley Arlen, who minded the family on Saturday and Sunday mornings so that I could finish this book, and prepare the index.

J.H.M.

This book is affectionately dedicated to my
two wonderful daughters,

Jessica Sanderson Moore
and
Alexandra Montgomery Moore

1

Cheyenne Origins

In seeking "Cheyenne origins" we need to determine who the ancestors of the Cheyennes were, and where they lived, as far back in history and prehistory as the evidence will allow. Currently the most reliable methods are provided by the fields of linguistics, archaeology, and human biology. The methods of all three fields, however, are based on premises which are open to criticism, and they yield results which, to a degree, must be regarded as uncertain. But the convergence of evidence indicates that the Cheyennes are among the Algonquian peoples of North America, and that they originated in the subarctic.

When historical linguists say that there is an Algonquian family of languages, they mean specifically that there was once a language community or tribe who spoke a common language which was later modified in many directions as tribes and bands split off, increased in population, and migrated away from the mother group. After hundreds or thousands of years of separation, these daughter groups could no longer understand each other's speech, but the evidence of their common origin remains imbedded in the phonetic structure, grammar, and vocabulary of each group, and can be detected by linguistic analysis. Knowing the phonetic rules by which languages change, it is even possible for linguists to reconstruct the original or "proto-" language of the mother group by comparing the daughter languages. In the case of the Algonquian family, the proto-language has been largely reconstructed and the vocabulary collected in a dictionary by George Aubin (1975).

When all the languages of a family have been studied, they can be sorted into sub-groups based on their overall similarities. The

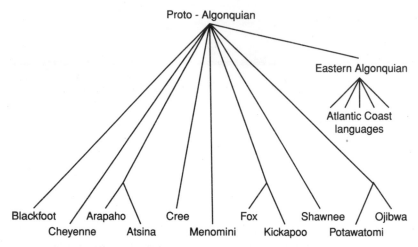

Figure 1.1 Historical relationships among languages in the proto-Algonquian family (after Goddard 1979: 95)

languages in a sub-group are also alleged to have a common origin, but later than that of the proto-language: that is, they are more closely related to each other than to other languages in the family. The only sub-group in the Algonquian family presently recognized by a consensus of linguists is the Eastern Algonquian group, which does not include the Cheyennes, the Arapahoes, or the Blackfeet, all of whom spoke Algonquian languages and lived on the plains in early historic times (figure 1.1). This means that the Algonquian language spoken by the Cheyennes is no more closely related to other Plains Algonquian languages than to languages in the central and eastern parts of North America, such as Shawnee, Ojibwa, or Cree.

By analyzing the names for plants and animals in the daughter languages, we can hypothesize an original homeland for a language family. This assumes that the daughter languages will have the same or similar names for the plants and animals they knew in the homeland, but different names for the plants and animals they saw for the first time after they migrated to a new area. Although he did not use Cheyenne words in his analysis, Siebert has hypothesized that an area north-east of the Great Lakes was the original home of all the Algonquian peoples, as shown on map 1.1. He notes that many Algonquian languages have similar names for such biological entities as evergreen trees,

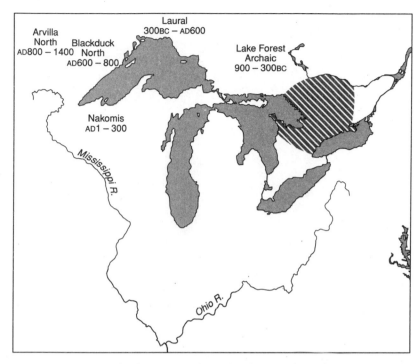

Arvilla
North
AD800 – 1400

Blackduck
North
AD600 – 800

Laural
300BC – AD600

Lake Forest
Archaic
900 – 300BC

Nakomis
AD1 – 300

Mississippi R.

Ohio R.

Map 1.1   Original Algonquian homeland according to Siebert (shaded area) and locations of possible proto-Cheyenne archaeological cultures (compiled from Siebert 1967: 35; Fitting 1978: 47; Brose 1978: 570; Schlesier 1987: 113–15; Ossenberg 1974: 18)

seals, and caribou, and he estimates that the early migrations of daughter groups from the homeland took place around 1200–900 BC.

Table 1.1 shows similarities in vocabulary among some of the Algonquian languages. Of course the words for some items are entirely different between any two languages, but these examples show the kinds of similarities that are important for placing languages in the same language family. It is also important to note that, in order to assert a historical relationship between two languages, the differences between them should be systematic, and not just occasional or accidental. By chance alone, words for the same lexical item can be similar between any two languages, related or not. For example, the Jaqaru word for "ask" is *ask"a*. The Aymara word for "water" is *uma*, while the Japanese word for "ocean" is *umi*. This does not mean that the

Table 1.1 Comparison of Algonquian vocabularies

	Cheyenne	Menomini	Fox	Ojibwa	Cree	Blackfoot
bone	heʔko	ohkaːn	ahkani	okkan	oskan	oχkini
duck	šiʔši	seːʔsep	šiːšiːpa	šiːšːiːp	siːsiːp	meksikatsi
bee	hahnoma	aːmoːw	aːmoːwi	aːmo	aːmoːw	namo
on high/ up above	—	espeːmiah	ahpemegi	išpiming	ispimihk	ispixtsiu
woman	heʔe	nekaːneseːhkweːw (woman's name – "Little Leader Woman")	ihkweːwa	ikkweː	iskweːw	ake
charcoal	hoʔkose	mahkaːhsiw	kahkešeːwi	kekkiše:	kaskaskisiw	osoχktsimokui
men	hitaniyoʔu	ineː¹ niwʌk	neniwagi	ininiwag	iyiniwag	unnasina
sticks	kahamaxeste	meʔtekwan	mehtegoːni	mihtigoːg	mistikwa	mistsists
fire	hoʔesta	iskoːteːw	aškuteːwi	iskude	iškuteːw	istsiu
dog	hotam	anɛːm	anemoːha	anim	atim	imita
kettle	kasoʔšk	ahkɛːh	ahkohkwa	akkikk	askihk	isk
ear	mahtowoːʔots	nɛhtaːwak	otawakayi	otawag	mihtawakay	moχtokis
day/sky	eše	keːsek	kiːšekwi	kiːšik	kiːsik	ksiːstsiko
moccasin	—	mahkɛːsen	mahkeseːhi	makkisin	maskisin	matsikin
trees	hoohtseto (sing.)	meʔtekwak	mehtegoːni	nihtigoːg	mistikwak	mistiks

Source; Aubin 1975: Bloomfield 1975; Uhlenbeck & Van Gulik 1930; Language Research Department 1976

Japanese and Aymara languages are distantly related; the similarity is only coincidental.[1]

To undertake historical linguistic studies, scholars must of course have good descriptions of the languages under consideration. In the Cheyenne case, there are two large bodies of language description from this century, as well as a score of shorter word lists and some brief phonetic and grammatical descriptions from the 19th century (Pilling 1891). For the Southern Cheyennes, now resident in Oklahoma, there is an enormous English–Cheyenne dictionary, a grammar, and various translations compiled by the Mennonite missionary Rodolphe Petter from 1891 until his death in 1947 (Petter 1915; 1952). More than just a linguistic enterprise, Petter's dictionary is full of detailed ethnographic observations as well as long definitions, translations, and examples. Equally impressive is the work of the modern linguist Wayne Leman who has worked primarily with the Northern Cheyennes of Montana. Working with Cheyenne-speaking linguists whom he has helped to train, he has published a series of dictionaries, workbooks, and descriptions, of which the most important from an ethnographic standpoint are his topical dictionary and his book of bilingual narratives (Language Research Dept 1976; Leman 1987). Following is a morning prayer from a chief named Teeth, published by Leman. It gives a sense not only of the sounds and structure of Cheyenne, but of the kinds of sentiments and morality which are even now a recurring part of Cheyenne culture.

Ka'eškonehasestse, méhotahtse,   néve'nesétamahtséme,   pehéve'tovahtse,
Children,   love each other,   don't be against each other, be good to each other,

vovóhnehešéhahtse,   véstahémahtse,   néve'eóoxo'eéhahtséme.
take care of one another,   help each other,   don't do things to spite each other.

Vovóhnehešeha ma'háhkeseho naa tó'hove ka'eškóneho tsééeohtsese
Take care of the old people and orphans who are wandering around,

tséháo'omenehese, netao'o vo'estane pehéve'tova.   Ka'eškonehasestse,
those who are poor,   to everyone be good!   Children,

toetanó'tome tséhetatsése.   Hó'ó'tóva nahtsevoneotse,
keep in mind what I have told you.   Someday I'll be gone,

nestseohkesáa'éveévanéhéme.
you will not hear me anymore.

(Leman 1987: 206)

Archaeology

Although Siebert's linguistic research is useful in establishing the location of the Algonquian homeland, and hence the Cheyenne homeland, he does not speculate on the movements of the Cheyennes, or more properly the "proto-Cheyennes," after about 900 BC. Consequently there is a gap in our knowledge from then until the beginning of ethnohistorical and historical evidence, about 3,000 years later. To fill this gap, we must look to the science of archaeology, which has the scholarly mission of reconstructing human history from the evidence of artifacts uncovered by excavation.

Fortunately or unfortunately, archaeological evidence occurs in the form of qualitatively distinct traditions ("cultures," "horizons," or "types"), each of which usually comprises several archaeological sites where the artifacts are similar and belong to about the same time period. That is, among the "strata" uncovered at one site, there may be one stratum which is very similar in content and age to a stratum in a nearby site. There are great difficulties to be surmounted, however, in tracing the historical and geographical relationships among different strata and sites, and in finding the common origins of cultural traditions as they appear and disappear in the archaeological record. Specifically, it cannot be assumed that each archaeological culture has one and only one mother culture; a specific tradition might be derived from several antecedent sources.

Looking at Siebert's location for the proto-Algonquian homeland as shown on map 1.1, the most likely candidates to be proto-Cheyennes seem to be the people living between that homeland and the Great Plains, around the Great Lakes. Ultimately, the proto-Blackfeet, the proto-Cheyennes, and the proto-Arapahoes (including the Atsina) all emerged from the proto-Algonquians at some point and moved west, but they did not necessarily emerge at the same time or take the same route in their migrations. For the Cheyennes, locations around Lake Superior are the closest to their first historically-recorded villages in Minnesota in the 17th century. It is also possible that the Cheyennes, as well as the Blackfeet and Arapahoes, were derived from proto-Algonquian locations south of Lake Superior, from the peninsula between Lakes Superior and Michigan, or even from north of Lake Huron.

Assuming that Siebert's dates and locations are approximately correct for the proto-Algonquians north of the Great Lakes, we can match his results to the developing archaeological interpretations of that area. For the period before 1000 BC, we find that the archaeological tradition north and east of the Great Lakes is called Archaic. In general across North America, Archaic cultures have been characterized as intensive foraging societies which utilized many varieties of food and natural resources, rather than concentrating on a narrow range of plant and animal foods, as was apparently typical in previous periods. The particular variety of Archaic tradition found north of the Great Lakes is known as the "Lake Forest Archaic" (Tuck 1978). As with other Archaic traditions, the Lake Forest economy was apparently not dependent on horticulture, but rather on tools and techniques which enabled the people to pursue a combination of foraging activities, including in this case hunting, fishing, and the gathering of plant foods.

Concerning their stone technology, James Tuck has characterized Lake Forest material as including "large, thick, more or less parallel-sided projectile points with concave bases (usually ground), well-defined side notches, and squared tangs; end scrapers with similar bases and possibly made on broken points; expanded base drills; and occasionally bifacial 'knives'" (Tuck 1978: 31). These kinds of artifacts define the Archaic cultures not only north of the Great Lakes but also down the St Lawrence River toward the Atlantic. From the sparse evidence left behind, these groups can be reliably described only as using some kinds of projectile points (for lances, arrows, or darts) living in roofed structures, and exploiting some combination of game, fish, and plant foods.

Toward the end of the Archaic period, north-west of the Great Lakes, an archaeological culture developed which carried suggestions of the definitely horticultural Woodland period which would follow. The Glacial Kame culture included elaborate burials which, along with pottery and horticulture, were the most important diagnostic features of Woodland cultures (Tuck 1978: 43). But no pottery has been found in Glacial Kame burials, and no living sites have been excavated either, leaving the culture as a puzzling isolate known only by its burials on the margin of the Archaic-to-Woodland transition.

In general the technology of later Archaic cultures leading to Woodland is better known than that of earlier ones, and has been described as comprising "distinctive thin triangular bifacial 'blades' modified into side- or corner-notched projectile points, knives, and end scrapers and stemmed points in later phases . . ." (Tuck 1978: 40). What this all means for Cheyenne origins is that if the proto-Cheyennes had stayed in the area north-west of the Great Lakes from about 900 BC to about 300 BC, they would have participated in Archaic culture and, consequently, at some point would have exchanged a rough tool kit for a more sophisticated one, although without adopting horticulture. Specifically, they abandoned large, thick projectile points in favor of thin triangular points which represented a more efficient use of their flint resources.

South of the Great Lakes, Woodland cultures began to accelerate in their development after about 300 BC, producing large populations based on horticulture, an elaborate technology, and long-distance trade, for example in the Ohio River Valley (Fitting 1978). If the Cheyennes remained in the Lake Forest region in this period, they were on the very edge of this florescent area (Coe et al. 1986: 51). In so far as the Woodland economy depended on horticulture, people of Woodland culture could only be marginally successful in the Lake Forest region, where the growing season was short and the harvest unreliable. And we do not know for sure whether the proto-Cheyennes themselves became Woodland people, or whether they were located farther north and west and continued a foraging existence, as Karl Schlesier has suggested (1987: 134–44; 1994: 308–81). He identifies the Cheyennes not among the Lake Forest peoples, but among the Besant peoples of the north-eastern Great Plains, until their movement back east to form the Arvilla culture.

If the Cheyennes were among the horticultural Woodland peoples in the period from about 300 BC to AD 1000, there are several regional cultures which might represent their presence. The Glacial Kame culture, mentioned before, may itself be an Early Woodland tradition but, whether or not this is true, there evolved by AD 100, in that area north-west of the Great Lakes, three quite successful Middle Woodland traditions called Lake Forest, Laurel and Nakomis, each with its own kind of ceramics, artistic style, and burial tradition (Fitting 1978: 44–51). Following these cultures, in the Late Woodland period, a tradition called Blackduck occupied the whole area north of the Great Lakes, from the tip of Lake Superior to the present Canadian province of Ontario (Brase 1978: 569–77). By this time, about AD 1000, we have a better picture of the life of the people who created the artifacts. The Blackduck people apparently lived in settled villages, keeping gardens, but also intensively fishing and gathering wild rice. It is interesting that when the Europeans first encountered the Cheyennes in the 17th century, the Cheyennes were still fishing, keeping gardens and gathering wild rice.

The last remaining archaeological tradition which connects the proto-Algonquians with the historical Cheyennes is the Arvilla complex of northern Minnesota. But to understand this connection we must turn to our third method of tracing prehistoric migrations – biological anthropology. We will find that the techniques of this field enable us to choose among several archaeological possibilities in selecting the most likely ancestors of the Cheyennes.

Biological Anthropology

The osteologist Nancie Ossenberg has measured several hundred skulls in museum collections, representing six archaeological traditions, and has tried to match the physical characteristics of these skulls with skulls from historic times which represent four different linguistic and political groups of the Great Plains (Ossenberg 1974). That is, she has tried to determine which modern tribes came from which prehistoric archaeological traditions by this means. The archaeological skulls were taken from excavated burials while the skulls representing modern tribes were collected in the 19th and early 20th centuries. The archaeological traditions all represent different phases of the Woodland period in the Great Lakes area – Mille Lacs, Arvilla South, Arvilla North, Laurel, Blackduck North, and Blackduck South. The historically-known tribes are the Cheyennes, Dakotas, Assiniboins, and Blackfeet.

After an elaborate analysis, Ossenberg found that the most convincing connection between an archaeological tradition and a modern tribe was between Arvilla North and the Cheyennes, and that there was also a connection between Arvilla North and a preceding Woodland tradition, Blackduck North (map 1.1). Her evidence indicates, then, that the proto-Cheyennes were cognate with the Arvilla North culture from AD 800 to 1400, and before that with the North Blackduck culture, which itself may have been derived from the Laurel tradition, a connection which has also been suggested on archaeological grounds (Wright 1981: 94). This of course contradicts Schlesier's theory that the proto-Cheyennes were derived from Besant rather than Woodland traditions.

If we wanted to construct a current best guess about Cheyenne origins then, we might postulate a series of migrations from the more eastern to the more western cultures shown on map 1.1. The dates are approximate, of course, and do not indicate the entire existence of these archaeological traditions but only the periods in which the proto-Cheyennes were likely participants in these cultures. In all cases, the geographical and chronological boundaries between any two traditions are fuzzy, and old traditions persisted in certain areas after some portions of the population had developed new traditions and moved to a new territory.

It is clear from comparing archaeological, linguistic, and biological evidence that an archaeological tradition, a language community, and a biological population are three different things. A single archaeological tradition might include several different ethnic groups, physical types, or distinct languages. It is also apparent that migrating ethnic groups change biologically because of intermarriage with their new neighbors, as Ossenberg noted for the groups she examined. What we have done in this chapter is trace the likely migrations of a language community, the proto-Cheyennes, from their geographical origins as established by linguistic techniques, across several millennia and hundreds of miles in North America. But we should be aware that the group called Cheyennes which arrived on the Great Plains in the 18th century was probably quite different, biologically and culturally, from the proto-Algonquian group living north of the Great Lakes in about 1200 BC.

At the start of the 20th century, after the Plains Indians had settled into reservation life, physical anthropologists undertook to determine historical relationships among them by examining biological similarities. To do this, they used the best methods available at the time – physical measurement or anthropometry. They measured sitting height and standing height of living people, and were especially interested in taking elaborate measurements of the head. They compared their results with a large museum collection of skeletal material which had been curated at the Smithsonian Institution (Hrdlička 1927).

Their conclusions, generally, were that American Indian physical types did not correspond precisely to linguistic or cultural types, and they decided that, biologically speaking, the Cheyennes should be classed with the Sioux as the "Prairid" type, later called "Siouan," and still later "Lakotid" (Neumann 1952: 29–31). The Lakotids are described as among the tallest populations in North America, relatively light-skinned, and with medium-sized skulls exhibiting a number of diagnostic features of the sort examined by Ossenberg.

In the 1920s the science of immunology developed with the invention of new techniques for determining blood types. Medically, the new science was directed towards the determination of blood compatibility for transfusion, but the genetics of blood type also served historical purposes. Since blood type had been shown to have a genetic base, it could be used to determine the shared ancestry of different populations scattered around the globe. And, in fact, analyses of blood type soon confirmed that American Indians were, as suspected, derived from Asia, since they were similar in many respects to the populations of east Asia and Siberia (Mourant 1954).

In their blood types as with bone measurements, physical categories cut across linguistic and cultural boundaries in North America. On the Great Plains, the Blackfeet and their northern plains neighbors, including the Cheyennes, exhibited a higher frequency of blood type A and a lower frequency of blood type O than any populations in North or South America (Mourant 1954: 138–43).

In recent years, genetic studies of DNA sequences, obtained directly from the chromosomes, have replaced blood type as the best way to determine historical relationships among tribal peoples. So far, the results obtained from these studies have not contradicted results from the analysis of blood type, which is, after all, merely an indirect method of studying genes. In the coming years, however, we can expect a much finer knowledge of genetic differences among Native Americans, as a result of the Human Genome Diversity Project now being planned.

2

Cheyenne Migrations

When the Cheyennes are first mentioned in historical documents, in the 17th century, they are said to be living just west of the Mississippi River in Minnesota, in the area between Mille Lacs and the River. Tracing their migrations from that location to the Great Plains is very difficult, however, because of two kinds of problems which all ethnohistorians must face. First of all, tribes, nations, and ethnicities frequently change their names to reflect a new geographical orientation or changed cultural or political conditions. This is universally true. The British settlers in North America, for example, became "Americans" in the 17th century and then "Canadians" or "Yankees," while citizens of the mother country vacillated sometimes between being English, British, or Scottish, depending on ancestry and social context. The second problem is that a nation is frequently known by different names to its different neighbors. The people English-speakers call Germans, for example, are called Allemands by the French, Duitser by the Dutch, and Niemiecki by the Poles, while the Germans call themselves Deutsch. In the case of the Cheyennes, the name they call themselves, often spelled "Tsistsistas," does not appear in print until 1884, 200 years after they were first mentioned in historical records.

"Cheyenne" is an approximate spelling of the term applied by the Dakota people (who are themselves most often referred to by their derogatory Chippewa name "Sioux" meaning "serpent") to nations who spoke a foreign language but were not regarded as enemies. And so those tribes whose language they understood they called "white-speakers," and those they did not understand they called "red-speakers." Serving as interpreters and hosts to

early European travelers, the Dakotas referred to their Algonquian-speaking allies and neighbors as "Cheyennes" or "red-
speakers," rather than using the kinds of derogatory names
which tribes reserved for their enemies, such as "Liars,"
"Thieves," "Smelly People," or "Incestuous People." Even in
modern times, the Dakota sometimes refer to their Cree and
Chippewa neighbors, no longer their enemies, as "Cheyennes,"
even though historical and official practice has now pinned the
name exclusively on the Tsistsistas.[1]

The tribal, ethnic, and band names used mutually among
peoples of the Great Lakes and North American Plains were not
only confusing at any one time, but also changed through the
centuries, so that there are literally hundreds of names used
between 1680 and 1880 to describe the peoples of that area.
With all this complexity of language, etymology, and history, it
is no wonder that a special science, ethnonymy, has grown up to
help maintain a systematic, scholarly control of the names which
groups have used to designate each other. Although some issues
of ethnonymy are very much in dispute concerning the Cheyennes, I will report here what I consider to be the best evidence
of the names used for people who became Cheyennes, and I will
describe the documentary evidence for tribal movements from
about 1680 until the time when permanent contact was established between Euro-Americans and Cheyennes on the Great
Plains, about 1833.

Early Accounts

Our best witness for the condition of the Cheyennes in the
earliest historical period is probably Louis (or Lewis) Hennepin,
a French Franciscan companion of Robert de la Salle (usually
referred to simply as La Salle in English sources), who set out
from the French camp at Crèvecoeur in Illinois in 1680 to
reconnoiter toward the north-west, where the Dakota, also called
Issati, lived at that time. According to the maps prepared by
Hennepin, and according to two maps prepared by Franquelin
in about the same period, incorporating information from Joliet,
the "Nation du Chien," "Chaienaton," or "Chaiena" lived

among the Dakota and occupied part of the area between the Mississippi and "Lake Issati," also called "Lake Buade," the present Mille Lacs (Moore 1987: 78–84; 1981). We know that the groups referred to in these terms by the Dakotas are not the Crees or Chippewas because at that time the Dakotas were at war with the Crees, who lived to the north-west, and the Chippewas were well-known trading partners of the French, referred to as Saulteurs in these early texts. It is possible that the term Chaiena, as used by the Dakotas at that time, also included the Algonquian-speaking Arapahoes, but linguist Ives Goddard derives the Arapahoes from the Miamis, who lived at least 300 miles to the south-east (1967). Hennepin commented on the linguistic diversity of the area as follows:

'Tis very strange that every Nation of the Savages of the Northern America should have a peculiar Language; for though some of them live not ten Leagues from one another they must use an Interpreter to talk together ... they us'd to send one of their Men to each of their Allies, to learn their Language, and remain with them as their Resident, and take Care of their Concerns. (1698: 141)

According to the maps prepared by Hennepin and Franquelin, the Cheyenne villages were located among those of the Dakotas, and although we do not have descriptions of villages which are explicitly labelled "Chiene," we can get some idea of what Cheyenne culture was like by interpolating from Hennepin's description of the Dakotas. These two peoples lived in the same geographical and ecological zone, and presumably had similar economies and lifestyles. Indeed there is nothing in the archaeological evidence to enable us to differentiate between the Cheyennes and the Dakotas in this period (Aufderheide et al. 1994: 256). In Cheyenne tradition, this period is remembered as the time when they "lived near a big lake" (Will 1914: 69).

Concerning their general technological level, Hennepin said: "They were altogether ignorant of Fire-Arms, and all other Instruments and Tools of Iron and Steel, their Knives and Axes being made of Flint, and other sharp Stones ..." (1698: 142). Using this technology, people of the area were concerned with two primary foraging activities – gathering wild rice and hunting. About wild rice (*Zizania aquatica*), Hennepin says:

This kind of grain grows in swampy land without being sown. It resembles oats but tastes better and has longer stems and stalks. The

Indians gather it in season, the women binding many stalks together with basswood bark to prevent its being entirely eaten by the flocks of duck and teal found in the region. The Indians lay in a store of it for part of the year, to eat when their hunting season is over. (1938: 91)

Although Hennepin described the hunting and consumption of several woodland game animals, the main target of his Indian hosts was apparently buffaloes, which ranged at that time through southern Minnesota and on toward the prairies of the present states of Illinois and Indiana. In this area of mixed prairie, parkland, and riverine forests, buffaloes were killed by stalking, by driving them into rivers, or by driving them by fire into an ambush. Hennepin says that the meat was preserved by cutting it into strips and preserving the strips either by jerking them on open racks in the sun or by smoking them over a fire:

They sometimes dry their meat in the sun. Frequently they keep meat three or four months; for although they have no salt, they cure the flesh so well that it does not spoil at all. Four months after meat has been prepared in this way, one would say on eating it that the animal was freshly killed. (1938: 126)

Other animals hunted for food by the people around Mille Lacs, according to Hennepin, were deer, bear, turkeys, beavers, porcupines, and elk (1938: 167). He also mentions fish and fish eggs being served to him while at Mille Lacs, and specifically bream, catfish, paddlefish, and carp (pp. 116, 118, 120, 121). At the end of his narrative, and discussing the food species of the Great Lakes in general and not just the Dakota area in Minnesota, he mentions the importance of salmon, "salmon trout," whitefish, eels, sturgeon, pike, and bass (pp. 140, 171–2). However, in these pages he does not say which groups collected which species, so it is not clear which other fish species might have been collected by the Dakota and presumably by the associated Cheyennes in this period.

Concerning shelter, Hennepin says that the people of the Mille Lacs area lived in wigwams or "cabins," rather than in long houses like the Iroquois. He does not say whether these wigwams were round, rectangular, or conical like plains tipis, although he mentions that some of them had "poles" (1938: 104–13). When a conical framework was used, the preferred covering material in the Great Lakes area was elm bark, instead of the buffalo

Map 2.1   Forest line and corn line in the Great Lakes area (from Tanner 1987; Aufderheide et al. 1994)

skins which would become typical for Plains Indians (Nabokov & Easton 1989: 60–4; Wedel 1961: 171).

The general state of Cheyenne ecology in this period, and their opportunities for migration to the prairies, can be better understood by looking at the maps of ecological resources prepared by Elden Johnson and Helen Tanner, combined here as map 2.1. Clearly the Mille Lacs area was optimally located for creating an economy which seasonally both collected wild rice and hunted buffaloes – wild rice in the summer and buffaloes in the spring and fall. Located at the edge of swampy Great Lakes habitat which was favorable for wild rice, the Mille Lacs area was only about a hundred kilometers from real prairies, not just mixed prairie parkland, with opportunities for hunting substantial numbers of buffaloes.

During the time of Hennepin, the Chippewas were allied with the Dakotas, serving as a source of French trade goods from Canada which were exchanged for beaver pelts. In their role of middleman and ally, the Chippewas were invited to share the hunting grounds of the Dakotas between Lake Superior and Mille Lacs toward the end of the 18th century, and to locate villages on the south shore of Lake Superior, on the Chequamegon and Keweenaw peninsulas. But soon the Chippewas, enriched by their role in the beaver trade, aspired to attain exclusive control of the rich area between Mille Lacs and Lake Superior, and made war against the Dakotas between the years 1736 and 1765 (Hickerson 1962: 65–72). With superior firearms received from the French, they drove the Dakotas south and west to a line approximating the edge of the forests (see map 2.1), a line which was stipulated in a treaty negotiated at Prairie du Chien under United States supervision in 1825 (Hickerson 1962: 28–9; Tanner 1987: 123).

The war with the Chippewas had forced the Dakotas and their allies the Cheyennes south and west, where Jonathan Carver found them in 1766 camped together on the Minnesota River, which he called the River St Pierre, as shown on map 2.2 (Carver 1956: 76–85). There Carver found "a great number of tents, and more than a thousand Indians. . . ." The groups he listed included the "Schians," and he was told that another group, the "Schianese," lived farther west. In my book *The Cheyenne Nation* (1987), I have argued that these were two separate proto-Cheyenne groups with different alliances, which later became part of a unified Cheyenne nation.

We should note that the area on the Minnesota River where Carver found the Cheyennes was beyond the range of wild rice and well into the prairies. Also, the people were said by Carver to be living in "tents," not cabins or wigwams. From this we can infer that the Cheyennes and Dakotas, or portions of these groups, were living in skin-covered tipis for at least part of the year, and were making a transition to a new style of life which was more mobile and emphasized buffalo hunting. This kind of

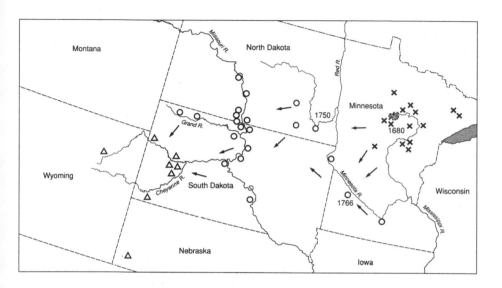

*Map 2.2 Cheyenne locations between Mille Lacs and the Black Hills
(from Moore 1987: 83)*

economy was embraced and elaborated by the Cheyennes and
the westernmost branch of the Dakotas, the Lakota or Tetons,
from then until the middle of the 19th century.

  Somewhere along the way, however, at least a portion of the
Cheyennes adopted a radically different lifestyle, which involved
farming and living in earthen lodges surrounded by fortifications.
The evidence for this comes from place names, archaeology, and
the oral traditions of the Dakotas, the Chippewas, and the
Cheyennes themselves. While these traditions, when published,
are not always carefully referenced concerning their source and
are somewhat contradictory, they seem to indicate that the
Cheyennes in the late 17th century, or some of them, lived in
earthen lodges along the Minnesota River.[2] George Grinnell
identified two traditional Cheyenne villages in the Minnesota
River watershed, one near Mankato on the river proper, and the

other on the Yellow Medicine, a tributary of the Minnesota about 100 miles upstream from Mankato (1918: 377).

As Waldo Wedel has pointed out, the existence of earthen lodges, and especially of fortifications, presupposes a productive agricultural base (1961: 168–9). Without that base, a group cannot live in the same place long enough to justify the work of building permanent timber and earthen structures. In the Mille Lacs area, although Hennepin reports some Indian gardens, horticulture was apparently not reliable enough to encourage a real dependence. Horticulture was only one among several activities for securing food, and he indicates that harvesting wild rice and hunting buffaloes were both more important as economic activities.

On the Minnesota River, however, the Cheyennes were located south of the "corn line," a line which geographers draw on a map defining a region where there are usually enough frost-free days for the corn to mature every year. In this more southerly region, farming was an activity which had hegemony over all others. That is, other economic and cultural activities were curtailed if necessary so that corn could be planted at the right time, properly weeded, and harvested.

Another advantage of moving south and planting corn was that a group could live much closer to the buffalo range. Hennepin reports that the people of Mille Lacs had to travel many miles by canoe and on foot to find buffaloes. But on the Minnesota River the Cheyennes lived in the riverine or "riparian" forests which traversed the very heart of the prairie. Even though much of their time was spent tending their gardens, when it came time to hunt buffaloes, the prairie was directly at hand.

It should not be assumed that the Cheyennes, in their earlier periods, knew nothing about farming, making tipis, or building earthen lodges. Like all humans, they utilized at one time only part of their mental inventory of cultural knowledge. In 1985, for example, I was amazed to see a large Cheyenne family build for itself a traditional "mud house" in Oklahoma, having been denied housing by the government housing authority. After consulting with elders, this Cheyenne family built their house without leaving a space for livestock inside. To do so, said the Cheyenne elders, would cause them to "live like Pawnees." It is interesting to note, too, that many of the techniques for building earthen lodges are retained in the building of the modern Sun Dance lodge (see chapter 8). The Cheyenne family building the mud house already knew, from their participation in the Sun Dance, how to set four posts and poles to provide structure and support for the walls.

In general, modern elders are the repositories of a great deal of latent cultural knowledge about traditional matters. They know how to train horses in an Indian manner and how to make Indian gardens, even though they have not done so for years. In the 1970s a Cheyenne woman, who has since died, told me how wild rice was collected and how to catch ducks in nets made of human hair. She had been told about this, she said, by her maternal grandmother, who was born about 1840. The general point I want to make, then, is that all peoples know how to do a great many more things than they actually demonstrate at any one time. So we should not be surprised if the Cheyennes, after moving south from Mille Lacs, quickly adapted themselves to new styles of life either as hunters living in tipis or as farmers and residents of earthen lodges, activities they knew about from their observations of other tribes.

Horticulture and the Biesterfeldt Site

Since Indian people in aboriginal times had no way of breaking through the thick sod and sun-baked soil of the plains proper, they farmed instead along the watercourses, where riparian forests shaded the ground leaving moist soil with a covering of leaf humus on the forest floor (Wilson 1917; Holder 1970). In selecting their garden spots along the rivers, Indian farmers tried to find sandy soils, which were more easily worked than clay soils. In a suitable area, the men usually assisted the women in girdling the trees to kill them and let the sunlight through. Then the underbrush, grass, and fallen branches were raked together and burned, while suitable spots of soil among the trees were loosened and raked together to form hillocks, using the kinds of tools shown in figure 2.1.

These hillocks were then planted in corn, beans, and squash, so that the roots of the cultigens formed a thick mass to hold the

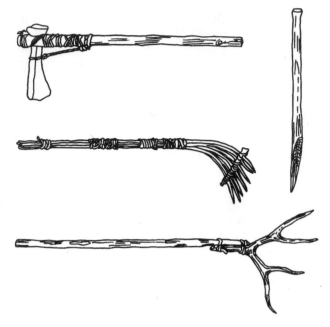

Figure 2.1 Tools used by Plains Indian horticulturists (redrawn by Wenqiu Zhang from Wilson 1917)

soil, and the nitrogen produced by the bean plants could serve to fertilize the other crops. On the major streams, each family planted several gardens on river terraces at different elevations, so that if the lower terraces were flooded, or if there were a drought and the upper terraces dried out, there would still be a harvest from at least some of the gardens. On the smaller streams there was usually only one terrace, and so the gardens were arranged along that terrace in a suitable area near the village. In both situations, some gardens were planted early and some later, as a hedge against a killing frost.

Many of the plains rivers were flanked by large areas of sandy soil along the terraces where gardens could be made. Near such potential garden sites, Indian people had to find a location for a new village which was easily defensible. These villages were usually located at the top of a steep riverbank, where enemy warriors would have to struggle uphill to attack from the riverside. On the other sides of the village, brush barriers, ditches, and palisades could be built to slow down the attackers and give defenders the advantages of concealment and protection from missiles.

One of the best-known fortified villages on the north-eastern plains happens to be a Cheyenne village, not surprisingly on the Sheyenne River in North Dakota, known in the archaeological literature as the Biesterfeldt site (Wood 1971: 55). Although the Sheyenne River is a tributary of the Red River, which flows north towards Hudson's Bay, at this point it is located only 50 miles from the Missouri River watershed and only 150 miles from the Missouri River itself. This village gives us our first good, direct look at Cheyenne culture, not only from the remains of the site itself but also from concurrent historical documents which describe the economy and politics of the Cheyennes at this time, and their motivations both for moving to the Sheyenne River and later for emigrating further west.

The earliest date which can reliably be assigned to Biesterfeldt is based on astronomical evidence. According to Cheyenne traditions collected by George Will, a Cheyenne war party setting out from Biesterfeldt once encountered a solar eclipse by which "the sun was blotted out in full day" (1914: 70). A calendar of solar eclipses indicates that this must have been in 1724, when a solar eclipse occurred just north of the Biesterfeldt site (Wood 1971: 55).

The role of this particular Cheyenne village in the economy and trade of the north-eastern plains was made clear about 1798 in a statement from the Chippewa chief, Sheshepaskut, who had led the war party which destroyed Biesterfeldt several years earlier. The reason that the Chippewas had tolerated the village for so long, he said, was that "they had Corn and other Vegetables, which we had not, and of which we were fond, and traded with them . . ." (Wood 1971: 56). The trader Alexander Henry reported that in these years the Cheyennes "were a neutral tribe between the Sioux and the Saulteurs . . . but the latter, who are of a jealous disposition, suspected they favored the Sioux" Wood 1971: 56). The best estimates of when the village was attacked and burned indicate a date no later than 1790.

Located in present-day Ransom County, North Dakota, Biesterfeldt in its heyday was a village of about 70 earthen lodges on a steep south bank of the Sheyenne River, protected by palisades and a ditch around the west, south, and east sides of the village. Map 2.3 shows the environment of the site at the time it was in

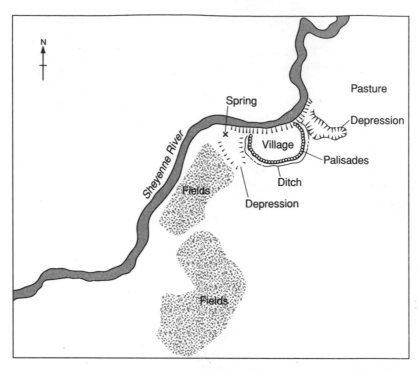

Map 2.3   The Biesterfeldt site and its environs (compiled from Wood 1971; Grinnell 1918; and current soil and topographic maps)

use, while figure 2.2 shows the arrangement of earthen lodges within the village fortifications (based on excavations of the site by William Duncan Strong in 1938, as reported by Strong and by W. Raymond Wood). Since the site was burned and then subjected to 150 years of weathering before it was excavated, some of the superstructural features are not known. We do not know, for example, how tall the palisades might have been, except by analogy with other sites recorded by graphic artists in their visits to Middle Missouri villages in the 19th century, which would indicate a height of about ten feet.

Not only was Biesterfeldt built on the edge of a river embankment for defense, but it was also located between two depressions which served to reinforce the ditch and palisade system, as shown in map 2.3. A nearby spring provided water for the village, and the locations of the gardens on the map (each field is comprised of individual gardens) are based on the

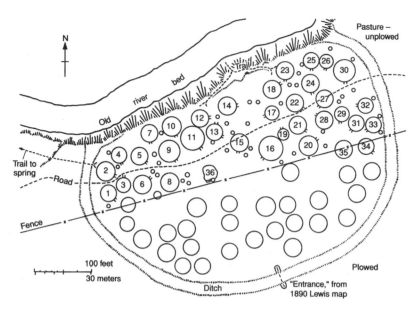

Figure 2.2 Layout of the Biesterfeldt site, a Cheyenne village of the 18th century (from Wood 1971: 7)

availability of sandy loam soils, in this case Sioux cobbly sandy loam and Fordville loam.[3]

The large quantity of stone grinders found at the site attests to the reliance of the Biesterfeldt people on corn and other vegetable foods in this period, as mentioned in the account of Chief Sheshepaskut. In addition, the remains of cultivated plants at the site confirm that the plants being processed were indeed predominantly domestic rather than wild species. The remains of other agricultural tools were also found, including hoes made of buffalo scapulas. Many other buffalo bones indicate the intensity of buffalo hunting in this period, although the remains of elk, deer, and bear were also found, as well as examples of the arrow points used for hunting, and domestic tools for processing meat, hides, and bones. Domestic tools also included mauls and hammers of various kinds, as well as a number of smaller flint and ground stone implements. Only a few trade items of European origin were found. In sum, the physical evidence shows that by the middle of the 18th century the Cheyennes, or a portion of them, had adopted a very common and successful economic strategy, devoting great attention to their gardens but scheduling buffalo hunts into the surrounding prairies when agricultural duties permitted. But the most exciting piece of evidence from Biesterfeldt is the remains of horses, indicating that during this period the Cheyennes had already acquired some knowledge of horse domestication. Confirming this, Chief Shesh-epaskut notes that his attack was conducted after "the Chyennes had collected their Horses and brought them to the Village" in preparation for hunting and after "a great many men and women had gone off a hunting, and very few remained in the Village." So we know that, during this period, the economic inventory of the Cheyennes included the means and knowledge for intensive agriculture, as well as for hunting buffaloes with the assistance of horses.

The Biesterfeldt site is also informative about the social organization of the Cheyennes at that time. The size of the individual lodges, about 20–30 feet in diameter, indicates that each was occupied by an extended family, comprising perhaps 12–20 people. Taking 15 people as a mean number of family members, we can estimate the total population of Biesterfeldt as approximately 900. Since total Cheyenne populations in the next 50 years were consistently estimated by travelers and traders at about 3,000, we can confirm that not all Cheyennes in this earlier period lived at Biesterfeldt.

Another feature of the Biesterfeldt site indicates a hierarchy in their social structure – the fact that one of the central earthen lodges (house 16) is larger and better-built than the others. By analogy with other Middle Missouri peoples, such as the Mandans and Hidatsas, this would indicate the presence of a chiefly family, who were perhaps religious leaders as well. House 16, with a diameter of 40 feet, could easily have accommodated all the senior men of the village for a meeting, or it could have served as the site of religious activities, or both. House 16 is also adjacent to a large open plaza area, about 60 by 100 feet, which could have served social and ceremonial purposes.

Concerning religious beliefs, it is generally dangerous to make inferences about such matters from archaeological evidence, unless there is ethnographic confirmation, but several features of Biesterfeldt are suggestive of Cheyenne religion in later times. As mentioned earlier, the basic structure of the houses, shown in figure 2.3, is the same as that of the modern Sun Dance lodge, except that the Sun Dance lodge is not covered with branches

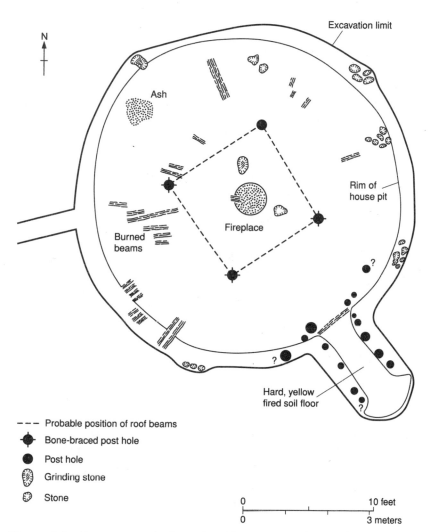

N

Excavation limit

Ash

Rim of
house pit

Burned
beams

Fireplace

Hard, yellow
fired soil floor

– – – Probable position of roof beams

Bone-braced post hole

Post hole

Grinding stone

Stone

0   10 feet
0   3 meters

*Figure 2.3   Basic ground plan of a Cheyenne earthen lodge or "mud
house" at Biesterfeldt (from Wood 1971: 13)*

and dirt. The orientation of most of the houses at Biesterfeldt is
the same as modern Cheyenne tipis, with the entrances facing a
semi-cardinal direction, south-east, except for House 16.

Several of the artifacts found at Biesterfeldt are also reminis-
cent of objects used in more recent Cheyenne religion and ritual.
Of these, catlinite tobacco pipes and bone whistles are still
widely used among plains tribes, as they were then. More

esoteric, however, are the fragments of mussel shell which Strong and Wood interpret as scrapers. Strong describes them as follows: "In shell, a very common but hitherto unique artifact type is a crescentic knife or scraper worn down from a heavy freshwater mussel shell that is very abundant at this site. Small triangular and rectangular forms are also present. These latter types seem rare in the Plains" (1940: 375). These kinds of shells, however, are included in some modern Cheyenne medicine bundles where they are regarded as symbols of the crescent moon. These crescent shell fragments are created by the action of streams which erode the rest of the shell away, leaving only a remnant of the thick part near the hinge of the shell. In the Cheyenne language, these are known as *màthōhevo* (the "claw" or "shield") and symbolize fingernails, animal claws, war shields, the crescent moon, and protection from death. As far as I know, this interpretation is unique to the Cheyennes. According to Strong, 51 shell objects were found at Biesterfeldt.

In addition to Biesterfeldt, the remains of several other 18th century agricultural villages in the northern plains have been attributed to the Cheyennes, all of them in the Middle Missouri watershed and none of them excavated. Of the six village sites discussed by Wood, only one was fortified, located at the mouth of Porcupine Creek near the present North Dakota–South Dakota boundary. This village was said to have been contemporary with Biesterfeldt, existing from 1730 to 1784. According to Dakota tradition, this was where the Biesterfeldt Cheyennes took refuge after their village was burned by the Chippewas (Grinnell 1962: vol. 1, 28). After staying a while they moved about 20 miles south, building an unfortified village on the west side of the Missouri. Both Cheyenne villages moved again soon afterwards, south and westward away from the Missouri proper and up the Grand River, in present-day Corson County, South Dakota. According to the Dakota people, the descendants of the Biesterfeldt village moved to a location where Dirt Lodge Creek enters the Grand River, about 45 miles from the Missouri, while the former occupants of the Porcupine Creek village relocated to a position about 20 miles downstream from Dirt Lodge Creek on the Grand River, as shown on map 2.2.

From these locations, the Cheyennes were poised for a migration onto the high plains and a grand transition from earthlodgedwelling agriculturists to nomadic, full-time buffalo hunters, under the impetus of the political, military, and economic events discussed in chapter 4. But first it will be useful and interesting to explore the technology, organization of work, and expertise which made this new style of life possible. The elements of this "culture of a new type" had been accumulating among the Cheyennes for about a hundred years, but had not yet been assembled to allow a radical cultural transformation which included the abandonment of agriculture and earthen lodges, and the apparent security of sedentary life.

3

Pastoral Nomadism

All human societies change through time. They might change for positive reasons, because of the availability of new tools or techniques, or because of the opportunity to occupy new territories. They can also change for negative reasons, because of the exhaustion of resources or competition from other societies, or they can change because of rapid increases or decreases in population. While cultural changes can occur gradually through time, sometimes they are sudden and dramatic. The word "ethnogenesis" is used to describe how human beings occasionally create novel and original new cultures and societies by combining the bits and pieces of pre-existing cultures in a fresh and enterprising manner. Ethnogenesis usually involves the invention of a new social and economic framework upon which all other aspects of the new culture are hung. In the case of the Cheyennes in the 18th century, the new framework was a type of pastoral nomadism, and was based to a large extent on hunting buffaloes on horseback. Patterned after the cultures of people who were already on the plains, such as the Apaches, Kiowas, and Crows, this new Cheyenne culture was based on commitment to a migratory style of life, in which every person had to be ready, at a moment's notice, to pack up all their possessions and move quickly to another location. There were two major kinds of advantages to adopting this style of life – economic and military.

Economically, a nomadic existence gave the Cheyennes access to buffaloes in all seasons. In one of their previous locations, at Mille Lacs, the Cheyennes, like their Dakota neighbors, had to wait every year for the buffaloes to move into a location where they could be hunted. Consequently, buffalo hunting was seasonal and required a great deal of preparation and marching on foot or traveling by canoe to the prairies of Illinois, Minnesota, and Iowa. If the hunters were successful, they had to dry or smoke their meat and carry it all the way back to their home villages, or load it into canoes for a difficult upstream journey.

Even when located at the Biesterfeldt in later times, out in the prairies and possessing horses, the Cheyennes were still limited in their hunting by the need to leave some people at home to defend their gardens and food from the forays of enemy tribes. These defensive efforts were sometimes unsuccessful, as when the Chippewas attacked the Biesterfeldt village, and later when the Arikaras raided Cheyenne villages on the Missouri, Grand, and Cheyenne Rivers to steal their caches of corn and other garden produce. A horticultural life therefore not only limited the number of available hunters, because of the need to leave some men behind, but also affected the geographical range of the active hunters: they dared not travel too far because of the possibility that they would have to return home quickly to fight or chase away foreign groups who came too close.

Some time in the 18th century the Cheyenne bands, probably not all at the same time, decided to put farming behind them and set sail across the great sea of grass which stretched from the subarctic forests of modern Alberta south to the deserts of Mexico, and from Minnesota and Missouri westward, all the way to the Rocky Mountains of Wyoming and Colorado. The advantages of this decision for hunting were clear. As a nomadic society, they could take the whole population with them on the hunt and have not only the maximum number of hunters engaged in the chase, but the maximum number of women in camp nearby to cut and dry a large quantity of meat quickly to prevent spoilage. Also, they would have better success finding buffaloes, since they could go anywhere the buffaloes could, without worrying about returning to a home base.

A collateral economic advantage for becoming nomadic was the opportunity for long-distance trade. While the Cheyennes had traded somewhat in their previous locations in Minnesota and the Dakotas, the transition to nomadism enabled them to serve as intermediaries for trade between riverine horticulturists such as the Mandans and Arikaras, who possessed guns from

Canada, and plains tribes such as the Apaches and Comanches, who were rich in horses. To assume this role of intermediary, they would of course make enemies and would need military alliances. But they already had powerful allies among the Dakota and Lakota groups, and they were well acquainted with Middle Missouri groups such as the Mandans and Arikaras because of their sojourn in that area as farmers.

Putting the whole society on horseback also had military advantages. For example, the village could be moved quickly, day or night, away from enemies and into a more secure location, and the whole population could be kept together. Also, if the Cheyennes could put all their warriors on horseback, they would have advantages of mobility in maneuver and of height in fighting warriors on foot. In addition, mounted Cheyenne warriors could be dispersed to gather intelligence about the location of enemies, reporting back to the main body at some pre-arranged rendezvous.

Even with opportunities for hunting and trade available in the 18th century, and with the promise of improved success in warfare, the Cheyennes must have been anxious about cutting loose from their home territories and gardens and setting out across the plains. But during such periods of stress and cultural tension, human societies frequently find their comfort in super-natural beliefs, and in the words and actions of prophets and cultural heroes. In the Cheyennes' case, the certainty of their success was provided by the prophet Sweet Medicine, or Mut-siev, who visited a sacred mountain in the Black Hills and returned with four arrows, two of which would ensure their success in the hunt and two of which would destroy their enemies. Encouraged by their possession of the arrows, and by the ceremonies and beliefs which accompanied them, the Chey-ennes bravely broke loose from the past and entered a new era where, as we shall see in subsequent chapters, they prospered in many ways and became a major force in Great Plains trade and politics.

To set out onto the plains, the Cheyennes had to have a special inventory of skills and equipment – everything had to be light and movable. Also, they had to become a horse-centered society, since rapid movement required that everything must be loaded on or pulled behind horses. Not only were earthen lodges and palisades left behind, but also heavy tools such as hoes, rakes,

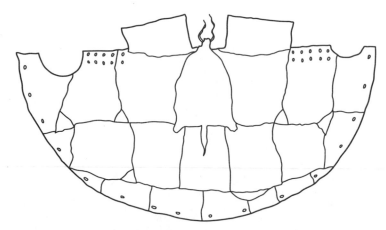

Figure 3.1   Design of Cheyenne tipi made of buffalo skins (redrawn by Wenqiu Zhang from Nabokov & Easton 1989: 155)

manos, and metates. In the new cultural inventory, the two most important items were tipis and horses.

Plains Tipi Construction

A tipi is essentially a skin or cloth covering supported internally by poles. In its general appearance and construction, it is similar to the bark-covered and skin-covered lodges of the Arctic and subarctic areas of North America, Siberia, and Europe.[1] But there are some features of construction which make the plains tipi unique. First of all, the skins of the cover are sewn together into a regular, pre-planned shape, as shown in figure 3.1, rather than being simply tossed onto a conical or hemispherical framework of poles. Secondly, this sewn cover is designed to produce a lodge shaped like a cone tilted backward, and with a large door, small holes in the front for fasteners, and smoke flaps. It is this combination of features which makes the plains tipi unique among tents.

Although the skins of elk or deer might have been chosen for lodge covers, the Cheyennes and other plains groups used buffalo skins because they were thicker, stronger, less grainy, and therefore less inclined to rip. To make the buffalo skins as light

Plate 3.1   Cheyenne tipis made of buffalo skins (taken by Will Soule at Fort Sill, Oklahoma Territory, in 1868, Western History Collections, University of Oklahoma)

and compact as possible, they were de-haired and scraped thin. So that the lodge cover would be waterproof, and could be folded into a squared, compact bundle, the skins were tanned and greased (Grinnell 1962: vol. 1, 213–17). The completed lodge cover might weigh from 100 to 300 pounds, depending on the size of the tipi and the thickness of the skins (see plate 3.1).

Each of the plains tribes adopted certain styles in tipi construction which made their camps visibly different from one another. An experienced traveler on the plains in the 18th century could tell at a glance the tribal identity of a village of tipis. The Cheyennes were noted for having tipis that were "white as linen" because they used a tanning process which produced white buffalo skins. This whiteness was enhanced by the application of white clay or of baked selenite, a form of gypsum. When selenite was used, the tipis were not only white, but actually sparkled in the sun. After a few months of winter use, the lodges became

Plate 3.2 A Cheyenne camp about 1890: these canvas tipis are still mostly white, but the older ones are smoke-stained at the top (Shuck Collection, Western History Collections, University of Oklahoma)

darkened around the smoke holes, but still the overwhelming impression of a Cheyenne camp was that the tipis were white. After they began to use canvas, the tradition of white tipis was still maintained by Cheyennes (plate 3.2), although some other tribes dyed the canvas in bright colors.

Another characteristic of Cheyenne camps was that among the white tipis were a few which were lavishly and colorfully painted with geometric designs, natural symbols, and scenes of warfare. In about 1902, the anthropologist James Mooney commissioned the construction of scale models of 18 of these traditional Cheyenne painted tipis. The most significant were those which housed the Cheyennes' sacred arrows, and their sacred buffalo hat. The tipi of Starving Coyote, shown in figure 3.2, combines geometric designs with realistic drawings of his horses.

Like the Parthenon at Athens, the dimensions and construction of a Cheyenne tipi are not as simple as they appear. Just as the Parthenon is not truly a rectangle and the columns not truly of

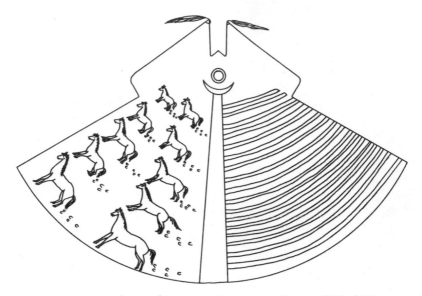

Figure 3.2   Painted tipi of Starving Coyote (see Fagin 1988: 272)

the same size for reasons of visual aesthetics, so does the Cheyenne tipi cover deviate from a conical shape and the base deviate from a circular arrangement for subtle reasons of comfort and stability. When properly erected, a Plains Indian tipi is stable in high winds, bending and squatting instead of blowing over. When properly buttoned up in winter, the tipi only needs a small fire to maintain a comfortable internal temperature above 50 degrees Fahrenheit.

The construction and pitching of the Cheyenne lodge were somewhat different from those of other tribes, although they used the same "three-pole base" as the Dakotas. The lodge poles used by the Cheyennes came from two different species of trees, one of which, the lodge-pole pine, is more northerly in its distribution. Southern Cheyennes, like other tribes in the south, used cedar poles, which were heavier although stronger and more resistant to rotting at the base where the pole was stuck in the ground.

Although Cheyenne families have differed somewhat in their techniques of tipi erection, there tends to be a standard Cheyenne procedure which has been described by Walter Campbell, and which is still in use among modern Cheyennes. The procedure begins with laying out three of the longest and straightest tipi

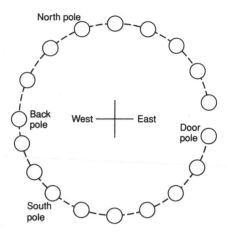

Figure 3.3 Position of Cheyenne tipi poles (redrawn by Wenqiu Zhang from W. Campbell 1915: 689)

poles and binding them together near the tips so that the front pole, laid and bound at right angles to the other two, is longer. The rope used to tie the tripod is about 30–50 feet long and is left dangling in the center as the tripod is erected with the door facing south-east (figure 3.3). The other front poles, perhaps six to ten in number, depending on the size of the tipi, are then laid in the crotch of the tripod created by the north and south poles, working northward from the door to the north pole of the tripod, and then southward from the door to the south pole. When the front poles have been properly arranged in a Cheyenne manner, the pattern should resemble your left fingers folded inside your right fingers. Then the side and back poles are added, the back poles on the outside of the front poles in the same crotch, and the side poles across the back poles, in front of where the north and south poles cross. A gap is left in the arrangement of poles opposite the door for the main back pole, which will carry the tipi cover.

With the poles thus in an approximately circular arrangement, but closer together than they will be when the cover is added, the dangling rope is taken out through the poles just west of the north pole, walked four times around the structure, and tied loosely to the north pole. Then a long, strong back pole is placed on the ground west of the pole structure, pointing toward the structure, and the cover is placed over it with the outside up, and the sides rolled up to meet in the center. The cover is then tied to the pole with a short cord and by means of a special flap attached for that purpose to the top of the cover. Then the pole and cover are raised into place, a job requiring the cooperation of several people, and the cover is unrolled around both sides of the tipi. Cheyenne women, who usually erect the tipis, use long forked sticks to lower the back pole into place.

Adjusting the poles inside the tipi requires a great deal of time. Ideally, the bases of the poles should be gradually pushed into the shape of an oval on the ground, with the long axis from front to rear. Since the cone of the tipi is bent backwards, this enables the fireplace to be placed toward the rear of the tipi under the smoke hole and leaves an open area toward the front. This is one of the subtleties of tipi design, and in anticipation of the oval shape of the floor and the tilting of the tipi, the cover has been sewn to have greater dimensions from apex to bottom of the door than from apex to back, and to have a sharper curve toward the back than toward the front.[2]

With the cover and poles loosely in position, the cover is buttoned in the front, south flap over north flap, using dogwood sticks. For the top sticks, a ladder or table must be found to stand on; in early times a crosspiece was tied across the two door poles, and someone stood on the crosspiece to button the top of the cover. After buttoning, the cover is ready for tightening. To move a tipi pole from inside the tipi, it is twisted slightly to loosen it from the rope at the top, and extended outward to tighten the cover. When the correct positions for the poles are found, each pole is set in the ground slightly, either by pushing the sharpened base into the soil, or digging a small hole with an axe.

The last three steps in erecting the tipi are to stake down the bottom of the cover, adjust the smoke flaps, and attach the door. Tipi covers made of buffalo skins had holes pierced around the bottom for the stakes, and the skins around the bottom were left thick at the edge to strengthen the area around the stakes. The stakes themselves are made of chokecherry wood, which tends not to splinter when driven. Each stake is made of a chokecherry branch which has a sidebranch near its base; the small end of the branch is the tip of the stake, and the stub of the sidebranch, which points down, is hooked around the tipi cover.

To position the smoke flaps, a long narrow pole is inserted in

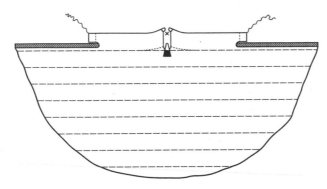

Figure 3.4   How canvas strips are sewn together to make a Cheyenne tipi cover (redrawn by Wenqiu Zhang from W. Campbell 1915: 686)

the pocket of each flap, bent around the tipi and set in the ground at the back. Cords attached to the bottoms of the smoke flaps are tied to stakes. By adjusting these flap poles and flap stakes in accordance with wind direction, a proper draft for the fire in the tipi is ensured, so that air comes in the door or under the cover and the smoke goes out the top. When it rains, the flaps are overlapped, south over north. Most Cheyenne tipis have round or oval doors, which are hung from the bottom-most dogwood stick used to button the cover. Sometimes there is merely a slit door in the cover, rather than a hole for a separate door.

When a tipi is erected for a special event, a meeting or ceremony, the front and back poles are alternated and inter-locked in the crotch of the tripod instead of nested as left fingers inside right fingers. Seeing this interlocked arrangement, visitors to a camp know that this tipi is not to be entered without special permission. Some families and organizations also have their own unique ways of stacking or interlocking the tipi poles at the top, although most people in modern times use the standard arrange-ment described here. Sometimes, for example at the annual ceremonies, a double or triple tipi can be erected around two cones of lodge poles with two or three lodge covers buttoned together.

Canvas tipi covers are of course much lighter than the old skin covers, and came into use in the middle and late 19th century. Figure 3.4 shows how the canvas strips are sewn together to make a tipi. The design and construction of the canvas cover are

approximately the same as the buffalo skin cover, except that
loops are sewn around the edge to accommodate the stakes,
since the light canvas cannot endure a stake being driven through
it. Some tipis, especially in modern times, have straps or cords
sewn to the cover about four feet from the edge, inside and out,
so that the cover can be rolled up and tied all around in warm
weather.

In reservation times towards the end of the 19th century, wall
tents began to replace tipis for summer living, while log cabins
and small frame houses were utilized for winter residence. Even
now, some Cheyenne families move into their tipis and tents for
the summer, erecting brush arbors for a cooking area, and at
their annual spring ceremonies and summer pow-wows hundreds
of Cheyenne families still erect their tents and tipis. The last
Cheyennes to live year-round in tents and tipis were some of the
Red Moon band of Hammon, Oklahoma. The last segment of
that band moved from "West Camp" to houses in town in 1968,
when a settlement was received for land in Colorado illegally
taken from the Cheyennes by the US government in violation of
the 1851 Treaty of Fort Laramie.

A great deal more could be said about the behavior which
accompanies the construction and use of Cheyenne tipis. In
particular there is an elaborate etiquette to be observed in
entering and leaving tipis. These topics will be considered in the
context of religion and social structure in subsequent chapters.
Here I have only tried to describe the basic technology, emphasizing the combination of features which is uniquely Cheyenne.

Horses – Training and Use

The tipis described above, when made of buffalo skins, each
required about three horses for transport. A tipi cover made in
aboriginal times from 11 skins weighed nearly 200 pounds,
required 18 tipi poles, and was slung for travel between two
large tipi poles dragged behind a horse as a travois. The other
tipi poles were not so much heavy as awkward to transport, and
were dragged behind two other horses, eight to a horse, four on
each side, often rigged as a travois with food or equipment

Plate 3.3 A travois built from tipi poles; a pack-horse can be seen behind the horse with the travois (Campbell Collection, Western History Collections, University of Oklahoma)

carried between the poles (plate 3.3). Obviously, the transport of the cover and the poles required horses – humans or dogs could not easily have carried or dragged a full-sized tipi very far. And so we see why horses and tipis are inseparable as we consider the technology adopted by the Cheyennes to become Plains nomads.

Horses evolved in the Americas during the Tertiary period, but had become extinct in the Western hemisphere by modern times, although they had migrated to Asia during the "faunal exchange" caused by the Bering Strait land bridge during the Pleistocene period. Ironically, the horses, which would ultimately become so important for the Cheyennes, were passing in the other direction between Alaska and Siberia as the ancestors of the Cheyennes migrated to North America.

The ancestors of the horses which became known as "Indian ponies" were mostly Spanish horses, some of which escaped to create herds of wild horses in Texas and New Mexico as early as the 16th century.[3] These horses were smaller than modern riding horses, and averaged perhaps 900 pounds in weight. A small female might weigh as little as 700 pounds, while a large, well-fed stallion might be as large as an average American saddle horse, about 1100 pounds. Recent research indicates, however, that the generally smaller size of wild horses and Indian ponies may have been a product of poor nutrition rather than a genetic adaptation to living in the wild. Indian horse herds were not only derived from wild herds, but also replenished continually by domestic stock obtained from Mexican ranches to the south and Anglo-Americans to the east. A herd of Indian ponies in the 19th century, then, might include some wild horses, some Mexican and Anglo-American domesticates, their offspring, and a number of mules as well.

The Cheyennes have at least two traditional accounts explaining where they acquired their horses, and both of them are probably accurate. Northern Cheyennes say that their ancestors got their first horses from the Arapahoes, and Southern Cheyennes say that the Apaches were the source. The fact that Cheyennes have two different words for "horse," as well as two different stories, might indicate that at least two different bands received them on different occasions from different sources. The Northern Cheyennes refer to horses as *mohéno*, the same word as "elk," while Southern Cheyennes refer to a horse as *nathoze*, meaning "my pet," a term which is also used for dogs. The Southern Cheyenne tradition also tells us that four medicine bundles were received from Apaches for training and ministering to horses, along with the horses themselves.[4] In my fieldwork, I have been privileged to consult with three of the last four holders of these medicine bundles – Henry Mann, Roy Bull Coming, and Edward Red Hat.

The traditional Cheyenne method for training horses is radically different both from Spanish and from Anglo-American methods. Horses born in Cheyenne herds were not customarily "broken" to their tasks of carrying riders or pulling loads; instead they were "gentled." From first foaling, the horses were attended by the boys who watched the herds every day, who stroked them, talked to them, and played with them. On occasion the owner of a colt, usually an adult man, would visit the young horse in the pasture and stroke it and sing to it, sometimes smoking a pipe and blowing the smoke on the colt's face. As the colt grew older, the boys would ride it, so that it got used to carrying a weight and associating with humans. At about 18 months old, in the fall of its second year, a horse's serious training would begin. This was conducted by the owner, sometimes assisted by a holder of one of the horse medicine bundles. The horse was sung to and smoked over, as before, and stroked with fans made from eagle wings. Gradually it was made accustomed to the saddle, soft rope bridle, and rider. If the horse was intended for use in hunting or warfare, the training was more intensive. If it was only intended to carry a pack or travois, the training was minimal, and was often done by women or girls. Stallions were usually chosen for war or hunting because they tended to be larger than mares and hence had more stamina when galloping under the weight of a rider. To be a hunter or war horse, a stallion had to have a suitable temperament. Hunters had to be willing to close with a buffalo on the run, and war horses had to be aggressive and indifferent to gunfire and arrows. Only a few special horses were capable of being trained for both tasks. Most men had both a "running horse" for hunting and a war horse.

Although the herd boys rode the young horses without saddles in the pastures, adults preferred pads or saddles when riding, both of which were equipped with stirrups. It is a myth that Indians customarily or preferably rode bareback; anyone who has tried to gallop bareback over rough ground knows that it is nearly impossible to keep your seat. So Cheyenne riders used pads and saddles. The pads were simply a leather oval or rectangular cover stuffed with horsehair or grass, most often tied with a rope around pad and horse, instead of a girth strap. Even without a girth or rope, a pad with stirrups could be centered by pushing on the stirrups. When riding any distance, however, or at a gait faster than a walk, Cheyennes looked for a saddle. Early Cheyenne saddles were patterned after Spanish saddles, with high wooden pommels and cantles, sometimes held together with dried rawhide and usually cinched over a buffalo skin or wool saddle blanket. Other skins or blankets were thrown on top of the wooden saddle to pad the rider. When the Cheyennes became involved in plains trading networks in the 18th century, Navaho and Mexican blankets were substituted for buffalo skins. Even later, they began to use American-style leather saddles, either acquired in trade or captured in warfare and raiding.

Since Cheyenne horses had been gentled rather than broken, the riders ideally did not have to lasso them for a day's riding, but simply approached them slowly, talking or singing, and placed a short lead rope around their necks, which was often tied to the pommel when the horse was saddled. To control the horse, a rope was tied around the horse's lower jaw in a clove hitch for a bridle, with the two ends of the rope serving as reins. Cheyenne riders, however, prided themselves on controlling their horses without touching the reins, but rather by the press of their knees. The very best Cheyenne horsemen (i.e. horse trainers), it is said, could control riderless horses simply by voice commands and hand signals. To call a horse in from pasture by voice and have it stand still for saddling, without being tied or restrained, was said to represent the very best of Cheyenne horsemanship and horse medicine.

Some Cheyennes trained and controlled their horses in a Spanish manner, especially the wild horses captured in Colorado beginning in the late 18th century. To break such a horse, it was hobbled and staked out, and its mouth muzzled or tied shut for a day or more. Then it was allowed to overfeed on green grass, filling its stomach and making it very uncomfortable. For breaking, it was led into a river or lake, if possible, to bloat on water and so that the water would cushion the fall of the "broncbuster," if necessary, and then it was mounted. When the horse ceased to buck under the rider and was "broken," it was ridden around by a series of riders for several hours until it was exhausted and so that it got used to the idea of being ridden. Sometimes a horse had to be broken several days in succession, and Cheyenne horsemen never trusted the behavior of such a horse as much as they trusted those which were gentled, according to modern consultants. Although spurs, whips, and metal bits were used by some Cheyennes, the most respected Cheyenne method was gentling and control by minimal restraints.

Two devices were used by Cheyennes for transporting their belongings with horses – packs and travois. Travois were used in the open plains, while packs were used in rough or rocky terrain. Both were simply scaled-up versions of devices used in an earlier period when dogs were the only animal used for transport. Packs were loaded in two or three sections. The first two sections were of equal weight and hung on the sides of the dog or horse, tied by two ropes under the chest and belly. In the case of horses, a third pack was sometimes added on top, if no one was riding the horse. A cinched riding saddle or pack saddle could be used to create a firm anchor on top of the horse, over which the packs were placed.

Dogs did not carry a third pack because they were a very unstable traveling platform, jumping over rocks and bushes, stopping to scratch, and otherwise constantly disarranging their load. Pack dogs carrying equipment were simply allowed to follow their owners when they travelled, but pack dogs carrying food were led by leashes to prevent their eating the food. Pack-horses were led by ropes if they were not ridden and were mostly very stable, although Cheyennes preferred mules for packing when they were available.

The travois was an ingenious Native American invention, remarkably appropriate for the roadless prairie. The fundamental idea of the travois was to tie a rope between two long poles near the tip, leaving about two feet of rope between the poles. The poles were placed on each side of a horse with the rope laid across its withers. Then two crosspieces were lashed across the poles behind the horse, and a rope or strip of leather wrapped around both crosspieces to serve as a platform for carrying food, people or equipment. The horse could then either be ridden or led.

A horse could drag about two or three times more weight on a travois than it could carry as a pack-horse. While a pack-horse or mule could carry about 200 pounds, a travois on hard, level ground could carry 5–600 pounds. Because the poles were pointed up and forward over the horse, they tended not to get entangled in brush but actually separated the brush so that it did not snag the load, unlike the packs carried by pack-horses. Cheyennes preferred not to use tipi poles as travois poles, since the bases of the travois poles soon began to wear down on one side because of the dragging. Instead, they preferred to construct permanent travois structures with shorter poles, which often were made of a hardwood like oak or hickory. The travois in plate 3.4 is built on special travois poles, not on tipi poles.

A permanent travois structure might also comprise a cage built from green willow branches. These, too, were scaled up from a dog travois arrangement, as can be seen by comparing plates 3.4 and 3.5. These cages were especially used to transport young children who were too heavy to carry but too young to walk for very long. The children could be dropped in the top of the cage, and a blanket or robe thrown over the opening. A Cheyenne elder in 1981 told me that she had regularly travelled in such a cage as a child, and "it always put me to sleep."

Plate 3.4 The family of Stump Horn photographed at Fort Keogh, Montana in 1889 (Smithsonian Institution National Anthropological Archives, Bureau of American Ethnology Collection)

When the nomadic Cheyennes packed their possessions to move, most items were simply laid on a buffalo robe, blanket, or canvas, which was then folded up from all four sides and tied to make a pack. Certain items, however, required special containers. Food, which mostly consisted of dried buffalo jerky, corn, flour, dried fruits, and vegetables, was usually packed in parfleches, which were flat bags made of rawhide. Similar to saddle bags in appearance, parfleches were folded up instead of sewn. Figure 3.5 shows the outside surfaces of a parfleche about six by three feet in size. The jerky or corn to be packed was placed in the center of the parfleche when it was turned over, and then all four sides were folded in like an envelope, exposing the decorated surfaces. The edges of the decorated panels were tied together using laces which passed through holes in the rawhide, as shown in the figure.

The most bulky items which had to be packed were the buffalo robes, stuffed mattresses, willow mats, and backrests, used for resting and sleeping. All of these were rolled up for transport, sometimes with fragile items inside. After they were obtained in trade, heavy metal cooking pots also had to be transported,

Plate 3.5 *The wife of Black Horse with a dog travois, about 1900 (Campbell Collection, Western History Collections, University of Oklahoma)*

along with traditional leather water bags and buckets of either leather or metal. These were usually tied on the outside of packs, up high to avoid snagging in bushes.

Tanned leather was used to make a variety of bags and sacks of various sizes, some beautifully decorated, to hold small objects such as tools, sewing materials, toys, and the like. They use a

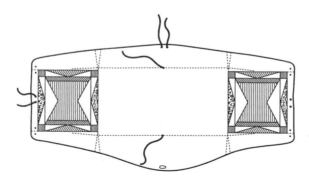

Figure 3.5 *A rawhide parfleche before folding (redrawn by Wenqiu Zhang from Laubin & Laubin 1957: 84)*

special container for their own personal medicine – a rectangular piece of tanned material with the long sides folded in, rolled up into a cylinder around the medicine objects and tied with two thongs near each end. When traveling, men of warrior age usually did not take packs on their horses, but carried their weapons with them as they preceded the main body and guarded the flanks. During a march, some warriors would drop out to guard the train of stragglers which inevitably developed as horses became lame, loads had to be repacked, or people fell ill.

The families in a band did not ride in a column as if they were following a road, but spread out to avoid each other's dust. Although they usually camped along creeks and rivers, they did not travel for long distances along watercourses because of the trees and heavy brush. Instead, they followed traditional routes on higher ground which connected their favorite camping places. Deserts, gullied surfaces, and boulder-strewn areas – known colloquially in English as breaks and badlands – had to be avoided. When moving, a Cheyenne band was an impressive sight – 6–800 people with over a thousand horses mounted, packed, or pulling a travois, preceded and flanked by a screen of mounted warriors, and followed by a train of stragglers and herds of extra horses being driven by mounted herdsmen, raising dust that persisted for hours and could be seen for miles around.

If they were packed and prepared to move at dawn, a Cheyenne band could travel 20 miles in a day if the terrain were not too rough. When they were in a hurry or escaping enemies, they could pack and move much faster. In the extreme, according to modern consultants, they could leave most of the tipi poles behind and be packed and out of sight within 15 minutes. If it seemed tactically advisable, a band could disperse in a hundred directions, gathering together later at some pre-determined camping spot. Dispersing, or traveling at night, meant that their dust would not betray their route or rendezvous.

A large Cheyenne band with a thousand horses required considerable space for pasture when they stopped to make camp and erect their tipis. Consequently, they tended to select their camps where grass was thick and nutritious and the pastures clearly visible from the camp to prevent horse-raiding. Because of the mosaic pattern of plains soils, grass can be five times thicker and of better quality in one place than another place close by; the Cheyennes selected those pastures near streams whcre the grass was thickest and best. In particular, they looked for three kinds of native wild grasses: grama (genus *Bouteloua*) bluestem (genus *Andropogon*) and buffalograss (*Buchloe dacty-loides*).[5] While there were scores of native grass species on the plains where the Cheyennes ranged, these three grasses were dominant before the proliferation of foreign grass species. They tend to grow not only in small homogeneous patches, but more often in huge, mixed-species communities covering perhaps hundreds of acres.

Although most Cheyenne horses ran free in herds tended by herd boys, some especially valuable horses – running horses and war horses – were staked out near to the owner's tipi or hobbled near camp. Herders were with the horses night and day, and in fact minding the horses was about the only kind of work assigned to boys under 14. The main difficulty in tending free herds is that the horses are very selective in their eating, and tend to range away from the camp to find preferred grasses or grasses in a preferred stage of development. Consequently there was a continuing struggle between herders and horses to keep them near enough to camp so that the warriors in the camp could respond quickly if the horses were raided by enemies.

The sedentary peoples of the Middle Missouri, such as the Mandans and Arikaras, could not keep large herds of horses because of the limited area of secure pastures near to the village. If the herds were too large, then the horses ate all the grass near the village and moved out onto the plains, thus becoming vulnerable to raiders. Consequently the ratio of horses to people for the horticultural tribes was about one horse for every two or three people (see Ewers 1955: table 2). For the Cheyennes to abandon their horticultural villages in the 18th century, they first had to accumulate enough horses at one time to put the whole society on horseback, a ratio of about one to one. To achieve this higher horse:person ratio, they went through a transitional period when they conducted "casual horticulture," planting their crops in the spring and then leaving to hunt for the entire summer, returning for the harvest. Thus they saved the grass near their village for winter grazing and could keep larger herds of horses than their horticultural neighbors, who tended their gardens continually through the summer and kept their horses nearby. It was in this period of Cheyenne casual horticulture that the Arikaras raided the vacant Cheyenne villages in late

summer and "stole their corn," which was undefended, and thus
encouraged the Cheyennes to give up horticulture altogether and
become plains nomads.

Hunting

Before they had horses trained for chasing buffaloes, the Cheyennes hunted on foot. They had to rely on techniques of stalking,
surrounding, and ambushing buffaloes on the open plains, so
they often took advantage of special geological and human-made
structures which had been used for centuries by generations of
pedestrian hunters. Some structures used especially for killing
buffaloes are called buffalo "jumps" – cliff faces nearly invisible
from above so that a stampeding herd of buffaloes could not see
them until it was too late to avoid being pushed off the cliff by
buffaloes coming up behind. Other special structures had been
especially built by various tribes for hunting pronghorn
antelopes.

The structures built for antelope hunting have been variously
called corrals, enclosures, or traps, and were located where
natural features of geography, such as creeks, rough terrain, or
lakes, tended to funnel animals into a restricted area (see Frison
1991; Grinnell 1962: vol. 1, 247–311). The construction of an
antelope trap took advantage of the animal's inquisitive nature,
its skittishness, herding tendencies, and unwillingness to push
through or jump over obstacles. The wings and fences of the trap
were most often merely piles of brush, cut and collected at the
site and piled in the arrangement shown in figure 3.6.

To begin the antelope drive, young men were sent by circuitous
routes far out onto the prairie to alarm the herds and move them
toward the trap. This was easy to do because of the generally
nervous nature of antelopes, and their unwillingness to let
humans approach very close. The opposite technique was to
attract the antelopes toward the trap by setting up something
strange and interesting between the wings, such as a small tipi,
an antelope decoy, a brightly decorated robe or blanket, or even
a person crawling on the ground painted and dressed to resemble
an antelope. When the antelopes were driven or attracted to a

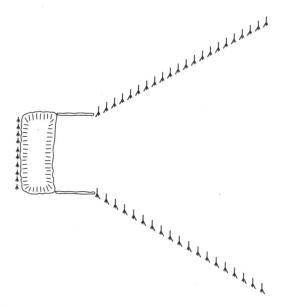

Figure 3.6 General configuration of an antelope trap; a buffalo jump was similar, except on a larger scale and ending at the top of a cliff rather than in a corral (redrawn by Wenqiu Zhang from Grinnell 1962: vol. 1, 279)

location between the wings, young men outside the wings would then run forward to frighten them into the neck of the trap. If the antelopes veered toward the wings instead of heading toward the corral, people hiding behind the brush on the wings stood up to scare them back. Once the antelopes were in the corral, people standing all around it endeavored to frighten the antelopes, which became exhausted from running around. As they stumbled into the killing pit, which was about five feet deep, they were attacked by people standing behind the pit with clubs and lances. One such hunt led by the medicine man White Faced Bull resulted in the slaughter of 600 antelopes, according to George Grinnell.

As a source of meat in quantity, antelopes were not as desirable a quarry as buffaloes. While a large antelope might provide 40 pounds of flesh, an average adult female buffalo can provide 400 pounds. Not surprisingly, it was buffaloes which were the main quarry of the Cheyennes, while antelopes were hunted only as a collateral activity, especially when a Cheyenne band happened to be near an area which had been used historically as a trap.

Buffaloes, too, were hunted by means of structures, but different techniques had to be used because the buffaloes were big and aggressive, not easily killed, and not afraid to push through a brush enclosure. The wings leading to a buffalo jump often comprised stone cairns instead of brush, with people stationed behind to frighten the buffaloes toward a jump, corral, or box canyon. The five-foot walls of a killing pit did not work for buffaloes because they could easily climb out, and when a corral was used, it was usually built of substantial logs, stones, and branches instead of brush. The killing, which was dangerous, was accomplished by lances and arrows; the hunters stood only on one side of the buffaloes to avoid shooting or lancing one another. When the buffaloes were herded over a jump, they were usually so injured that they were easy to approach and kill, if in fact they were not killed by the fall.

In addition to traps, Cheyennes used ambushes and surrounds to kill buffaloes in the years before they had buffalo horses. A surround was accomplished when a group of hunters stealthily moved up on a buffalo herd in a long rank abreast, from downwind, and slowly enveloped the herd on all sides. Then the circle was gradually closed until the buffaloes at last were alarmed and tried to escape. The hunters herded them back toward the center for as long as possible by waving arms and blankets, until they could approach close enough to shoot them with arrows, about 20–40 yards.

An ambush could be accomplished by a single hunter or group of hunters simply by hiding near a trail where buffaloes were known to pass, for example near a creek or pond. Buffaloes could also be stalked by a single hunter or a few hunters crawling toward the herd with a blanket or animal skin draped over the head and torso for concealment. Since buffaloes are so big and aggressive, they are often indifferent to the movements of small animals, even wolves and coyotes, and so even if they noticed the hunters they might not be alarmed. Groups of humans, or especially humans on horseback, however, did alarm the buffaloes.

With trained horses, beginning in the 18th century, buffaloes could be chased instead of trapped, surrounded, or stalked. The most productive mounted hunts were the large communal expeditions, since the more hunters there were present, the less chance there was that buffaloes would find an avenue of escape among the horsemen. The communal hunts were usually conducted in the spring and early summer, when there were large congregations of buffaloes on the new grass, and the success of the hunt depended on Cheyenne "wolves" or scouts who could find these congregations and report back to the camp without alarming the buffaloes. Unlike antelopes, buffaloes when alarmed might travel long distances before they once again settled down to graze.

When the buffalo herd was located and reported, no one was allowed to hunt prematurely. Instead, all the hunters of the camp, perhaps several hundred of them, moved out together, followed at a distance by women leading horses, carrying meat racks on their pack-horses and travois. Leading their hunting horses or lying flat down in the saddle, the Cheyennes approached into the wind and tried to envelope the buffaloes on two or three sides. They tried to leave one avenue open, away from the camp and assembled women, so that the buffaloes would run in a straight line as they were approached by the mounted hunters, rather than dodging and changing direction. As soon as the herd showed the first signs of alarm, the hunters leaped on their horses and charged. The success of this kind of hunting was based on the fact that a sprinting fresh horse, even carrying a rider, can overtake a running buffalo, at least for the first three to five minutes of the chase. After that, the horses become tired and the buffaloes pull away. So the hunters tried to kill as many buffaloes as they could, as quickly as possible.

Different tribes of Plains Indians used different weapons for killing buffaloes from horseback, but the Cheyennes preferred a short, stiff, wooden bow three or four feet long, and thick, strong arrows about 20–25 inches in length. The flat arrow point, of stone or metal, was set at right angles to the nock, so that when the hunter bent forward to shoot down on the buffalo's back, the point would slide between the ribs, hopefully penetrating to the heart and lungs. The appearance of blood on the buffalo's nose and mouth indicated to the hunter that the lungs had been pierced and the animal was dying, and was his signal to move to the next buffalo. Good hunters could kill two or three buffaloes in a single chase.

With the buffaloes dead and dying on the prairie, the women

came forward, and once again there was a race against time. In the heat of the summer sun, the meat could spoil within 24 hours, and so the buffaloes had to be skinned and dressed quickly. The Cheyennes have a unique manner of dressing buffaloes, which they still demonstrate yearly at their ceremonies. With the buffalo turned on its stomach and its legs folded up, it is cut down the back from head to tail and the skin peeled back on both sides. This immediately exposes two choice pieces, the hump and the kidneys, which some people like to eat raw. Then the skin is rolled down both sides of the carcass, so that strips of meat can be cut for jerky. The meat is cut in two ways, as strips or flayed panels. To produce the panels, a large chunk of meat is cut off the carcass in the shape of a cylinder. Then a shallow cut is made down the length of the cylinder, and a long knife inserted in the cut so that a continuous panel of meat can be cut off as if one were unrolling it from the cylinder. The meat is then spread to dry using wooden splints, as shown in plate 3.6. The resulting jerky is thinner, dries more quickly, and is not so tough as the jerky cut in strips. When as much meat as possible has been flayed, the rest is cut in long strips about the thickness of one's little finger.

If the buffalo skin was needed to make robes, shields, or lodge covers, it was cut and removed from the animal in a different manner. If only the back skin was needed, the buffalo was laid on its side and "caped." This was done by cutting the skin across the back of the neck and extending the cut to the base of each leg and the tail. This produced a cape which contained only the section of buffalo hide which was thickest and had the longest hair. If the whole skin was required for a robe, the buffalo was cut down the belly, and then the head, feet and anal area were circled. Then the skin was removed across the back, as if removing an overcoat, and laid on the ground still attached to the underside of the buffalo. When most of the meat had been removed, the carcass was lighter in weight and could be lifted or rolled and the skin detached from the other side. Buffalo skins, hair side down, were used as convenient work areas for cutting and stacking the meat as it was cut from the buffalo.

To dry large quantities of meat quickly, it is important to have a large number of drying racks. In aboriginal times, these mostly consisted of forked sticks about six feet tall set in the ground, with crosspieces set in the forks and tied across the shafts of the

Plate 3.6   A Cheyenne woman hanging meat which will dry into jerky (Smithsonian Institution National Anthropological Archives)

uprights. Tipi poles, ropes, and nearby tree branches were also used. The incentive for all this hard work is that a single buffalo can provide all the calories that an adult needs for about 200 days. Consequently, the people worked night and day to jerk the meat until they were finished, or until the meat had begun to spoil.

Cheyenne people still jerk meat, and some even build special screened porches on their houses for this purpose. In the dry, windy environment of the Great Plains it is interesting to note that flayed meat can dry completely on a rack in about two hours and strips of jerky in about four hours under ideal conditions. The meat of course is considerably lightened in weight by drying, and thus a whole buffalo with 400 pounds of meat can be converted, with a few hours of optimum drying weather, into about 120–160 pounds of jerky, depending on humidity and drying conditions (see Frison 1991: 316).[6] This was the attraction, then, which nomadic life held for the Cheyennes. With the nomadic technology of horses and tipis, they could continually raid the buffalo larder of the Great Plains and be well fed on a protein-rich diet.

There have been many attempts to find patterns in the migrations of the buffaloes which the Cheyennes depended on in the 18th and 19th centuries. Some scholars have said that there was an annual migration toward the south in winter, while others have said that the winter migration was toward wooded areas, such as the Black Hills and riverine forests. But scientists cannot agree that there were buffalo migrations which followed the same patterns year after year.

It is more certain, however, that buffalo migrations each year tended to follow the pattern of rainfall, which generated the grasses on which they fed. But every year the pattern of rainfall is different, so that an area rich in grass one year can experience a drought the next. Buffaloes, then, had to keep moving to find good grass and, when they found it, they stayed until it was gone or until they were frightened away by hunters. Looking for grass, they could sometimes accumulate into herds comprising thousands of animals, which were described in amazement in the accounts of early travelers.

The total number of buffaloes on the Great Plains when the Cheyennes arrived there was enormous. Estimates range from 5 to 75 million animals, perhaps enough to feed the whole 1850 population of the United States for more than a year. It is not known whether the horseback hunting of the Plains Indians had any impact on the buffalo population, but it is clear that the opening of the Oregon Trail about 1845 created a separation between what were called the "northern herd," north of the Platte River, and the "southern herd," south of the Platte. Until the 1870s both Indian and American buffalo hunters exploited the herds for their hides and meat until the species became nearly extinct.

Gathering

Although the nomadic Cheyennes traded with horticulturalists for corn and vegetable food when they could, there were wild plant resources on the plains which were of considerable interest.[7] Prominent among these were three starchy roots: (1) prairie turnips or breadroot (*Psoralea esculenta*), (2) Jerusalem artichokes (*Helianthus tuberosus*), and (3) Indian potatoes (*Glycine apios* or *Apios tuberosa*). They were collected by women using digging sticks as shown in plate 3.7. There were two kinds of digging sticks – long, forked sticks such as are shown in the photo and short, heavier sticks with a knob on the end for digging to greater depths. Although the sticks themselves were simple, the knowledge required to find the tubers in the correct season was not. Prairie turnips, for example, mature in June and quickly lose their tops, becoming nearly invisible. But by knowing the kinds of rocky soils and moisture conditions preferred by the plants, Cheyenne women could find them.

Jerusalem artichokes are a kind of sunflower and are now cultivated commercially and sold in grocery stores. They have also become a common garden vegetable in the United States, a perennial plant grown from thick beds of roots. In the wild, they are nearly indistinguishable from many other kinds of sunflowers and yellow-flowered plants which do not have an edible root. Cheyenne women, however, looked for the plant in moist basins on the plains and could recognize its flower in all stages of development.

The last of the three most important tubers, the Indian potato, grows in moist areas along streams on the prairie, and provides an edible seed as well as a tuber.

Although there were many fruits and berries available to the Cheyennes in the northern plains, they focussed on three species which were very plentiful and productive. These were buffaloberries (*Shepherdia argentea*), elderberries (*Sambucus racemosa*),

Plate 3.7 *Northern Cheyenne women foraging for prairie turnips, about 1900; the soil is rocky and the plants have lost their tops, making them nearly invisible (Grinnell Collection, Museum of the American Indian)*

and chokecherries (*Prunus virginiana*). Later, when the Cheyennes moved to the southern part of the plains, they emphasized the harvest of two additional species, sand cherries (*Prunus angustifolia*) and wild plums (*Prunus americana*). Each of these was harvested in season, eaten fresh, and preserved by drying for later consumption.

Of the plant foods mentioned above, two became important trade items – prairie turnips and chokecherries. Prairie turnips became commercially important in the 18th century when the Cheyennes were living near the Black Hills. No longer farmers themselves, the Cheyennes became specialists in finding these roots and drying them into flour. They not only used them to replace corn in their own diet, but also traded the flour with other nomadic tribes and even with the riverine tribes, who apparently welcomed a change from their usual corn meal.

The other wild plant food which became a trade item was

chokecherries in the form of flat, round cakes dried in the sun. To prepare these cakes, Cheyenne women pounded the cherries to pulp, seeds and all, and fashioned them into cookie-shaped patties about 3–4 inches in diameter. Prepared in this manner, dried chokecherries did not spoil as easily as other fruits and berries, and the patties were hard and did not crumble when carried in parfleches. These chokecherry cakes are still prepared in a traditional way and traded among the tribes of the Great Plains as special, traditional foods.

In their seasonal movements across the plains, the Cheyennes were guided not merely by their search for buffaloes, but also by a desire to harvest the tubers and berries mentioned above when they were ripe, and before they spoiled or were eaten by animals. In general, they tried to schedule their hunting and collecting activities to maximize the overall quantity and variety in their diet, and to secure food items which could be traded. Beginning in spring, the first food quest was usually a buffalo hunt, as soon as the horses were recovered from the hardship of winter. This was followed by the collection of minor berry crops and then the harvest of prairie turnips in June, which required several weeks. Chokecherries began to mature in July and August, followed by Jerusalem artichokes in late summer and buffaloberries after the first frost. Although buffaloes were hunted opportunistically all summer, another major hunt was in the fall, after plant foods were put away. This hunt was usually conducted at the band level and was not on the scale of the huge communal hunts of the spring.

If all the hunting and collecting had been successful, the Cheyennes were set for the winter. It only remained to break into family groups and find some secluded pasture along a creek or river. Although plains winters were harsh, protection from the storms could be found among the trees of the riverine forests, and camp could be moved during the periodic warm spells of winter if necessary. Since the entire camp was mobile, an extended family could pack up and move 20–50 miles in a few warm days, leaving behind their exhausted winter pasture, as well as their own garbage, camp refuse, and human waste.

Robes and Hides

When a family group was settled in for an extended period, one of the primary activities was tanning buffalo robes, since the process requires access to running water and a week or more of continuous work. Although the Cheyennes originally prepared buffalo robes for their own use, in the early 19th century these robes became their most important item of trade with Americans. This was because European buffaloes, bears, and other wild animals had become nearly extinct as sources of furry robes. The American buffalo robes, like the robes made from the European bison or wisent, were used on beds or as lap robes in the open wagons and carriages of the day. Looking for a new source of robes, commercial interests began to buy large quantities of raw buffalo hides and native-tanned robes from Plains Indians in the 19th century (Chittenden 1935; Gregg 1968(1844)). In the years 1830–50, it was the tanned and decorated robes which attracted attention, not the rawhides.

By that time, Cheyenne women had developed a technology for making robes which was very clever, although labor intensive (Grinnell 1962: vol. 2, 213–17; Mooney 1903). To make a robe, they preferred the skin of a buffalo killed in the fall, which had not only long, black, glossy guard hairs, but also a warm, reddish-brown undercoat. They also preferred a whole skin, although they would later trim off the edges where holes had been made to stake out the hide, and where it could not be properly scraped or tanned. The initial work on a fresh hide had to be accomplished quickly, before it spoiled and the hair became loose. When cut from the buffalo, the rawhide was simply folded up with the hair outside and brought back to camp. Ideally, in the next day or two, it was staked out for fleshing while still moist.

The hide was not staked out directly on the ground but several inches above it, on chokecherry pegs which had a notch near the top to hold the hide in the proper position. With the hide suspended on the stakes, it could be fleshed or scraped without touching the ground and thereby risking damage when caught between the ground and a sharp-edged scraper. Suspended under some tension, the hide continually stretched, and so the women

Figure 3.7 Tanning buffalo skins as portrayed by a Cheyenne artist: scraping and thinning the skin with an elk-horn scraper (top left); cracking bones to remove marrow (top right); dressing the skin to give it a proper texture (bottom left); softening the skin by pulling it over a rope tied to a post (bottom right) (Mooney Sketch Book No. 2, Anthropological Archives, Smithsonian Institution)

working on the skins had to periodically move the stakes further and further apart. Hides could also be stretched on a frame for work, as shown in a drawing made by a Cheyenne artist (figure 3.7).

Fleshing could be done with a variety of tools made of bone,

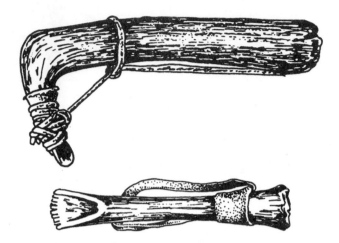

Figure 3.8   Elk-horn scraper (top) and flesher (redrawn by Wenqiu Zhang from Nagy n.d.: 106)

stone or steel, all of which had smooth, dull, and serrated working edges (figure 3.8). The purpose of fleshing was to remove the "fleshy" parts of the buffalo from the skin. This especially included the sticky, translucent tissue which connected the skin to the body, as well as any adhering meat, fat, and blood vessels. The fleshing tool was designed to work its way between these undesirable parts and the surface of the skin, which is very homogeneous and light-colored in appearance when exposed. When all the flesh had been removed from the hide, it was allowed to dry completely in the sun to prepare it for scraping. When the skin was dry it became very hard and essentially consisted of rawhide with the hair still attached. Modern Cheyenne women who still tan skins say that the skin at this stage "still has the glue in it."

Before the tanning solution could be applied, the skin had to be scraped and grained. The scraping was done in aboriginal times with an "elk-horn scraper" which was built around the carved fork of an elk's antler, to which was lashed a sharp blade, originally of flint but later of steel (figure 3.8, plate 3.8). With this tool, the skin was scraped down to a uniform thickness, especially thinning the thick skin at the hump and shoulders. The progress of the thinning was checked periodically by wetting

Plate 3.8 A Southern Cheyenne woman with an elk-horn scraper, about 1900 (Grinnell Collection, Museum of the American Indian)

the skin in one spot and pinching it to see how thick it was. The purpose of the scraping was to make sure the tanning solution could penetrate entirely through the skin, and to make sure that the finished robe would be equally supple everywhere.

Tanning is essentially a chemical process for turning the "glue" of the skin into substances which either are flexible or will crumble as powder from the skin when it is rubbed and twisted in its final stages of preparation. The tanning solution used by Cheyennes consisted entirely of natural products of the plains – brains, liver, soapweed, urine, and grease. Before the tanning solution was applied, the skin was grained – rubbed with a rough bone, stone, or piece of metal – to rough up the slick places created by the scraping and to allow the tanning solution to penetrate easily through the skin. After the solution was applied and rubbed in by hand, the robe was folded up overnight to prevent its drying out. Next day the skin was laid out again on stakes, allowed to dry, and checked by folding and scratching to see if the tanning had been even. If not, it was grained and treated again.

When the tanning was judged to be complete, the skin was rinsed with water to remove the excess tanning solution, dried, and then "worked" by being rubbed, bare side down, over poles, bones, or a rope, as shown in figure 3.7. The purpose of "working" was to allow the "glue" loosened or transformed by tanning to fall out of the skin as a powder or as tiny grains. Some of this material stays in the hide but is so broken and crumpled by the "working" that the skin is nonetheless supple. The powder contributes to the white color of the skin side of the completed robe. After many hours of working, the robe is judged to be finished, and the outside edge is trimmed off to make a symmetrical robe with the back of the buffalo in the center. The robe could then be sold as it was or decorated with quillwork, beads, or paint.

Sometimes raw folded buffalo hides were traded to other tribes who did not have good access to buffaloes, and in the mid 19th century large quantities of such hides were traded to American merchants. To store or transport a rawhide, it could not simply be folded up as it was removed from the buffalo, both because the inside surfaces would stick together, and because a wet, folded hide would spoil from bacterial action. To preserve it and fold it properly, a rawhide was first laid out to dry completely, hair side down, until it was hard and stiff. To fold it for transport, it was wet with water at the creases and folded over into a small rectangular package, hair side out. The creases soon dried out without harm to the hide. To unfold a hide properly, water had to be applied at the creases. Then the whole hide could be soaked in water and staked out for fleshing and scraping as described above. If Cheyenne women did not want to proceed immediately with tanning a skin after skinning and butchering a buffalo, they could dry and fold it to work on later.

Elk, deer, and otter skins were tanned in much the same manner as above, except that elk skins were usually dehaired and smoked when finished to give them a beautiful brown-orange color, and deer skins were dehaired and worked diligently until they turned white and were as supple as silk. Otter skins were often tanned with the hair on, cut into strips, and worked into hair braids. When Cheyennes lived in skin tipis, hairless buffalo skins, as a final step, could be worked through a hole made in the buffalo scapula, or shoulder blade, until the skin was nearly white. These skins, when tempered with white clay or baked selenite, gave Cheyenne tipis their unique white appearance.

Before they obtained cloth through trading, clothing was made of tanned leather, from the very lightest antelope skins to heavy buffalo skins. Men wore a breechclout of deer or elk skin, hanging over a belt in front and back so that it could serve as an outer garment. Women wore a breechclout which was of lighter material, and did not hang so far over the belt. As an outer garment, they wore a dress of elk or deer skin which hung just below the knees. In colder weather, men added a buck-skin or elk-skin shirt, while both men and women wore leggings tied to the belt (see figure 3.9). Moccasins were of two designs, one of ankle length for winter and low moccasins for summer.

The major protection against the cold, however, was the buffalo robe, which was not only a cover for the bed but was worn as a blanket or cape around the camp. There were many different kinds and sizes of buffalo robes, some with hair, some without, some highly decorated, some not, and each adult had to have at least one robe. Beds frequently had two or more robes, some under the sleeper and some on top. When temperatures in the northern plains went below zero degrees Fahrenheit, people did not stir much from their beds, except to tend the fire.

In addition to manufacturing skins for clothing, the skins and body parts of many other animals were and are often preserved to be worn by men for religious purposes, but these items are usually just spread or arranged into the desired configuration and dried in the sun with no special tanning. Items prepared in this way include eagle and hawk wings, stuffed crows and ravens, porcupine tails for combs, woodpecker heads, bear claws and feet, and the head skins of various mammals. To protect skins and hair from insects, they are stored in cedar boxes and occasionally exposed to the sun for a day at a time.

Minerals and Other Resources

Before they received metal as trade goods, the Cheyennes depended on flint to make their sharp-edged tools and weapons. Although obsidian, flint, and chert are common on the plains, they can be quarried easily in only a few locations. If a tribe could not enter a flint-mining area because of hostilities with the local tribe, they had to trade for the flint. There are no traditions

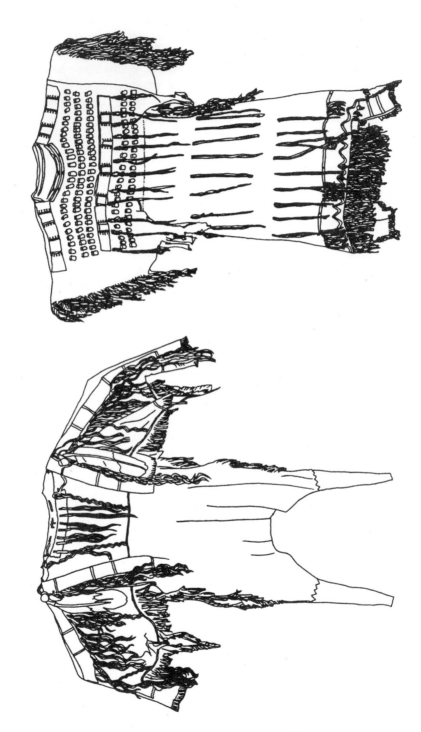

Figure 3.9   Man's shirt and woman's dress (drawn by Wenqiu Zhang-from photographs in Conn 1961)

of flint-mining among the Cheyennes, so they apparently obtained their materials only by trade. Flint was usually received in the form of cores or flakes which Cheyenne craftsmen would work into tools of their own design.

Other minerals were required for Cheyenne ceremonies, especially red Catlinite to make ceremonial pipes, a material which was mined in south-western Minnesota by Dakota Indians, who traded the soft, moist stone wrapped in deer or elk skins continually sprinkled with water. The Cheyenne carver also kept the stone wet while he worked on it. When dried, the stone becomes very hard and can be polished, and is very difficult to wet again clear through.

Cheyenne ceremonies also require colorful mineral paints for the body and for decorated robes, tipis, and tipi liners. Cheyenne white paint, which they loosely refer to as "mica," is in fact a form of gypsum, called selenite, which is found in exposed beds in the southern Great Plains. The bright red paint pigment used in aboriginal times is red ochre or hematite, the best of which comes from northern New Mexico. The best blue paint pigments and yellow ochre come from the Black Hills.

There was also an aboriginal trade in fossils, odd-shaped stones, and archaeological artifacts among Plains Indians. These materials were used for ritual purposes and are prominent in Cheyenne medicine bags. Fossil materials especially include teeth, tusks, and horns, but also shells. Odd-shaped stones come especially from the gravel beds of swift-moving streams in the Rocky Mountains, and Cheyennes favored those which resembled animals and birds. Archaeological artifacts particularly include arrowheads and lance points washed into streams from archaeological sites. Also, the skulls of antique species of buffaloes, such as *bison antiquus* and *bison occidentalis*, were sought at ancient buffalo jumps, since the skulls and huge, wide-spreading horns are much more impressive than those of the living bison. Because of their respect for and avoidance of the dead, Cheyennes did not dig for human-made artifacts, although they dug for the paints they needed. When toys shaped like animals became available in the 20th century, many were purchased by medicine people and included in medicine bundles. Even now, medicine people buy glass and plastic animals for use in serious rituals.

Wood for bows was required by Cheyenne bowyers and

hunters. The two most desirable species were the Rocky Mountain juniper (*Juniperus scopulorum*), colloquially called a cedar, and the Osage orange (*Maclura pomifera*), colloquially called bois d'arc or bodark, both of which have ranges on the borders of the plains, the former where the central Rockies meet the plains in the present states of Wyoming and Colorado, and the Osage orange on the south-eastern border of the plains in Missouri, Arkansas, Oklahoma, and Texas. In both cases, the wood was traded as bundles of unfinished staves. Cheyenne bowyers either carved and tillered these staves into a single one-piece or "self" bow, or else made a compound bow by combining strips of wood with horn and sinew (Wallentine 1988; Laubin 1980); the horn was obtained by trade from Rocky Mountains tribes. Sometimes finished bows were received from Shoshone craftsmen.

The Yearly Cycle

Human societies in general, especially those which hunt and gather, name their seasons and their months in terms of the natural events which are important to their culture. In English we preserve some of these sentiments in our terms for "spring," when new leaves, buds, and sprouts "spring" from the earth or from dormant branches, and "fall," the season when leaves and fruit "fall" from the trees. In the Cheyenne case, the annual cycle was usually divided into six to eight seasons (Glenmore & Leman 1984: 194–5). There has been some variation in the names used for these seasons, and there are periodic attempts to simplify or elaborate them to make them correspond to the 'white man's' four seasons or twelve months, but the translations of the original eight names of the seasons are approximately as follows:

New Leaves and Berries	March–April
Animals Getting Fat	May–June
Fruit Season	July–August
Animals Breeding	September
Dust in the Face	October
Ice Forming	November

| Cold, Hard Faces | December |
| Hoop Games | January–February |

The most important social transition for the Cheyenne people was in spring, the season of New Leaves and Berries, when the dispersed extended families left their winter camps and gathered at some pre-arranged location, formed a tribal circle with their tipis, conducted a massive buffalo hunt, and held their annual ceremonies. Following that, there was a period of large-scale warfare to establish territories or take revenge against aggressive neighbors. The tribe then split into bands of several hundred people each, who followed some recognized, successful leader through the summer and fall months of smaller-scale hunting and collecting, the season of Animals Getting Fat and the Fruit Season.

During these seasons, each band would return to its own recognized territory, usually the valley or drainage area of a particular river (see map 6.1 on page 147). While other Cheyenne bands were welcome to hunt in this territory, it was generally recognized that the home band had first rights to the plant, animal, and mineral resources of the area. This was the area where the women knew exactly where the useful wild plants were located, and the hunters knew where local, non-migratory game like deer and elk were likely to be found. On the basis of this local knowledge, the band augmented the food resources gained in the spring communal buffalo hunt, and accumulated special products that could be exchanged with relatives in other bands, or traded to foreign tribes.

In late summer the Cheyennes would go horse-raiding against the horse-rich tribes to their south, followed by a period of intensive trade and traveling when the dust would blow in their faces, the seasons of Animals Breeding and Dust in the Face. Although some trade was conducted throughout the year, the intensive trade was in the fall and early winter, when the various bands and tribes were rich with the produce of the summer and fall. As the Ice Forming and Cold, Hard Faces seasons came on, the extended families of 20–50 people would once again disperse to some sheltered spot along one of the creeks or rivers of the plains, waiting for spring and for yet another repetition of the annual cycle.

4

Trade and Politics

Plains Indian history has suffered a great deal from interpretations which emphasize which tribe had the greatest leaders, which was the bravest, or which had the best horsemen. While it is true that such factors might influence the outcome of certain battles, alliances, or treaties, the long-term sequence of events on the plains depended much more on concrete factors such as the location of each tribe, its population, its productive capabilities, and its access to trade – the factors emphasized in "geopolitics" and "political economy."

It is hard to exaggerate the importance of European trade for the histories of Plains Indian societies, beginning in the 18th century. Without European-made guns, the tribes could never have initiated the patterns of warfare which affected all the tribes of the plains and surrounding areas. Without a market for their horses and buffalo robes in the colonial and European economies, the plains tribes could not have traded these commodities for the guns, kettles, and other goods they came to depend on. Although the plains tribes were located far away from Europe and the American colonies, they were not unaffected by events in those economic spheres. Had it not been for the disappearance of European sources of robes, the trade in buffalo robes would not have boomed; or if the wool market in Europe had permitted the manufacture of cheap, thick blankets for carriage robes and beds, the trade in buffalo hides from America would have collapsed. Concerning horses, if the Mexicans had been free to trade with Louisiana, there would have been no horse shortage in the area of the Lower Mississippi, or if California and Oregon had not been opened to American immigrants, there would have been no horse market in St Louis selling mounts and draft horses to wagon trains setting out on the Oregon and Santa Fe Trails. But as it happened, the demands for both robes and horses were increasing at the time the Cheyennes entered the plains, and they entered by a geographical route where they could assume a central role as this trade developed (Chittenden 1902; Phillips 1961). The particular role taken by the Cheyennes, however, cannot be understood without a general discussion of the geography of the plains, plains tribes, and the historical events of the 18th and 19th centuries. Cheyenne culture did not develop in a vacuum, but in response to other cultures and other peoples in the same area. The tribe was merely one among several characters who played off one another in a great historical drama which included 20 or more other tribes, the traders and trappers of three European countries, and powerful armies comprising thousands of Indian warriors and uniformed soldiers. All of this was set in a breathtaking landscape of immense distances, powerful rivers, towering mountains, and forbidding deserts.

Plains Geography and Geopolitics

Except on its western boundary, which is the Rocky Mountains, the grasslands of the Great Plains have fuzzy edges (map 4.1). Toward the south-west, in northern New Mexico and West Texas, the plains gradually fade out into desert, except for scattered mountainous areas which constitute oases of water, grass, and wild game all the way from southern Colorado to northern Mexico. Toward the east and south-east, in what is now Texas, Oklahoma, and Kansas, the plains are bounded intermittantly by crosstimbers and thick scrub, and penetrated periodically by fingers of deciduous forest along rivers which stretch from the eastern woodlands. These riverine or "riparian" forests continually broaden and gradually merge as one travels east, until they constitute a continual and complete forest only passable to horses by following certain discrete and restricted roads and trails, in what are now the states of Arkansas, Missouri, Iowa, and Minnesota. Toward the north and north-west, in Montana and the Dakotas, the plains become wetter,

*Map 4.1 Schematic map of the major rivers and landforms of the
Great Plains*

with more and more timbered areas around ponds, lakes, and permanent streams, until one reaches uninterrupted expanses of aspen and pine forest in Canada, where canoes rather than horses become the preferred means of transportation (Webb 1931; Kraenzel 1955).

Map 4.1 shows the major rivers and landforms of the Great Plains, especially in the areas where the Cheyennes lived in the 18th and 19th centuries. It is essentially a myth that the plains are treeless or featureless, although one can find areas in eastern Colorado or western Kansas where there is not a hill or a tree in sight. But the riparian forests form stringers of deciduous growth all the way across the plains from east to west, especially along the Missouri, Platte, and Arkansas Rivers, and there are forested hills, mountains, and escarpments scattered throughout the prairies. Even in the Texas and Oklahoma panhandles there are scattered groves of Ponderosa pine. Typically, even in areas of low rainfall, such as the Wichita Mountains, the run-off from mountains and cliffs enables trees to grow wherever there is convergent drainage.

The permanent rivers which cross the plains are very different from one another. At one extreme, the Missouri is one of the major rivers of the world, occupying a drainage trough which in some places is several miles wide, with an enormous flow of water, huge annual floods, tiers of natural terraces along the sides, occasional steep cliff faces at the water's edge, and large groves of hardwood and softwood riparian forests. At the other extreme, the Niobrara in northern Nebraska is hard to see until you are right upon it – a small, deep, swift-flowing, steep-banked river which the Cheyennes called "The Surprise River." Another unique river is the Platte, where most of the water flow is underground, through miles and miles of deep, porous sand. The Arkansas River and the South Canadian River are much like the Platte, but smaller, and they are discontinuous during the dry part of the year, flowing entirely underground in some places. The Cimarron River is even dryer than these, and for most of its course, most of the time, it is a river of sand. Indian people, however, knew where to dig in the sand to find water for themselves and their horses. After the spring rains, sandy riverbeds like the Platte, Arkansas, Cimarron, and South Canadian swirled with quicksand and were dangerous to cross. In modern times these rivers are still dangerous; each year livestock as well as careless people and their vehicles are lost in the shifting, flowing quicksand.

The wide, timbered plains rivers, as well as the forested mountains and hills, were desirable camping areas, although some of them also constituted barriers to travel. Other barriers were presented by areas which are rough and rocky, or heavily eroded, such as the Canadian Breaks or the Dakota Badlands, which were hard to travel across and thus tended to deflect equestrian traffic out onto the level plains. Consequent to all these factors, certain convenient routes across the plains became heavily traveled by Indian people, although they were not "roads" comparable to the Indian roads and pathways of the eastern woodlands. Only after wagon traffic began along the Oregon and Santa Fe Trails could one detect permanent road-ways on the plains, except for the deep pathways worn by buffaloes in their travels from grass to water and back to grass. When European immigrants first came onto the plains, they soon discovered that these "buffalo roads" did not necessarily lead to any place that humans wanted to go.

Peoples of the Plains

Those Native American tribes who arrived earliest on the plains naturally took for themselves the most desirable territories. The Middle Missouri was a prime location, and when the Cheyennes arrived there in the middle 18th century the area had been continuously occupied by Indian farmers for over a thousand years. The advantage of the location was the opportunity to engage in horticulture on the fertile natural terraces of the Missouri, with vast supplies of timber nearby for firewood. There were also defensive possibilities offered by the steep riverbanks, to protect one side of a fortified village, and there were opportunities for trade up and down the river. But when horses became available, the Middle Missouri agriculturists discovered that pasture opportunities along the Middle Missouri were somewhat limited. When the Cheyennes arrived there, the occupants of the prime locations of the Great Bend of the Missouri were the Mandans and Hidatsas, both Siouan-speaking groups. The Mandans had been on the Missouri for about 400 years and the Hidatsas somewhat less, perhaps 300 years (see map 4.2).[1]

South of the Great Bend, various tribes representing the Caddoan language family had been practicing agriculture along plains rivers for a long time. The most northerly of the Caddoan tribes were the Arikaras, who had separated from the Pawnees somewhat earlier to occupy villages spread from about the mouth of the Cheyenne River to the mouth of the Platte. The Pawnees, a complex and populous assortment of Caddoan-speaking tribes, lived mainly on the Loup River, west of the Missouri and right in the midst of the buffalo herds, although they had earlier lived further east and south, on the Republican River. The Wichitas, known for their grass houses, and the Caddoes, who are more properly considered south-eastern woodland Indians, lived even further south, as shown on the map. The Caddoes, like the Mandans, Hidatsas, Arikaras, and Pawnees, lived in earthen lodges most of the year, although they kept tipis to use in summer when they went buffalo hunting.

Of the fully nomadic buffalo hunters whom the Cheyennes met on the Great Plains in 1780, the Blackfeet and Apaches had probably been there the longest. In fact it is thought that both tribes had originally been pedestrian buffalo hunters on the plains before they acquired horses (Hyde 1959; Wood & Liberty 1980). In the case of the Blackfeet, known in Canadian documents as "Blackfoot," they managed to stay in the same territory after the arrival of horses, taking advantage of their position on the edge of the north-western plains to exploit both mountain and prairie resources. By contrast, the Apaches soon found themselves pushed out of the central plains and to the south-west by the Comanches, linguistic cousins of the Utes and Shoshones, who streamed out of the mountains onto the plains to acquire horses and hunt buffaloes beginning in the late 17th century. The Kiowas, who originated somehow among the Pueblo Indians of northern New Mexico, originally emigrated as horse nomads all the way to the northern part of the plains in the late 17th or early 18th centuries, where they allied themselves with a group of Athapaskan-speakers known as the "Kiowa-Apaches." Later, they too were driven south by the new arrivals on the plains.

The Crows had hived off from the Hidatsas about AD

Map 4.2   Locations of major tribes and their populations, about 1780 (after Ubelaker 1992)

1000–1200, and migrated west to an especially benevolent region of the grasslands called the Big Horn Basin. From this position they traded intensively with the Hidatsas in a manner which has been described as "symbiotic." That is, each group could not survive without the other, the Hidatsas depending on the Crows for meat and buffalo products while the Crows depended on the Hidatsas for agricultural produce. The Assiniboins, like the Crows and Hidatsas, represented the Siouan language family, but they had taken a more northerly route onto the plains in the 18th century and did not farm. They became a major factor in the fur trade as it developed in Canada, both in the woodlands around Lake Winnipeg and onto the plains along the Saskatchewan River.

Close cousins of the Assiniboins, linguistically, were the Dakotas and Lakotas, who came onto the plains at about the same time, although by a more southerly route from Minnesota. These tribes, each of which had important divisions and sub-tribes, were closely allied among themselves and cooperated in making war against contiguous groups. In modern usage, the term "Lakota" is used for the more westerly groups, also called the Teton. In some historical documents the term "Dakota" is used to designate the western as well as the eastern groups. The "Dakota" language of the eastern groups is only dialectically different from Lakota, and typically has a "d" sound where Lakota has an "l." Collectively they also appear in early documents as the "Sioux," which is what the Chippewas called them, and in the 18th century they were a numerous and aggressive group just entering the plains. By the beginning of the 19th century they had become the most important group on the northern plains, politically and militarily. The Lakotas or Tetons ultimately moved to the Black Hills and west, while some of the Dakota groups remained as far east as Minnesota.

Around the edges of the Great Plains lived a number of tribes who were not full-time residents of the grasslands, but came there seasonally to hunt buffaloes. All of these, such as the Osages to the east, the Utes and Shoshones to the west, the plateau tribes to the north-west, and the Crees and Chippewas to the north-east, had other seasonal concerns which kept them beyond the plains for much of the year. For the plateau peoples, their other main concerns were the annual salmon runs from the Pacific Ocean and horse husbandry, which they pursued in the

mild climates of the Snake and Columbia River valleys of Idaho
and Oregon. Appaloosa horses were first developed by one of
these plateau tribes, the Nez Percé. The Crees and Chippewas to
the north-east of the plains were north of the corn line and were
not horticultural, and in winter they hunted the forests for
moose, caribou, and other game, harvested berries, and
especially trapped beavers for trade with Europeans. Later,
portions of both groups became full-time buffalo hunters,
dubbed the "Plains Cree" and "Plains Chippewa," respectively.
Here again there is a difference between Canadian and US
nomenclature. In many Canadian documents, the term "Ojibwa"
is substituted for "Chippewa," referring to the same people.

The Osages and related Dhegiha and Chiwere tribes in Iowa
and Missouri, all sometimes called "southern Sioux," were
somewhat agricultural and scheduled their buffalo hunting
around the demands of their gardens, as the Cheyennes had done
in earlier times. The Osages in particular became notorious
traders and raiders. With a population of about 7,000, they
enjoyed military advantages over all their neighbors except the
Dakotas. To secure territorial and trading privileges, they raided
tribes far out onto the plains, as far as Texas.

Map 4.2 shows the populations as well as the locations of
Plains Indian tribes at the time the Cheyennes became full-time
pastoral nomads, about 1780. The relative numbers are important because they indicate the approximate economic and military
strengths of the various groups. For the agricultural groups, the
population of women indicated the tribe's capacity to produce
corn and vegetables for trade. For the nomadic groups, the
population of women was directly related to the amount of
jerked meat, prairie turnips, and buffalo robes available for
trade. For all groups, the number of men was related to their
military strength, although military strength also depended on
the number and quality of war horses, as well as organizational
and psychological factors which we will discuss in the next
chapter. For the nomadic groups, the number of warriors was
taken to be approximately two per tipi, or about one third of the
total population, figures which excluded women, children, and
old men.

Map 4.2 shows that the Cheyennes suffered a serious disadvantage of numbers when they first entered the Great Plains.
They were a small group, and could not afford to confront such

formidable military forces as the Blackfeet or Assiniboins. Also, even though they were long-time allies of the Lakotas, they could not afford to stand in their way as the Lakotas expanded westward across the Missouri and into the Black Hills. But the Cheyennes developed a brilliant solution to their military and geopolitical problems, as we shall see.

Patterns of Trade

During the 18th century, the centers of trade on the northern plains were the villages of the Middle Missouri horticulturists – the closely allied Mandans and Hidatsas at the Great Bend and the Arikaras to the south (Jablow 1951). The basis of their trade was agricultural produce, which they exchanged with plains nomads for horses and the products of the hunt, especially jerky and robes. These tribes traded horses, robes, meat and agricultural products to the woodland tribes toward the north-east and to the French, supplies which helped support the personnel of the fur trade. In the 18th century, the fur trade on the northern plains was contested between the French, trading from Montreal through the Great Lakes and its tributaries, and the Hudson's Bay Company, which traded up the rivers flowing into Hudson's Bay, which notably included the Red River of the north and the Saskatchewan River (see map 4.1).

In the south, the Wichitas were the nexus of trade, supported by resident French traders in a major trading town located in northern Texas where the Wichita River flows from the south into the Red River, east of the modern city of Wichita Falls, Texas (Hoig 1993; Kenner 1969). In addition, there was an east–west trade in horses and agricultural produce farther to the south between the Comanches and the Caddoes (map 4.2). The Comanches in the early 18th century also captured members of enemy tribes for a slave trade which developed among the tribes living in Texas, Louisiana, and New Mexico. Military affairs on the southern plains were dominated by the Comanches, who constituted a formidable barrier to trade between Louisiana and Mexico, and to any European occupation of the whole area between the major French trading post at Natchidoches, in

Louisiana, and the Spanish settlements in south-western Texas and New Mexico.

Map 4.3 shows the locations of the permanent trading posts and sedentary villages of the Great Plains and surrounding areas. In addition, it shows the locations of traditional "rendezvous" areas which were dominated by Indian–Indian trade, although European traders were increasingly present at these affairs in the 18th century. At these locations, certain tribes gathered annually to exchange their products, to feast together, and sometimes to arrange strategic marriages among the sons and daughters of chiefs of different tribes.

Although it was not on the plains, the Dalles Rendezvous generated several significant items for the plains trade. Located at a constriction of the Columbia River where salmon fishing was easy, the rendezvous was held in the fall and attracted many of the coastal, plateau, great basin, and even plains tribes. The items traded included jerky, buffalo robes, deer and elk skins, bows made of horn, clothing, shells from the Pacific Ocean, dried salmon, fish oil, root and seed foods, and later, horses and guns. The Shoshones traded at Dalles, as did various plateau tribes who hunted seasonally on the plains, and the Shoshones also sponsored their own rendezvous in the spring, in their home territory in what is now south-western Wyoming. The Shoshone Rendezvous attracted a large number of plains tribes, most notably the Crows, who in turn traded items from the Dalles Rendezvous, via the Shoshone Rendezvous, to their Hidatsa brethren on the Middle Missouri. From there certain items, especially shells, oils, and other luxury goods, were traded to the tribes of the central and north-eastern plains, such as the Assiniboins, Lakotas, and Arikaras.

The Lakotas and Dakotas also had a traditional annual rendezvous, back toward the east originally at the Falls of St Anthony, near the present site of Minneapolis-St Paul, but later moved to the Minnesota River, the site of Jonathan Carver's visit in 1766. Here the plains hunters exchanged horses, jerky, robes, and other products of the hunt for European goods as well as for agricultural and forest produce from the woodland tribes. One reason for the success of the Lakotas in expanding their territory out onto the plains was the maintenance of a secure source of European goods, especially guns and powder, in Minnesota.

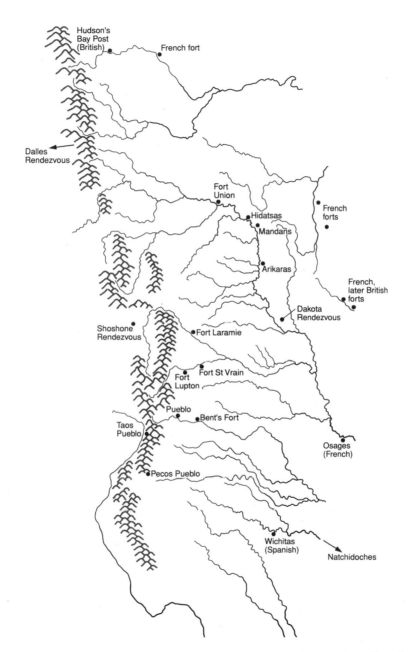

Map 4.3 Locations of major trade centers in the late 18th and early 19th centuries

At the south-west edge of the plains, Taos Pueblo had long entertained plains hunters at its annual trade fair, which still continues every summer in modern times, both for Indian–Indian trade and for tourist entertainment. At an earlier time, the Pecos Pueblo in eastern New Mexico at the edge of the plains was a center for trade between Pueblo Indians and plains hunters. With the coming of the Spanish, trade between Pueblo Indians and Plains Indians became even more important, since European goods became available at the pueblos. But the Spanish, Mexican, and New Mexican governments did not allow guns to be traded to Indians. The guns of Spanish manufacture which appeared on the plains were not obtained in open trade, but were rather stolen during Plains Indian raids on Spanish settlements, or else obtained in an illicit trade with "Comancheros," semi-legal merchants who traveled out onto the plains from Texas and New Mexico to trade with the southern tribes, especially the Comanches. We should note in passing that Plains Indians have traditionally recognized a difference in nationality between the colonists who began to fill up the area near the Gulf Coast, in Texas and western Louisiana, whom they called "Texans," and the people who lived along the Rio Grande, whom they called "Mexicans" whether they were Spanish, Mexicans, or Pueblo Indians. The term "American" was reserved for migrants from the east who settled across Kansas, Nebraska and the Dakotas.

The major, permanent French presence on the southern plains was at Natchidoches, where the official policy of the French government, and later the Spanish government, from 1762 to 1800, was represented through an Indian agent. Elsewhere in the southern and central plains, although the traders occasionally built forts and trading posts, the French presence was mobile. The traders tended to move around year to year in response to patterns of alliance and enmity among their client tribes. The permanent French establishments for the Missouri River trade were much farther east, at Cahokia and St Genevieve, near what is now St Louis, Missouri.

Across Canada, French trade was originally organized from Montreal and from trading posts in the Great Lakes area, all the way to the Pacific Ocean. In general, the social backbone of French trade was the group of hardy, waterborne traders known as voyageurs. Setting out in the spring with canoes or pirogues full of trade goods, French traders undertook to return in the fall with boats and rafts loaded with beaver skins and other products of Indian labor. If they had to winter in Indian territory, they preferred to stay with the Indians, supplementing their store of furs by continual trading. Sometimes the traders arranged to meet with Indian groups at designated spots where trade could safely be conducted.

French trade was especially significant with the Osages, who insisted on maintaining a middleman role between the French on the lower Missouri and the plains tribes. At various times the Osages were at war with all their neighbors, as well as with the French, to maintain their hegemony in Missouri and what is now eastern Kansas and north-eastern Oklahoma. As a numerous, powerful tribe, the "imperial Osages" sought to control the trade in French goods on the southern tributaries of the Missouri, and on the Arkansas River where it turns south from Kansas into Oklahoma and becomes a large, permanent, navigable waterway.

After a treaty signed in Paris in 1763, the Missouri River Valley was added to Spanish territory, and Canada became British instead of French. At first, this had little consequence for plains trade, which was conducted mostly by the same French traders from New Orleans, St Louis, and Montreal, although operating under Spanish or British franchises. In the north, however, the British-controlled Hudson's Bay Company soon displaced French traders, trading from their permanent trading posts on the Saskatchewan, as shown on map 4.3. By 1780, both the French traders and the Hudson's Bay Company had permanent trading posts on the northern plains.

The Louisiana Purchase of 1803 brought the whole Missouri–Mississippi drainage under United States control, and meant that both French and British traders were displaced from the center of the Great Plains, although the British continued to trade from Canada, and the Spanish from Texas and New Mexico. The Lewis and Clark Expedition of 1804–6 and the Atkinson Expedition of 1825 both undertook to organize and mobilize Plains Indians for American purposes so that they would (1) inhabit particular territories recognized by the US, (2) trade only with American traders and only at designated places, and (3) arrest or expel any Spanish or French traders who entered territory claimed by the US.

The earliest items produced by native labor which attracted European interest, beginning in the early 17th century, were beaver pelts, from which the fur was shaved to make felt hats in Europe and America. Since beavers are forest animals, requiring permanent streams and softwood trees for food (aspens, poplars), the trade in beaver pelts mostly bypassed the plains. From among the Plains Indians during their equestrian period, only the Blackfeet and Assiniboins trapped beavers to any significant extent. This was because beaver trapping, for most tribes, was incompatible with a nomadic style of life. Beaver trapping was accomplished by setting out a line of traps several miles along mountain streams where beaver dams and houses were found. To exhaust the beaver supply along a trap line required several weeks or months of work, visiting the traps daily, or at least every few days. The nomadic buffalo hunters could not afford to stay in one place that long. For one thing, the small pastures of mountain grass were usually grazed to the ground in a few weeks, and the nomads had to move constantly to follow the buffaloes and exploit the berry and root crops they depended on. So it was only on the fringes of the northern plains that certain tribes could figure out how to schedule beaver trapping among the other activities which were important to their economy. Generally speaking, the beavers of the northern Rocky Mountains were not heavily exploited until the first few decades of the 19th century, when American and Canadian traders and trappers entered the area in large numbers.

Buffalo robes, however, had an entirely different place in the economy of Plains Indians. These were products of an animal that was their prime target in hunting, and they already knew how to produce robes, although not in great numbers. As the number of beavers began to diminish in the 18th century, as well as the demand for beaver pelts, the European traders of the plains area began to turn their attention to acquiring buffalo robes, and they encouraged plains tribes to produce them.

In this period, the French traders from St Louis began to move their trading sites farther down the Missouri River, toward the center of the plains, rather than concentrating their attention on the beaver-producing Missouri tributaries near the Rocky Mountains, in the area of modern Montana. Canadian traders in Manitoba and Alberta were already suitably located, and simply turned their attention from the woodlands to the plains.

In the southern plains, the beaver trade had never been extensive, and the trade in buffalo robes soon surpassed it. After the "factory system" was abolished for Indian trade in United States territories in 1826, American traders were not required to have special franchises and were free to trade with Plains Indians. Consequently, several important American-owned trading posts grew up on the Arkansas, Platte, and Missouri Rivers.

For the Cheyennes, the most important trading post became Bent's Fort on the Arkansas, which has been rebuilt as a historical landmark in its original position near La Junta, Colorado. The importance of this fort and trading post was enhanced by its special relationship to the city of Taos in New Mexico (Lavender 1954; Garrard 1955). After the American occupation of New Mexico in 1846, Charles Bent, long-time trader and resident in Taos, was appointed Governor of New Mexico, while his brother, William Bent, continued to manage Bent's Fort. Mexican goods, especially wool blankets, food, and the remains of the trade in beaver pelts, traveled in this period to Bent's Fort and were either traded to Indians or sent east on the Sante Fe Trail to St Louis. From St Louis came manufactured goods, especially guns and kettles. And from the Plains Indians came buffalo robes and horses, sent east to St Louis, while St Louis goods were sent south-west to New Mexico.

The two most important items traded on the plains, however, were guns and horses, which followed a natural pattern of exchange from south-west to north-east. The pattern was natural because horses bred better and were more numerous in the south-western part of the plains, while guns were only available from French, British, and later, American sources on the north-eastern fringe of the plains. Guns were scarce not only because they were forbidden to the Indian trade by the Spanish colonial government, but also because the Osages and other tribes on the eastern fringe of the plains forbade French and American traders from trading guns to their enemies on the plains proper. The Osages, for example, insisted on their right to inspect all boats going up the Missouri, and they took the guns for themselves, not wanting to arm their enemies, especially the Lakotas and Pawnees. While the Lakotas had their own supply of guns from Minnesota, the Pawnees had none, and suffered terribly in warfare because of this.

Horses owned by Indian tribes on the south-western plains

came from three main sources: (1) raids on domestic herds in Texas, New Mexico, and Mexico, especially those conducted by the Comanches, (2) wild horse herds in eastern Colorado and western Nebraska, and (3) the natural increase of horses held by Indians. In their early days on the northern plains, the Cheyennes had to rely on raiding the Kiowas and Comanches for horses. When they moved further south, the Cheyenne herds were more fertile and produced a net increase in horses each year. When they moved to what is now eastern Colorado, certain bands of Cheyennes became accomplished catchers of the wild horses in that area, trading the captured horses to other bands of Cheyennes, to other tribes, and to Bent's Fort. And last, after the great alliance with the Kiowas, Comanches, and Apaches in 1840, the Cheyennes joined them for horse raids on ranches in Texas and Mexico.

Guns were used mostly for warfare, not hunting, although when revolvers became available just before the Civil War, they were used to kill buffaloes from horseback. The first guns available to Cheyennes were muzzle-loading flintlocks, patterned after the classic French design of 1763. During the 19th century, however, guns with percussion caps and with a breech-loading capability became increasingly available from American sources.

Although patterns of trade were complex on the plains, the trade in horses was generally from the south-west toward the north and east. Guns came from the French in the north and east, and were traded onto the plains toward the west and south. Buffalo robes and hides originated on the plains, and were traded in all directions. Blankets, saddles, and food were traded onto the plains by the Pueblo Indians and their Spanish and Mexican co-residents in New Mexico in a north-eastern direction. Knives, kettles, other metal goods, beads, and many smaller items were traded onto the plains by all the European sources. The most significant of all the items, in terms of dollar value, were guns, horses, and buffalo robes. Toward the end of the 18th century, a gun traded nearly evenly for a good horse at Middle Missouri trading sites, and a gun or a good horse was worth about 6–10 buffalo robes. However, on the southern plains a gun might trade for 6–10 horses, while among the Assiniboins in the north a good horse was worth perhaps 2 or 3 guns. Buffalo robes were worth $2–5 cash at Bent's Fort in the 1830s, but upwards of

$10–20 in St Louis. Plains trade, then, was based on the significance of these differential values, and so was plains warfare.

Corridors of Trade and Warfare

In a classic essay, Patricia Albers has developed a model for explaining the historical patterns of trade and warfare on the plains (Albers 1993).[2] It is not surprising that she finds trade and warfare so closely connected, since this has often been noted on other continents, in other situations. For example, it is beyond debate that both before and after World War II the Japanese were a major trading partner of the United States, and the war was fought, to some extent, to determine which country would enjoy political and economic hegemony on the Pacific Rim. Among geopolitical scholars, the slogan is "You trade with your enemies;" if you defeat your enemy, you can either expel them from trade or dictate to them the terms of exchange. And this was the basis of warfare on the North American Plains.

Yet another myth about American Indians must be dealt with in this context, and that is the idea that each of the plains tribes had "traditional enemies" and "traditional allies." In most cases, a tribe fought both alongside and against all its neighbors some time in its history. For an extreme example, within two years of engaging in genocidal war against the Kiowas at the Battle of Wolf Creek, the Cheyennes were embracing them and giving them guns during the celebration of the great alliance of 1840. It may surprise some to learn that the Cheyennes were heavily intermarried with three of their most intransigent enemies, the Blackfeet, the Pawnees, and the Crows. So the patterns of warfare on the plains must be regarded as temporary and devoted to certain restricted, strategic purposes, rather than being eternal and "traditional."

The purpose of plains warfare, according to Albers, was to dominate certain corridors of trade, each of which was characterized by a "chain" of contiguous tribes trading with one another. For example, there was an east–west corridor of trade along the Missouri between the Dalles Rendezvous and the

Hidatsa villages on the Middle Missouri. Historically, this trade route had been dominated by the Crows, because of their special relationship and shared language with the Hidatsas. Parallel to this corridor, to the north, was another corridor of trade from the Blackfeet to the traders on the Saskatchewan River and east to the woodlands. This was historically dominated by the Blackfeet, but in the 18th and 19th centuries, Atsinas, Assiniboins, and Lakotas migrated onto the plains north of the Black Hills and tried to insert themselves into these trade connections.

To understand the migrations of the Cheyennes and their role in plains history, we must first understand in general the competition among plains tribes for a trading position. Albers uses the analogy of a chain, which I will explain briefly here. In all situations where trade is desirable, an item is worth less where it is produced than it will be worth elsewhere; if this were not the case, no one would have any motivation to trade. In the case of horses, for example, we have seen that a horse was worth perhaps ten times more on the Saskatchewan River than in Texas. Generally speaking, the value of a horse was proportional to its distance from its origins. Each time a horse was traded toward the north-east, then, it became more valuable, and the trader took as profit the difference between what he traded for the horse nearer its origin, and what he got for it when he traded it to someone farther from the origin.

If a horse was traded six times between Texas and Canada, each trader got approximately one sixth of the total difference in value, but if it was traded only three times, then each trader got one third of the difference. And so it was to the advantage of trading tribes to ensure that there were as few links as possible in the chain within which they were trading. Consequently they tried to knock other tribes out of the chain. Before other tribes arrived on the northern plains, both the Crows and the Blackfeet enjoyed maximum profits. But when the Assiniboins, Atsinas, and Lakotas tried to insert themselves into the trade chain, it diminished the profits of the Blackfeet and Crows.

Another strategy of the trade wars north of the Missouri, in addition to knocking competitors out of the chain, was to dominate two different chains of trade, causing them to converge on the dominant trader. This strategy was pursued, for example, by the Assiniboins, who sought to control both the Saskatchewan and Missouri River trade chains by dominating all the trading posts on the north-eastern edge of the plains, so that all goods had to pass through them.

For the tribes who constituted intermediate links on a chain, such as the Atsinas and Lakotas in the late 18th century, and the Plains Crees and Plains Chippewas later, the strategy was both to knock other tribes out of the chain and to control direct access to the trading posts. That is, both here and to the south, where the Cheyennes entered the plains, the goal of all competitors for trade was to minimize the number of links in their own chain, and to occupy locations where different chains of trade converged.

The Cheyenne Solution

Map 4.2 shows that when the Cheyennes first came onto the plains in about 1780, their population was about 3,000 (Ubelaker 1992). The village of Cheyennes burned out at Biesterfeldt probably housed about 900 people, judging from the architecture of the site, and the Cheyenne village in which they took refuge on Porcupine Creek was probably about the same size. For reasons concerning the economy of scale, in fact, nearly all the villages of riverine horticulturists in this period were of about this size. So the combined Cheyennes at Porcupine Creek numbered about 1,800, including about 600 warriors. But circumstances were percolating on the plains which would soon augment these numbers. For one thing, an intermarried band which the Cheyennes had left behind among the Lakotas, known to the Lakotas as the Sheo Band but to the Cheyennes as the Masikota Band, became involved in a dispute with other Lakota bands and joined the Cheyennes west of the Missouri. Soon afterwards, four bands of a tribe speaking a slightly different Algonquian language, the Sutaios, also joined with the Cheyennes, bringing their total numbers up to about 3,000, including 1,000 warriors, enough for a respectable military showing.

The Cheyennes were not alone in trying to augment their numbers in these years. The Kiowas, as we have seen, had taken in the Kiowa-Apaches, and all groups were engaged in capturing the women and children of enemy tribes to increase their own populations. The Comanches and Kiowas began adopting adult Mexican men to augment their own numbers. Some tribes were becoming enriched by trade, warfare was becoming intense, and all parties realized that success in large part depended on how many warriors a tribe could put in the field on a single battlefield.

Unlike some other tribes, most notably the Comanches, the Cheyennes went to great lengths to integrate their bands into a Cheyenne Nation. They inaugurated the Sun Dance, which has the political effect of requiring all allied bands to come together once a year and act out their political and military solidarity; and they had their four sacred arrows, which were the center of elaborate ceremonies of renewal. These arrows were associated with tribal laws which forbade murder among the bands and required them all to make war together once a declaration of war had been legally made. So, unlike other tribes, such as the Lakota, in which a band or division might or might not respect the declaration of war made by other bands, the Cheyennes absolutely required every band to participate. A full-scale war involved "moving the Arrows" against an enemy, and all men, women, and children had to be present at the battle site. Warriors reluctant to participate were beaten or had their tipis burned or their horses killed. By such means the Cheyennes by the end of the 18th century were well on their way to creating a ferocious, disciplined, and efficient war-making machine.

At about this time, the Cheyenne leadership made another geopolitical move which was strategically brilliant and which ultimately ensured their success in carving out a territory on the plains – they concluded an alliance with the Arapahoes. The Arapahoes, like the Cheyennes, suffered a deficiency in numbers. Split off from the Atsinas in about 1700, they were endeavoring to enter the north–south trade chain at the foot of the Rocky Mountains by keeping the Utes and Shoshones at bay within the mountains and separating the Kiowas from their trading partners the Crows. At that time, the Blackfeet were gaining more guns and horses, and were pressing the Crows from the north. The Arapahoes, then, were in a dangerous situation, with no allies nearby and furiously at war with all their neighbors. The Blackfeet, potential allies, were too far away to help, and their Atsina brothers had problems of their own, trying to enter the trade chain along the Saskatchewan by making alliances among the Blackfeet, Crows, and Assiniboins.

Both the Cheyennes and the Arapahoes recognized the advantages of alliance. With a combined force, they could perhaps dominate the trade corridor leading from horse-rich areas near the Arkansas to the villages of the Middle Missouri, at the point where the corridor narrowed between the Rocky Mountains and the Pawnees. Although the Pawnees were not well armed, they were still formidable because they lived in fortified villages and were very numerous. By driving the Kiowas southward, the Cheyennes and Arapahoes could displace them as special trading partners of the Arikaras. This was consistent with the existing Cheyenne alliance with the Lakotas, who were the trading partners of the Arikaras toward the east.

The new alliance between the Cheyennes and Arapahoes had three strategic purposes, the first of which was to gain control of the most productive buffalo pasture on the entire plains, the area from the forks of the Platte south to the Arkansas. Without good access to buffaloes, the tribes would have nothing to eat and only horses to trade. Second, the alliance had to aggressively pursue the existing Arapaho agenda, which was to push back the Utes, Shoshones, and Crows, so that those tribes were forced to participate in either the intermontane trading corridor, north and south through Utah behind the front range of the Rockies, or the Dalles–Hidatsa corridor, roughly along the Upper Missouri River. The third part of the emerging Cheyenne–Arapaho military agenda was to develop a participation with the Lakotas in their invasion westward. This involved cooperating with the Lakotas in their attacks on the Pawnees, while encouraging the Lakotas to help in the Cheyenne–Arapaho effort to push the Kiowas southward.

In the first years of the Cheyenne–Arapaho alliance, the primary area of military activity was on the Upper Platte, where the Shoshones and Utes were accustomed to enter the plains for their seasonal buffalo hunting. The Utes, after some initial battles with the alliance, decided to pursue a more westerly and southerly route onto the plains, along the Upper Arkansas River where they would encounter the Comanches and, later, the Kiowas, instead of the Cheyennes and Arapahoes. The Shoshones in this period were already being punished by the rejuvenated and well-armed Blackfeet, and finally gave up their efforts to become full-time buffalo hunters on the plains. When the Cheyennes moved the sacred arrows against the Shoshones in 1817 to engage them in genocidal warfare, they couldn't find them.

The war against the Kiowas was much easier than expected, simply because the Comanches, who were south of the Kiowas, had decided to invade Texas for a better raiding and trading position between the Spanish settlements, to the south and west, and the Wichitas, Caddoes, and Louisiana, to the north and east. After some initial hostilities between them, the Kiowas settled in with the Comanches as allies in 1790, around and south of the Arkansas. A relatively small group themselves, the Kiowas welcomed an alliance with the Comanches as a protection against the Cheyenne–Arapaho alliance, and as partners for raiding into Mexico. So the Cheyennes had their way in the central plains, beginning to dominate the legitimate trade in horses from the south, as well as continually raiding the southern tribes for horses and dominating the trade southward from the Middle Missouri in guns, kettles, and other goods of European or colonial manufacture.

The Cheyennes, then, caused two of the important trading chains on the plains to converge on themselves. First there was the corridor at the foot of the Rockies from the Kiowas to the Blackfeet: they placed themselves in that chain between the Crows and the Kiowas. And second, there was the more easterly corridor from the Comanches to the Arikaras: here the Cheyennes had to neutralize the Pawnees and enter the chain between the Arikaras and the Pawnees and Kiowas to the south. To maintain their enviable position at the convergence of two chains, however, the Cheyennes and their Arapaho allies had to continually tend to several military chores: (1) they had to keep the Pawnees off the plains and cooped up in their villages on the Loup, (2) they had to keep the Utes, Shoshones, and Crows in place, and (3) they had to discourage the Kiowas and Comanches from hunting or trading north of the Arkansas. Between 1790 and 1840 they accomplished all these goals, and soon the Cheyennes became known among their neighbors not only for their ferocity in war, but for their great wealth as exhibited in the luxury of their tipis and their large horse herds. But several factors were conspiring at about this time to upset the status quo of the plains – these were the unexpected intensity of the trade in buffalo robes, the invasion across the Missouri of their ostensible allies, the Lakotas, and recurring epidemics of infectious disease among the riverine horticulturists. All of these combined to disorder and reorder the pattern of trading chains and military alliances on the plains in the early 19th century.

Invasion and Disease

Whether the Lakotas drove the Cheyennes out of the Black Hills or whether the Cheyennes allowed them in is a matter of dispute among Lakota and Cheyenne elders. This issue arose in 1980 when a group of Lakota traditionalists approached the Northern Cheyenne tribal government, asking them to stake a legal claim to the Black Hills as a way of blocking a proposed payment of $17 million cash to Lakota tribal governments in settlement of the Lakota claim to the Black Hills. The traditionalists did not want the tribal governments to accept the money – they wanted the Black Hills back. The Northern Cheyennes, in turn, hired me to interview Cheyenne elders about their own claim, which resulted in the publication of an ethnohistorical document in 1981 for legal purposes (Moore 1981). My conclusion was that as late as 1840 the Cheyennes were in full possession of the Black Hills, and that if any military actions had accompanied the emigration of the southern bands from the Hills and the Lakota occupancy, it was very little. As we have seen from a discussion of trade, the southern Cheyennes in fact had good motivation for moving south voluntarily, to assume a very privileged position in plains trade.

At about the time of the Lakota invasion across the Missouri, catastrophic events were occurring among the riverine agricultural people which would fundamentally change the political economy of the Great Plains. Beginning in the late 18th century, and terminating with the great smallpox epidemic of 1837, riverine populations were halved repeatedly by recurring outbreaks of fatal infectious diseases (Trimble 1986). The Mandans were hit the hardest, and only a few hundred were left after the 1837 epidemic, from a 1780 population of approximately 5,000. The Arikaras lived in villages which were more dispersed, and therefore suffered somewhat less, although they were diminished to about 1,500 people by 1840. The Hidatsas, some of whom were semi-nomadic by the early 19th century, were diminished to a population of 1,500, although some Hidatsas took refuge with the Crows. The remainders of all three riverine tribes, although they were different in language and culture, combined themselves for defense against the Lakotas into a single village called Like-a-Fishhook, in 1845, where the reservation of Fort Berthold is now located.

Confounding the difficulties of the riverine peoples at that time, the Lakotas began a period of serious and sustained warfare against them. Having bypassed the riverine peoples in their migration across the Missouri, they no longer needed them for trade and decided to exterminate or expel them, so that they could have uncontested access to the river trade from St. Louis, which was becoming more important because of the introduction of large river boats. Since the populations of the riverine groups had diminished so dramatically, they could no longer produce the surplus of agricultural products which was the basis of their role in plains trade, especially in their trade with the Lakotas.

The Pawnees, another sedentary agricultural tribe, were also hard hit by infectious disease. By 1840 their numbers were diminished by about half, to a total of 4,500. The Osages and their neighbors were similarly affected, and the Osages were no longer the potent military force they had been several decades earlier. By 1850 they were too weak to intercede effectively in the military affairs of the plains, and increasingly all the groups near the Missouri River came under the influence of European and American traders, political agents, and military forces.

By comparison with the sedentary tribes, the truly nomadic peoples of the plains did not suffer terribly from the epidemic diseases of the 18th and 19th centuries. The main reason for this was their dispersal in bands across the plains and the fact that infectious diseases were not as quickly or as thoroughly transmitted among the dispersed bands. Although some bands were infected with smallpox and cholera at various times, their immediate response, to flee onto the plains in small extended family groups, was an effective defense against infection of the whole band. In the cholera epidemic of 1849, for example, only one Cheyenne band, the Masikota, was seriously affected, suffering mortalities of about 50 per cent. These same rates of mortality were suffered by entire tribes of riverine agriculturists, not once but over and over, and hence their decimation.

By 1840, then, there was a new political situation on the plains. The riverine groups were essentially gone, and the Lakotas dominated the area from the Missouri to the Black Hills and south to the Platte. The Cheyennes and Arapahoes dominated the central plains, and in 1840 had arranged a great alliance with the Kiowas, Comanches, and the few remaining Apaches of the southern plains. The Comanches had expanded south and driven back the settlements of the Texans, and they hunted, raided, and traded freely from the Rio Grande to Natchidoches. On the northern plains, the Lakotas were expanding north-west as well as south, and were so numerous and powerful that they had little need of alliances. Having removed most of their competitors from northern plains trade corridors, they traded freely from the north Platte to Minnesota. Allied with the Cheyennes and Arapahoes to their south, they still punished and persecuted the weakened Osages and Pawnees when they could.

At this time, several new factors were emerging in the territory controlled by the Cheyennes. First of all, well-armed Delaware, Shawnee, and other eastern Indian tribes were migrating onto the eastern plains, displaced by the Indian Removal Act of 1828, which had established reservations for them in Kansas and Indian Territory. Well armed but poorly mounted, they hunted on the plains not just for food, but for hides to trade eastward. Further south, the Texas Republic had been founded, and in the 1840s the Texans were organizing themselves for an invasion and war of extermination not only against the Comanches, but against displaced eastern Indians, especially the Cherokees and Shawnees, who had entered the eastern part of the Republic. The Mexican War of 1845, ended by the Treaty of Guadeloupe Hidalgo in 1848, meant that New Mexico as well as Texas became part of the United States. And so the Plains Indians, from Minnesota to Texas to Montana, were now surrounded by a single unified political entity, the United States of America. No longer could they exploit differences in political attitude and trade policy among Spanish, Canadian, French, and American neighbors to their own advantage.

More ominously, the American frontier and its immigrants were encroaching onto the center of the plains, toward Cheyenne territory. Not only were farms and ranches moving up the Red and Brazos Rivers to the south, pushing the Comanches north-ward, but settlements of "Americans" were moving westward up the Kansas, Republican, and Smoky Hill Rivers, directly into the Cheyennes' most valued hunting reserves. In addition to permanent settlers, thousands of emigrants were crossing the plains through Cheyenne territory, along the Platte and Arkansas Rivers (Gregg 1962; Parkman 1903).

The Santa Fe Trail along the Arkansas River had been of some commercial importance for a long time, but when Mexico became independent from Spain in 1821, the door was opened for trade with the United States. The Santa Fe Trail from Independence, Missouri, was the most important route for this trade, and had two main sub-routes, one southern route across the desert and directly to Santa Fe, and another easier and more northerly route through Bent's Fort, where the Cheyennes traded, and then to Taos and Santa Fe.

The Oregon Trail along the Platte River had not been com-mercially important, but was opened entirely for the immigrant traffic in the 1820s. Like the Santa Fe Trail, it was flooded with immigrants when gold was discovered in California in 1849. For many immigrants, however, the "gold rush" was only symbolic of the move westward; most of the immigrants were farmers, ranchers, and merchants, headed for northern California and the Oregon Territory. Both immigrant trails experienced another brief flood of immigrants in 1859, when gold was discovered in Colorado, leading to the establishment of the city of Denver, a settlement which blocked historic Indian trade routes at the foot of the Rockies.

By 1860, over 100,000 immigrants and their livestock had passed along the Oregon and Santa Fe Trails, and their effect on the landscape was devastating. Buffaloes had been driven away from the Platte River, the route of the Oregon Trail, so that they were permanently separated and came to constitute a "northern herd" and a "southern herd." The immigrants, as well as commercial hunters and "mountain men," had also devastated one of the best buffalo ranges on the plains, the area between the forks of the Platte. The best remaining buffalo area controlled by the Cheyennes was at the headwaters of the Republican and Smoky Hill Rivers. Immigrant traffic had also taken away some of the best camping areas of the Cheyennes, along the Platte and the Arkansas.

The Cheyennes coped with the new situation as best they could. Ironically, the coming of immigrants coincided with the height of the market for buffalo robes, although the Cheyennes were now trading their robes at some new places. In addition to Bent's Fort, the Cheyennes traded at the new forts and trading posts on the South Platte, and with the "ranches" which had grown up along the Oregon Trail to service the immigrant traffic. With the increase in river-boat traffic, the more northerly bands of Cheyennes began to trade directly with the St Louis traders, rather than through Arikara intermediaries. To this end, they established new and stronger alliances with Lakota bands who controlled access to the trading posts along the Missouri River.

The new trading and hunting situation, and the immigrant traffic, undermined the national solidarity of the Cheyennes in the period 1840–60 and caused them to split into three groups. Of these, the largest and most stable faction were the bands which comprised the Southern Cheyennes, still deeply involved in the production of buffalo robes and the trading of horses, and ranging from Denver south and east where there were still buffaloes. Several of the northern bands, however, still resident around the Black Hills, had been geographically split from the Southern Cheyennes by the Platte River and the Oregon Trail, and increasingly cast their lot politically and militarily with the most north-westerly Lakota bands, especially the Hunkpapa and Sans Arc. A third group of Cheyennes, who became known as the Dog Soldiers, were originally a military society but had become a fully-fledged band, heavily intermarried with the most southerly Lakota bands, the Oglala and Brule. Increasingly, these bands were adopting the same kind of raiding lifestyle as the Comanches, eschewing trade and attacking immigrants, traders, and frontier settlers in Kansas and Nebraska to get what they needed.

By the 1860s, Indian–American relations in general and the Cheyenne situation in particular had reached a state of crisis. Most Americans on and around the plains no longer wanted to trade with the Indians or respect their territory – they wanted the land. The settlers in Kansas, the Colorado miners, and the citizens of Denver saw no use for the Cheyennes; they wanted them out of the way – dead or expelled. The traders who had benefited from good Cheyenne relations, and who were in fact married among the Cheyennes – Bent, Prowers, St Vrain, Lupton

– were trying to use their political influence to create a reservation for the "peace faction" of Southern Cheyennes in eastern Colorado, where they could return to an agricultural life and be protected from friction with American settlers. Meantime the militant Dog Soldier faction of Cheyennes had formed and was increasing its attacks on settlers and immigrants along the Platte. In 1864, all the anger and misunderstanding between whites and Indians on the plains led to a devastating landmark event in Plains Indian history – the Sand Creek Massacre.

Enraged by the Dog Soldier attacks, Colonel John M. Chivington, a Methodist minister, militia commander, and aspiring politician, organized an expedition of 100-day volunteers from Denver to retaliate against the Indians. Either unable to find the Dog Soldiers, or afraid that he might find them, Chivington and his rowdy "volunteers," along with a few regular US troops, attacked the peace faction at the Sand Creek crossing in southeast Colorado, where the Cheyennes had been told to camp by the Indian agent at Fort Lyons. At the time of the attack, most of the warriors were either out hunting or raiding with the Dog Soldiers, so the camp largely consisted of women, children, and elders. Before the attack was over, more than 250 Cheyennes, mostly women and children, had been killed, many of them tortured, murdered, and dismembered in the most brutal fashion imaginable. To their credit, some of the regular Army soldiers refused to participate in the butchery, and later testified against the offenders at an official inquiry into the affair.

Even from the standpoint of American self-interest, the Sand Creek Massacre was a terrible mistake. With the Civil War raging in the east, the Union did not have soldiers to protect the frontier from the inevitable retaliations by enraged Indians. Not only the Cheyennes, but all the plains tribes were convinced by the Sand Creek Massacre that the United States truly intended to exterminate them all, and they engaged in what they regarded as peremptory raids throughout the plains for the next three years. Undermanned at its frontier forts (Fay, 1977), the Army largely stood by as the Cheyennes and their allies closed the Platte River and Smoky Hill roads, burned farms and ranches in Colorado, Kansas, and Nebraska, and essentially rolled back the frontier several hundred miles.

Treaties and Forts

When the Cheyennes signed a treaty in 1865 which contained compensation for the attack at Sand Creek, this was only the most recent in a long line of treaties which supposedly guaranteed their sovereignty and territory. Their first treaty had been written with General Henry Atkinson in 1825 and was almost entirely about trade, which was the primary concern of US interests at that time. In his narrative, Atkinson recognized that the Cheyennes "occupy the country on the Cheyenne River, from near its mouth, back to the Black Hills. . . . Their principal rendezvous is towards the Black Hills, and their trading ground is at the mouth of Cherry River, a branch of the Cheyenne, 40 miles above its mouth."

The Cheyennes' next treaty was written 26 years later, after a portion of the tribe had moved south to trade at Bent's Fort, beginning about 1833, and after immigrant traffic had begun on the Oregon Trail. The purpose of the 1851 Treaty of Fort Laramie was largely to define tribal territories and protect immigrants, and in fact the fort itself had been established in 1849 to accommodate traffic on the Trail. After stating in the treaty that the Cheyennes "do not abandon or prejudice any rights or claims they may have to other lands," the treaty further describes their territory as stretching from the Platte to the Arkansas, as shown on map 4.4. Unlike the Atkinson Treaty, the treaty of 1851 is not mainly about trade, but rather about the right of the United States "to establish roads, military and other posts" within Cheyenne territory.

Three treaties, written in 1861, 1865, and 1867, were intended to establish a reservation for the Southern Cheyenne peace faction. The 1861 Treaty of Fort Wise established for them a supposedly safe, exclusive territory which included the site of the Sand Creek Massacre three years later. The 1865 Treaty of Little Arkansas apologized for the Sand Creek Massacre and established another supposedly safe area, this time in southern Kansas and northern Oklahoma, between the Arkansas and Cimarron Rivers. It was in Oklahoma that the peace faction was attacked yet again, this time by General George Custer in the 1868 Battle of the Washita. Like Chivington, Custer was frustrated in his

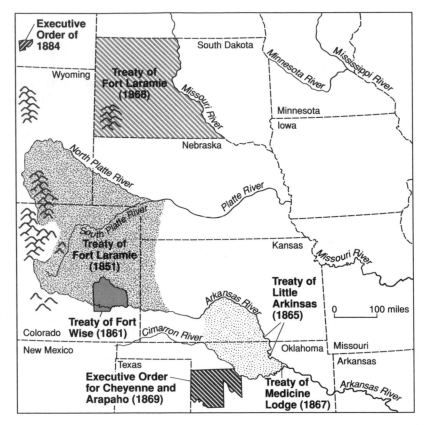

Map 4.4　Territories guaranteed to the Cheyennes by their treaties with the United States (adapted from Berthrong 1963: 11)

efforts at finding the militant Dog Soldiers, so he attacked the peace faction instead while they were on their way to their assigned Indian agency at Fort Sill.

In 1867–8, separate treaties were signed by the United States with the Northern Cheyennes and the Southern Cheyennes. The 1867 Treaty of Medicine Lodge included both the Dog Soldiers and the peace faction, and essentially guaranteed to them the same territory defined in 1865. The treaty was written in weakness on the part of the United States, and contained a considerable number of gifts and annuities in exchange for the cessation of Cheyenne hostilities. Although the Civil War was over by 1867 and a large number of US troops had been sent to the plains, the war against the Plains Indians was not going well from the American standpoint. Not only had frontier roads been closed and settlers burned out as the aftermath of the Sand Creek Massacre, but the Army discovered it could not defeat the Cheyennes and other plains warriors in mobile, face-to-face combat, and could not protect settlers and merchants, or surveyors sent out to blaze a trail for the trans-continental railroad. While it was considering its options, the United States decided to sign treaties which were very generous to the Indians, both in guarantees of land and in gifts and annuities. But, as we shall see, agents of the United States government apparently had no intention of honoring these treaties once they had gained a military advantage.

The military situation of the United States was even worse in the northern plains in 1868. The Northern Cheyennes and Northern Arapahoes, as part of a Lakota alliance, had not only closed the Bozeman Trail, which led north along the Powder River from the Platte River road, but had laid siege to the Army forts along the road, holding the soldiers hostage. Admitting defeat, the US government in the 1868 Treaty of Fort Laramie guaranteed to the Indians a huge tract of land between the Middle Missouri and the Rocky Mountains, including the Black Hills, and promised many gifts and benefits. In return, the Indian side agreed to allow roads and railroads to be built south of their reservation and, especially, to allow the troops to leave their forts on the Bozeman Trail. As they vacated their forts, the Army troops had to suffer the humiliation of passing by thousands of cheering Indian warriors, who quickly looted the forts and set fire to them.

With the treaties in place, the United States began to build up its supply system and chain of forts on the plains in preparation for an invasion of the Great Sioux Reservation, from which they had been expelled. A large number of forts were built along the Missouri, up the Platte, and along the Arkansas and their tributaries (Frazer 1972). Seeing the build-up at the forts, the Cheyennes acted immediately. After the peace faction had been twice attacked, the balance of the southern warriors joined the militant Dog Soldier faction, which after a series of engagements was finally defeated at the Battle of Summit Springs in eastern Colorado in 1869. After that, some of the Dog Soldiers joined the peace faction on the reservation in Oklahoma Territory where they received rations of food, while the militants joined the Lakotas and the Northern Cheyennes who were still fighting north of the Platte.

The events surrounding the breaking of the 1868 treaty and the invasion of the Great Sioux Reservation are complex and somewhat in dispute, but one key event was the Custer Expedition into the Black Hills in 1874, looking for and finding gold. To the Indian side, this was a clear violation of their treaty, and led to hostilities which culminated in the Battle of the Little Big Horn in 1876. Although the results of that battle were dramatic, with General Custer and all 254 members of his command killed, the battle with General Crook a week earlier was strategically more important. With a supposedly dominant force of cavalry, mounted infantry, and adequate supplies, General Crook was turned back on the Rosebud River by the harassing tactics of the Lakotas and their allies, including the Northern Cheyennes and the Southern Cheyenne militants. Flushed with success, the returning warriors were resting and recuperating in their camp on the Little Big Horn when they were attacked by Custer. As it happens, Custer attacked the combined camp at the point where the Cheyennes were located, and they were prominent among the warriors who reacted, surrounding and ultimately killing the Custer regiment. The purported scalp of George Custer lies among the sacred objects of the Northern Cheyennes.

Although the Indians won the battle, the retaliation of the United States troops was so massive that the Lakotas, Cheyennes, and Arapahoes dispersed all across the northern plains to escape them, and finally began to move to their assigned reservations in small groups during 1877 and '78. The Northern Cheyennes were originally moved to Oklahoma to join the Southern Cheyennes, but after a dramatic escape and a massacre of Dull Knife's band at Fort Robinson in 1879, they were permitted to occupy a separate reservation in Montana.

During their period of sovereignty and freedom on the plains, from 1780 until 1879, the Cheyennes were central to many events which still occupy the minds of American historians. Although a small group, they dominated a geographical area nearly as large as that of the Lakotas or the Comanches. Inveterate traders and politicians, the Cheyennes met Lewis and Clark, lent their auspices to the building of Bent's Fort, and for a century manipulated alliances with all the other central plains tribes to maximize their advantages in trade and politics.

When hostilities with the Americans began, different factions of Cheyennes tried both militancy and reconciliation. Strangely, the peace faction became renowned for its wisdom and desire to accommodate American designs at the same time as the militant faction was building a reputation as the most feared obstacle to westward expansion. The Cheyennes faded from view as a sovereign nation with two dramatic events, the Custer battle and the escape of Dull Knife, both of which are now staples of American history and folklore.

In all of the battles against American Indians officially listed in Army records from 1837 to 1891, a period which includes the Seminole Wars and the flight of Chief Joseph, 21 battles resulted in the killing of ten or more United States soldiers (Adjutant General's Office 1979). Of these, the Cheyennes were the antagonists in nine cases. So the question naturally arises as to what exactly was the temperament, and what were the weapons, organization, and tactics which made the Cheyennes so formidable in plains warfare, both against other tribes and against the US Army. We will explore these subjects in the next chapter.

5

Cheyenne Warfare

My friend John Greany, who was born in 1918 and became a chief of the Bowstring Soldiers, liked to talk about Cheyenne warfare in the form of a long battle narrative, which he had apparently compiled from stories he heard as a youth. The narrative was not about any battle in particular, but rather constituted an idealized battle between the Cheyennes and an enemy nation, a story which incorporated all the elements of traditional warfare which he thought were important. It serves as a good introduction to the subject, not only because it alludes to many of the topics we will consider at length later in this chapter, but also because it exhibits the perspective and attitudes which John, his ancestors, and his descendants have brought to battlefields from the Black Hills in the 18th century to the Persian Gulf War in 1991.

When the Cheyennes were going to war against other tribes, like the Kiowas or the Crows, it took the warriors a long time to get ready. First they had to check their war pony and make sure it was in good shape, ready to run, and that its hooves were clean and trimmed. If it was a medicine pony, they had to sing to it, and maybe brush it with an eagle wing or with sage, or apply some paint or some kind of medicine. The warriors had to check their own medicine bundle, to make sure it was all there and that they had plenty of paint. Maybe they had to fast or abstain from women for a while before they took off, as part of their medicine. They had to check and repair their weapons, their saddles, and their equipment. If they had a medicine lance or a medicine shield, they had to lay them out and smoke or maybe sing some songs. Maybe they had to talk with the man who made the shield or lance, or who gave it to them, and maybe give them a present. They had to get the food they would need, and the clothing they would wear into battle. It took a long time to do it right.

When they took off, they would leave quietly, so as not to disturb their medicine. They would take some spare horses, and maybe a boy to hold them, or a woman to cook for them, if it was a group. Usually they would go with their relatives, and with other members of their soldier clan. They didn't ride their war pony all the time, just part of the time, so it would be fresh for the fight. Everybody was supposed to be serious and quiet when they rode to war. You didn't want to bother anybody, because you didn't know what kind of medicine they had, and you didn't want to spoil it.

When they got close to enemy territory, they would send out scouts, they called them "wolves," to find their camp. When they found it, they would gather all the warriors together for the attack, and then they would stop to dress and make their paint. Different warriors had different paints. Maybe one person would paint his face like an eagle, with a black mouth, or another would paint like a wolf or a hawk. Some face paints were different, maybe half black and half white, or red streaks across the forehead, like splashes of blood, or lightning, or just some bright paint to frighten the enemy. There were lots of different kinds of paint.

Then the warriors would dress up, just as you would dress up a person who had died. They would wear their very best buckskin shirt and leggings, fancy moccasins and hair ornaments. Some men had a scalp-lock, a small braid which would be easy to cut off. That was the way we dared the enemy to try and take it. Last would come the weapons. Everybody carried a knife as a last resort. If you had fired your gun or lost your lance and club, you still had your knife. Everybody was very busy, and very quiet.

When everyone was ready, they got on their war ponies and headed slowly toward the enemy. The different soldier clans would ride forward together. The boys and women came slowly behind with the extra horses and other equipment. When somebody saw the enemy, they let out a yell so that everyone would know where they were, and then all the warriors would ride up. If we surprised the enemy, then we attacked immediately, but if it looked like the enemy was ready and alert, and if they were painted up and looking for us, then we would find some good place to line up, like on the top of a hill or a ridge. The enemy would form up facing us across a valley or a ravine, and we would start yelling at each other. If it looked like they were outnumbered, then we would charge, or if they thought they had the advantage, they would charge. But if it looked about even, everyone would sit there on their horses, taunting each other and singing soldier songs. There could be maybe a hundred or more warriors on each side. Sometimes the Cheyennes would charge a little way at the enemy, just to make them show themselves so we could see how many there were. They didn't sing death songs yet, that came later.

While they were lined up, some of the Cheyenne warriors would ride out front and challenge the enemy to shoot at them and test their medicine. Roman Nose used to do that. He would ride up and down the whole line of enemy and let them shoot at him. They never hit him. A warrior named Cloud Rider had medicine that would confuse the enemy; they couldn't see him. He would ride back and forth and they would be looking off in all directions. He blinded them with his medicine.

If the Cheyennes recognized some famous enemy warrior, maybe by his paint and costume, someone might ride out and challenge him to personal combat, yelling and taunting. Or some enemy warrior might come and challenge some famous Cheyenne warrior, like Roman Nose or Tall Bull or Little Hawk. They didn't come out and fight right away, but if one warrior challenged another, when the fighting started they would head for each other, and other warriors would get out of the way.

If there were some suicide boys who had made a vow, they were allowed to start the battle. They went to the front to fulfill their vow. They had no medicine to protect themselves. They were naked, and there was nothing on their bodies or their horses that the enemy could take as loot. They gave their bodies to the enemy for different reasons, maybe to honor someone, or to take revenge, or because they had a dream or because they were sick or unhappy or tired of living, or because some girl had turned them down – different reasons. But they all knew that when they started fighting, no one would help them. The other warriors all honored their suicide vow and tried to help them to die honorably. The warriors shouted encouragement to the suicide boys as they attacked the enemy, naked and without any weapons.

The suicide boys would trot their horses toward the enemy and sing their death songs. There were many different death songs, most ran in families; singing the song showed that a suicide boy was brave, and ready to die. They were simple songs, like

"Tell the girl in white buckskin that I love her."

"My grandfather killed Kiowas and I will kill some too."

"Today is a good day to die; only the stones live forever."

And then the Cheyenne warriors all yelled and the suicide boys charged among the enemy, hitting them with their fists, pulling them off their horses, choking them and biting them until the enemy gathered around them and at last all the suicide boys were dead. That is when things got more serious. Of course all the Cheyenne warriors were angry to see their kinfolk die, and they were ready to die to avenge them. So all the warriors began to sing their death songs. The warriors with dog ropes, most of them Dog Soldiers, rode out midway to the enemy, jumped off their horses and drove their stakes into the ground, so we had a line of maybe 20 dog men out in front.

The dog men vowed that once the stake was driven in the ground, they would not pull it up. One end of their sash was tied to the stake, the other looped around their shoulder. To the enemy, the dog men looked like easy targets, but they weren't. They were close enough together so that only one horse could pass between them, and they could help each other. Also, standing on the ground, they could shoot a gun or arrows more accurately than the enemy could, charging on horseback. Some of the dog men had long lances for fighting against warriors on horseback, and some had a big, heavy club they used to hit the enemy's horse in the head and bring it down. Most of them had shields to deflect an enemy's lance or club.

The dog men were like the bait in the trap. Behind the dog men were the rest of the Dog Soldiers. When an enemy warrior got through, they would chase him down and kill him. The dog men on foot broke up the charge of the enemy, and forced them to fight one on one.

The Bowstrings usually stayed behind until the enemy charged, and then we went to where the fighting was the worst. If the enemy tried to charge around the dog men, right or left, then the Bowstrings rode to meet them. Sometimes the enemy forgot about fighting and tried to charge around the battlefield and get to our horses in the rear. That was when the boys and women had a chance to fight. Even a young boy could count coup[1] on an enemy trying to steal his horses, just by touching him or hitting him with a whip.

After a while the enemy would give up and try to get back to their horses. If they managed to get to a fresh horse, we couldn't catch them. When the boys holding the Cheyenne horses saw that the battle was about over, they would bring some fresh horses up front so that we could chase the enemy and kill some more of them.

About this time, when the battle was won, the warriors would scalp the dead enemies, taking their scalp-lock if they had one. Also they would talk to each other about who had struck which enemy warrior first. The first coup was more honorable than the later coups; you could count three coups on each warrior. Before they went back to camp they wanted to have straight in their minds who had counted which coup, since not everyone could see the whole battle. If you struck an enemy, you didn't always know if someone had already struck him. You could also count coup on dead enemies, if they hadn't been struck three times.

About this time the victory songs began. These were joyous, quick songs, about how good it felt to be victorious and to be alive. They had words like:

Brother, pull up my dog rope. I will clean it and use it again.
Where are the enemies who taunted me? They are dead now.
I will see one more sunrise; it's too soon for me to go.
I will surprise my sweetheart; she thinks that I am dead.
I have another scalp for my mother; she will be proud.
My son, my son. You are gone now, but I have killed a Kiowa.

Sometimes women went along on the war party because they wanted to fight. Maybe they had lost a brother or husband to the enemy, and they wanted a coup or a scalp. Women who had lost relatives were entitled to take the horses, weapons, and other belongings of enemy warriors killed in battle. They were also responsible for gashing the bodies of dead enemies to release their spirits.

The Cheyennes were never defeated in war; their medicine was strong. Although hundreds of Cheyenne men served in the Vietnam War, none were killed. As long as we Cheyennes perform our ceremonies and keep our medicines, we will be a strong people.

The narrator of this story, John Greany, Jr., was not just a tribal historian, or a man interested in traditional warfare. He was a warrior and a war hero. During World War II on Iwo Jima and Guadalcanal, he was a fearless and ferocious infantryman, who was much decorated for his bravery and self-sacrifice. In May of 1945, Greany received special leave to attend a ceremony in his honor in Oklahoma (plate 5.1). The following story then appeared in the government magazine, *Indians at Work*:

Near El Reno, Oklahoma, during early May, 600 Indians, representing twelve tribes of the western part of the state, held an all-day victory celebration in honor of their tribesmen in the war. Chief among the honored was John Greaney [*sic*], Jr., a Cheyenne on furlough from the South Pacific, where he had been cited for bravery.

In an ancient sacred ceremony conducted by Ralph White Tail, a holy man of the Cheyenne, Greaney's Indian name was changed from Red Tooth to Little Chief in recognition of the warrior's valorous deeds. This was followed by a "give away," and many valuable presents, including three horses, were distributed through the honored one. Later there was a victory procession in the traditional manner, led by Greany and other service men. Then came the victory dance led by the hero, in which representatives of twelve tribes joined.

Thereafter special victory dances, also led by the hero, were performed for the War Mothers, upon whose brilliantly-colored shawls the names, ranks, and organizations of their warrior children were written that the world might see.

Not only John Greany but most of the prominent men of his generation were warriors – soldiers, veterans, and war heroes of World War II. Their experiences gave them high status in Cheyenne society, and led to their prominence in religious as well as civil offices. Roy Nightwalker, Cheyenne chief, camp crier, and religious leader, was a hero of the European theater in World War II. One dark night at the ceremonial grounds at Seiling, Oklahoma, he showed me the scalps of German soldiers he had killed in the war. Roy Bull Coming, Dog Soldier chief and ceremonial leader, was a highly-decorated infantryman who counted coup on surprised German soldiers in the days following the D-Day invasion of France.

During the Vietnam and Persian Gulf Wars, Cheyenne soldiers carried war medicines, performed rituals in the battlefield, sang death songs and painted their faces when they could. When they returned home, they joined the traditional soldier societies and participated in a host of special veterans groups for Indian people which have grown up in the last several decades (see plate 5.4). For all of them, their frame of reference as warriors and men has been not so much the recent traditions of bravery and sacrifice, as in World War II, but the oral traditions of Cheyenne warfare in the 19th century. In idealized form, such as the narrative of John Greany, these stories perpetuate a warrior tradition in which Cheyenne men rely on their war medicines and are brave to the point of being indifferent to the threat of death. These are the values imparted by the stories and by the death and victory songs.[2]

How remarkable it is that traditional Cheyenne warriors, as they approached a battlefield, did not prepare for victory so

Plate 5.1   John Greany (courtesy of John Greany, Jr.)

much as they prepared for death. They said goodbye to their relatives, they dressed themselves for their own funeral, they watched passively as the suicide boys were killed, they sang their death songs, and then they charged the enemy. Roy Bull Coming put it this way:

When a Cheyenne warrior enters the battle, he counts himself as dead already. Although he fights as hard as he can, he does not expect to survive. If he lives through the battle, he is surprised. I never expected to come back from the war. I simply wanted to die in a manner that would bring honor to my family, and to my people.

Although other Plains Indian tribes had some of the same war practices as the Cheyennes, I would argue that the Cheyennes centralized and institutionalized these practices and made them explicit to a greater extent. Their success in warfare testifies that they took these practices very seriously. One can only imagine the psychological effect on other tribes of engaging the Cheyennes in war and facing them across a battlefield. Lined up in proper Plains Indian fashion, the tribe first had to face the humiliation of taunting, and seeing Cheyenne warriors ride up and down in front of them with apparent magical immunity to bullets and arrows. Then there were the suicide boys, galloping across the battlefield and leaping on them with tooth and claw, desperately trying to kill them with their bare hands. Seeing that the other Cheyenne warriors made no move to help the suicide boys, the enemy tribe must have been convinced that the Cheyennes were not concerned about casualties, that they were truly trying to die.

Next were the dog rope men. Disdaining the mobility afforded by their horses, they not only fought on foot but confined themselves to the radius of their dog rope. Singing their death songs and shaking their scalp-locks, they dared the enemy to attack them. Next came the attack of the main force of the Cheyennes, who did not maneuver around the flanks seeking tactical advantage and did not try to steal horses, but charged headlong into the thickest part of the fighting. And last, the Cheyennes saw the benefit of pursuit in warfare. Instead of stopping to congratulate themselves on a victory or being content to count coup, the Cheyennes pursued the enemy as long as their horses lasted, bringing up fresh horses when possible.

Many of the Cheyennes' enemies were not so serious about

warfare. In a battle, they were often content to confront the enemy, count coup, and steal their horses if possible. By contrast, the Cheyennes' intention was to destroy the enemy, sometimes to the point of genocide. In their plains warfare period, they claim to have exterminated one entire tribe, the Owuqeo, and they killed women in their battles against the Crows and Kiowas. In the face of this ferocious behavior, it is no wonder that other tribes moved aside as the Cheyennes invaded the central plains, and that the Cheyennes came to occupy a much larger tribal territory than one would expect from their total numbers.

Weapons and Their Use

In the museums of North America and Europe, there are hundreds of examples of Cheyenne weapons used in the pre-reservation period. Although they come in many varieties, I will describe six classes of weapons: bows and arrows, firearms, lances, clubs and axes, knives and whips, lariats, and coup sticks. Each of them was used only in certain contexts of battle and in conjunction with certain tactics. I will also discuss war shields, which have had special meaning in Cheyenne warfare.

Bows and arrows

Among the Cheyennes there were certain older men who special-ized in the manufacture of arrows; some of them also made bows. The bows used for warfare were the same as those used in hunting. Most of them were short, stiff staves of Osage orange, or some other stiff, resilient wood, but the best were the compound bows of horn, wood, and sinew traded from the Shoshones and other mountain Indians. These compound bows had one of the same useful casting characteristics as modern wheel-and-pulley bows – the pull required at full draw was less than that required at mid-draw. Thus the bow was easier to hold on target, and the arrow accelerated rapidly through the middle period of casting the arrow. Compound bows would shoot perhaps twice as far as simple or "self" bows – 200 meters or more.

War arrows were made differently from hunting arrows. First of all, the flat stone or metal point was set parallel to the cock feather, so that it was at a right angle to the bow when it was nocked. The rationale for this was that it would pass between an enemy warrior's ribs more easily if it was fired with the point horizontal. To kill a buffalo, on the other hand, the point had to be vertical at firing to pass between the buffalo's ribs. Of course this rationale discounts the fact that arrows usually spin in flight, but we should note that the feathers on Cheyenne arrows were usually set straight, and the arrow was envisioned as lacking spin when it was shot.

War arrows were also a little longer than hunting arrows, so that they could be drawn more fully and shoot further. They were made of willow rather than dogwood or chokecherry, and were usually fletched with eagle or hawk feathers, rather than turkey, goose, or duck. This was to gain the medicine powers of the predatory birds, which was accomplished by rituals invoked by the arrow maker. Four "blood grooves" were also incised along the shaft of war arrows, so that an enemy would bleed to death if shot. In earlier times, the Cheyennes used flint for their arrow points, but in the late 18th century they began to use steel to make points, especially the barrel hoops which were traded to them for that purpose. One interesting source of material for arrow points was the glass insulators used on telegraph lines, which produced beautiful green, yellow, and blue arrow points, found in some museums.

Cheyenne arrow makers were full-time specialists. Each band comprised a few such men who manufactured hunting arrows in groups of ten and war arrows in groups of four to supply the whole band. In return, they received gifts of meat and produce from hunters, and horses and other captured goods from warriors. For the 1880 US Census, conducted early in the reservation period, some older Cheyenne men proudly listed their "vocation" as "arrow maker" (see plate 5.2). Each of them had his own style and trademarks, and they often deviated from the more-or-less standard practices described above.

Plate 5.2   Wolf Face, one of the last Southern Cheyenne arrow makers (Grinnell Collection, Museum of the American Indian)

Firearms

Although guns and rifles were rare among Cheyennes in their early years on the plains, and were difficult to use, they none the less made the crucial difference in warfare. They were usually brought to bear at long range in an initial volley, and they were intended both to inflict casualties at the beginning of the battle, which might have a discouraging effect, and to intimidate the enemy by showing them the number of firearms they were facing. After the initial volley, however, a Cheyenne warrior was faced with problems of reloading.

The muzzle-loading flintlock and matchlock rifles used initially by the Cheyennes required a charge of powder in the chamber, a patch between powder and ball, an over-sized ball which had to be rammed down the muzzle with a rod, a splash of powder in the powder pan, the cocking of the hammer, and possibly the relighting of the match. This was impossible to do from horseback if the horse was moving. Consequently, horsemen had to stop to reload, and they usually dismounted. Firing a muzzle-loader from horseback was difficult, since a rider might lose the fire from his matchlock or blow the powder from his pan while trying to engage the enemy. Consequently, Cheyenne riflemen behaved more like mounted infantry than cavalry early in the battle, firing an initial volley and perhaps one or two more rounds before engaging the enemy in hand-to-hand combat.

It was only toward the middle of the 19th century that Cheyennes had breech-loading and repeating rifles which could be easily fired and reloaded from horseback. These were used in warfare against the US Army, but were not used much against other Indians in the warfare characteristic of the late 18th and early 19th centuries. These repeating weapons were used throughout an engagement, although they had to be sheathed or thrown aside when the fighting became close and crowded.

Pistols, especially revolvers, also came into use just before the Civil War. The early versions, however, had to be reloaded with powder, ball, and cap chamber by chamber, which could not be done under battlefield conditions. So here, again, the pistol became a weapon of early engagement, while the last part of the battle was fought with hand weapons.

Cheyenne rifles, shotguns, and pistols were often highly decor-ated – carved, incised, painted, and hung with feathers and beads. The same kinds of designs were painted and carved on rifle stocks as on shields and tipis – medicine birds and animals to make the bullet strike true and to prevent the rifle from misfiring. On some museum examples, the metal parts are carved and incised as well as the wooden parts. Sometimes marks or notches were made on the stock or barrel to indicate an enemy killed or a coup counted.

Lances

Although Cheyenne bows and firearms did not carry much evidence of special ritual significance, Cheyenne lances did. Some of them were medicine lances only, intended to count coup and not to pierce the bodies of enemies. These include the bow lances carried by Contrary Warriors, Bowstring Warriors and others, and the crooked lances carried by Elk Warriors and others (see

Figure 5.1   A bow lance (left) and a crooked lance (redrawn by Wenqiu Zhang from Nagy n.d.: 15, 90)

figure 5.1). The bow lances were extra-long bows with a non-functional bowstring and a lance head set at one end. The crooked lances were regular pointed lances with the butt end of the shaft curved into a semi-circle and connected by a thong to the main shaft. Both the bow lances and the crooked lances were covered with strips of otter skin, beaver skin, or blankets for decoration, and some had feathers or enemy scalp-locks attached at the end. Some of the crooked lances were functional and could be used as weapons, but most of these were intended to be symbols of office in a military society or emblems of personal war medicine or personal status.

The straight lances used as weapons were between six and nine feet long, depending on personal preference, and were used primarily for stabbing and thrusting rather than as missiles. The longer lances were used to engage the enemy at a greater distance, although they were more unwieldy than the shorter ones. Although the lances were most often used from horseback, there are indications from battle accounts that they were not

clutched under the arm in the manner of a medieval knight, but
rather were held overhand for short jabs and thrusts. Neither
were they struck sideways in a sweeping or slashing manner,
since they lacked a cutting edge except for a few inches near the
point.

Clubs and axes

The essential difference between a club and an axe is that an axe
is intended to slash or cut an enemy while a club injures by
percussion. Some Cheyenne hand weapons were clearly axes,
some clearly clubs, but others were somewhere in between (see
figure 5.2). The most emphatic clubs were made of stone and
could be of any weight. Small clubs were attached to a wooden
handle by shrunken rawhide and usually had a wrist loop. These
were intended for close hand-to-hand combat, either on foot or
horseback. The longer clubs were intended for use from horseback and usually had a medium-sized head, a long, flexible
handle, and a wrist loop. Some exceptionally long examples in
museums have slender, flexible handles like polo mallets, and
exhibit a stone head ground to conical points at each end. There
were also some especially large and heavy clubs, with handles
about three feet long, which were used to attack horses as well
as enemy warriors.
   Stone club-heads were both found and manufactured. The
found heads came from mountain streams which, as they bend
and twist through the mountains, periodically deposit beds of
smoothly-ground stones of uniform size. Cheyenne warriors
simply selected from these beds the size and shape of stone they
desired for a club, usually choosing symmetrical round and
oblong stones of basalt or granite. Club-heads washed from
archaeological sites were also found and re-used if a warrior
thought he had the proper medicine to mollify the spirit and
medicine of the previous owner. Club-heads could also be
manufactured or modified by grinding a stone against another
stone with the assistance of sand and water. The double-pointed
club-heads mentioned above were modified from a found stone
in this manner.
   A variety of pointed, vicious-looking, club-like weapons were
constructed by Cheyennes in their period of warfare, with knife

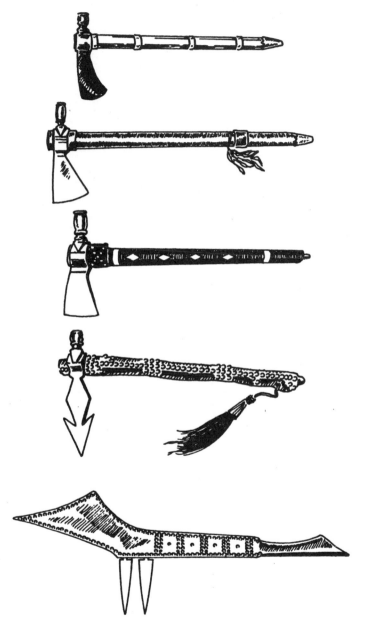

Figure 5.2 Clubs and axes (redrawn by Wenqiu Zhang from Nagy
n.d.: 105)

blades, stone points, nails, or spikes set on both edges of a hardwood handle about three to four feet in length, for a foot or more from the end of the weapon. These were cutting and slashing weapons and could be used either from horseback or on foot. Some weapons exhibit both a stone head and a sequence of spikes or knife points down the handle.

In the 17th and 18th centuries, decorative brass, iron, and steel axe-heads of small size were traded to the Cheyennes by French and British traders. Some were used merely for decoration, as medallions or breastplates, but some were actually used as weapons. Other, larger trade axe-heads intended for use as tools also became weapons, mounted on a wooden handle about 18–24 inches in length. Most of these war axes were intended as cutting rather than percussive weapons, although some had a flat or bulbous butt end, which could be used as a percussive weapon.

Knives

The original Cheyenne war knives of the 17th century were made of flint and were short, only six or eight inches in length. Short flint knives did not make good weapons and longer flint knives tended to break. Metal trade knives, however, were much longer, did not break easily, and could not only be used as knives in close combat, but could also be set in wooden club handles.

Cheyenne knife scabbards were tube-like leather holders long enough to cover the entire knife instead of just the blade, and had a flap which could be tied over the top of the handle. This was to prevent losing the knife when riding on horseback or running and jumping while engaged in battle. When personal, close combat was imminent, the knife was removed from the scabbard and stuck in a belt or sash. As mentioned previously, a knife was the weapon of last resort, and no one went to battle armed primarily with a knife. While elaborate medicine ways were often attached to the primary weapons of war, such as lances and clubs, there were no medicine knives and no knife rituals, as far as I know.

Whips, lariats, and coup sticks

A minority of Cheyenne warriors carried whips in battle. There were two kinds – the short, stiff kind for slapping the flank of the horse you were riding, and long "bull whips" between eight and ten feet in length. The short whips, which some men carried to speed up their horses, were used merely to count coup on an enemy by slapping him on the arm or across the body. The bull whips were used primarily to wrap around an enemy's neck, arm, or torso and pull him from his horse. The danger of this tactic, however, was that the enemy might grab the whip and pull the Cheyenne warrior from his own horse. To prevent this, the war whip had no wrist strap.

Lariats were used much like whips. Coiled in the hand, they could be used to count coup by slapping the enemy with the rope. Twirled over the head, they could be used to lasso and unhorse an enemy. Only a very few Cheyenne warriors used lassoes or whips.

Much more common, and in fact nearly universal, were coup sticks (see plate 5.3). These were usually made of light wood, and many had whiplashes at the end and a wrist strap. Some warriors used coup sticks only at the beginning of a battle to intimidate the enemy, and others throughout the battle as in the case of warriors with special medicine, but the general pattern was to use them at the end of the battle, when the enemy was on the run, as a method of humiliating them. While it was difficult or dangerous to chase and wound an enemy warrior with a lethal weapon, many enemies could be whacked and humiliated in their retreat by a Cheyenne warrior on a good horse using a coup stick. In this way, a Cheyenne could count many coups for later recitation.

Shields

Between the head and hump of a buffalo, there is an area of skin which is very thick, and can be made thicker by a process of heating and wetting the skin and then letting it dry and contract on a flat surface. To make a shield, the resulting flat plaque of skin is trimmed until it is round or oval in shape with a diameter

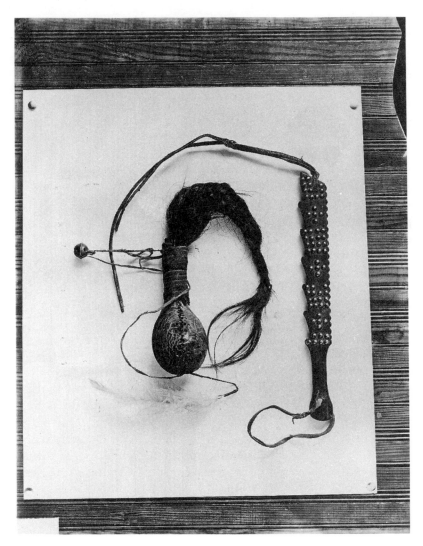

Plate 5.3   Dog Soldier rattle and coup stick (Smithsonian Institution National Anthropological Archives)

of 18–30 inches. Two thongs are attached to the back of the shield, through holes in the edge, so that it can be slipped onto the forearm. A right-handed Cheyenne warrior, then, would normally enter the battlefield with a shield over the left forearm, and a lance, club, axe, or coup stick in the right hand. Other weapons could be stuck in the belt or tied to the saddle.

Figure 5.3   Cheyenne shields (redrawn by Wenqiu Zhang from Nagy n.d.: 87 and Nagy 1994: 21)

Most Cheyenne shields had medicine powers derived from the dreams or vision quest of a warrior. Typically, the originator of a shield would paint the front with symbols of his medicine experience (see figure 5.3), and might also inaugurate an accompanying medicine bag. The bottom of the medicine shield was often hung with eagle or hawk feathers, or perhaps strips of otter or beaver fur. Medicine shields normally had a cover of elk or deer skin, which was similarly painted and decorated. The shield itself was taken from the cover and exposed only at the moment of battle.

If a man inaugurating a medicine shield was successful in battle, he had the right to instruct four other warriors in making the same kind of shield. These were usually younger men to whom he was related only through male lines – what anthropologists call "agnatic kin." These were also very likely members of his military society (discussed below), since sons tended to join their father's society. When a man had instructed four younger men in making shields, he usually retired from active life as a warrior and became primarily a medicine man or chief. In addition to the medicine shields, there were among the Cheyennes simple, functional, undecorated shields of the same size and shape carried by warriors who claimed no special medicine.

Counting Coup

French traders and explorers used the word *coup*, or "touch," to describe the basis upon which Plains Indian war honors were calculated. This word was carried over into English in the phrase "counting coup," since it made a difference whether the coup "counter" was the first, second, or third person to touch an enemy warrior. Although different plains tribes counted coup differently, for the Cheyennes the first three touches on an enemy warrior could be counted in the system of war honors.

There were good, practical reasons for making a coup the basis of war honors rather than having a system based on whether one killed, wounded, or scalped an enemy. First of all, it was not always clear whose blow had killed an enemy and whose merely wounded him. Second, it was frequently the case that a first blow was serious enough to cripple an enemy so that he could be killed easily by a second attacker. It was more clear who had touched or struck an enemy first, second, and third, and hence the Cheyenne system of war honors was organized on this basis. In this system it did not matter whether the blow was lethal or not: it was getting there first which mattered, and the system encouraged quick aggressive attacks by Cheyenne warriors.

Additional war honors were in fact based on whether one had killed an enemy, if it could be verified, or who had taken an enemy's weapon or horse. In addition, the circumstances of the confrontation were considered. For example, a Cheyenne who faced two or three enemies was given higher status than a warrior who had faced only one. A warrior who had killed a famous enemy warrior was given higher honors than a warrior who had killed a young, inexperienced enemy.

These additional war honors were acknowledged when the coup was "recounted" in a public war narrative. Immediately upon returning to camp, a chief, crier, or elder relative of a warrior might be recruited to ride about the Cheyenne camp announcing the coup or war exploit, if it was significant, for example as follows: "In the battle with the Comanches my grandson Blue Eagle was the first to strike a Comanche warrior, and here is the Comanche's scalp."

Scalping an enemy was not particularly honorable, and in fact men were not encouraged to stop fighting, dismount, and scalp an enemy before the battle was over. Scalps were regarded merely as souvenirs, and sometimes were removed by the noncombatant boys and women who accompanied the warriors. They were displayed on poles around the camp and during dances and religious ceremonies after the battle, especially if the scalp incorporated a highly-decorated scalp-lock.

Coups have to be recounted, or as Cheyennes now say, "war stories" have to be told on numerous special occasions. On these occasions, the warrior himself is required to tell the story, flying in the face of the customary Cheyenne requirement of personal modesty. And the story must be parallel, or relevant, to the special occasion being celebrated. For example, when a new tipi, made by a distinguished woman, was dedicated in Canton, Oklahoma, in 1983, a Vietnam veteran was invited to count a coup and receive a gift. Approaching the door of the tipi, which no one had yet entered, he spoke as follows: "In 1967 I was in the Mekong Delta and we came upon a village. I walked up to the first hut and could not see anybody inside, so I kicked the door in like this!" Whereupon he struck the tipi pole nearest the door with a decorated coup stick and the assembled people exclaimed loudly in unison, "Hwah!"

On another occasion I witnessed in 1971, a dancer at the Ashland, Montana, pow-wow had lost an eagle feather from his costume, a very bad omen. The dance was immediately stopped and the audience canvassed to see if there was a veteran present who could tell a war story. Reluctantly, an older man was pushed forward by his family, took a drumstick from one of the pow-wow singers, and approached the feather. He related the following story: "On Okinawa we were chasing a bunch of Japs through the jungle, shooting at them. We ran out of the trees into a clearing and I saw that one of the Japs had dropped his rifle. I went over and picked it up like this!" At this point the veteran struck the feather with the drumstick and the people shouted "Hwah!" And the feather was returned to the dancer, who was disqualified from the dancing competition.

In modern times, the war stories are not always so specific. On some occasions, for example at a giveaway, it is sufficient for a veteran to state his branch and time of service. Only occasionally do modern Cheyenne warriors claim that they counted a first or second coup in some engagement of World War II, Korea, Vietnam, or the Persian Gulf War. While in the past a group of warriors could be convened to confirm a coup, in modern times it is difficult to present verification, unless the actual events of a battle are included in a document, for example in the citation which accompanies a medal for bravery.

Military Societies

The Cheyenne military societies, also called soldier societies, were similar among themselves and similar to the societies of other plains tribes. Many of these societies were inspired by those of the Mandans, who served as tutors as well as trading partners to many of the tribes who moved west and south onto the plains in the 18th century. Among the societies of these tribes, one finds a similarity in the names, origin stories, symbols, and organization, although each is usually imprinted with some cultural elements which are unique to a tribe.[3]

Generally speaking, the Cheyenne military societies had between one and four big chiefs, between four and sixteen little chiefs, some unmarried women who have been described as "mascots," "princesses," or "servants," and a full complement of special emblems, songs, weapons, and war practices. Although the names and number of societies changed through time as some waxed or waned, became reorganized, split in two, or merged together, the usual names attributed to Cheyenne societies, along with some of their cultural attributes, are as follows:

Bowstring Soldiers – bow lances, bear totem, war bonnets, war shirts
Wolf Soldiers – wolf totem, straight lances with eagle feathers, fire dance, spear dance
Crazy Dogs – Northern Cheyenne version of Bowstrings, crazy dance
Red Shields – bull dance, informal behavior, red-painted shields
Dog Soldiers – crow-feather head-dresses, sawtooth coup sticks, doughnut-shaped rattles, dog ropes
Fox Soldiers – flint, sacred fox pelt
Elk Soldiers – hoof rattlers, elk-horn scrapers, crooked lances, hoop game

This list of traits should not imply that every member of a society exhibited all the traits, or that any trait was limited to a particular society. That is, if you had lined up all the Dog Soldiers going to war at a particular time in the 19th century, they would not look like a group of men in some kind of distinctive uniform. Cross-cutting all the symbols and attributes of a particular society were the personal medicines of a warrior, which might mean that a Dog Soldier would carry a crooked lance or a Fox Soldier a bow lance. Some warriors who were not Dog Soldiers might wear crow feathers, for personal medicine reasons, or have a dog rope. There were hundreds of personal medicine ways which were passed down through the generations of warriors which made each man distinctive in his dress, paint, and behavior in battle. Only the officers of the societies made some attempt to embody the distinctive emblems of their society in their battle dress. Sometimes a particular lance or other weapon, a head-dress, or a war shirt went along with the office to which a man was elected.

In modern times, the members of a military society make some effort to wear the same kind of clothing on special occasions. Sometimes they all wear red shirts and jeans, or white cowboy hats for an outdoor pow-wow. More emphatically, a society will occasionally authorize the printing of T-shirts or the manufacture of jackets which say, for example, "Dog Soldiers," or "Bowstring Memorial Dance 1989." Both the Bowstrings and the Dog Soldiers have occasionally made traditional war lances and coup sticks and carried them ceremonially on special occasions in recent years (plate 5.4).

In aboriginal times, all men were expected to join a military society when they approached adult status. Usually, a young man first went along on war parties, holding horses or otherwise assisting the warriors, before he joined a society. Although young men normally joined their father's society, legally they could join any society they chose. Sometimes there was competition among societies to attract the best and bravest young men as members.

Throughout the 20th century, the traditional sector of Cheyenne society has maintained the soldier societies, or "soldier clans" as they call them, and respectable young men are expected to join them when they are about high school age. The opportunity is presented annually in the few days preceding the major ceremonies, when the military societies erect tipis at the ceremon-

Plate 5.4   *A grand entry into a local pow-wow is led by two Vietnam veterans, Johnny Botone, carrying a crooked lance, and Colbert Cole, in 1986 (photo by Darrell Rice of the* Watonga Republican*)*

ial grounds and initiate their new members. In Oklahoma, the Bowstring and Elk societies are closely associated and initiate their members together, as do the Dog Soldiers and Foxes. The following narrative, from Birdie Burns, describes the recruitment of new members about 1920. In addition to showing recruitment procedures, the narrative also shows the gentle and humorous manner in which Cheyenne people participate in some of their most important institutions:[4]

> So when these old members die away the young ones carry on. And they used to encourage all these young boys at a certain age to go and join some clan. They said, "That's the only way you'll be recognized – if you join a clan. Otherwise you will not be recognized. People don't know who you are – your name and your parents. If you go there you get to introduce yourselves." These little boys.

I know mostly about these Bowstrings. I don't know about these other clans. Maybe they're about the same. My father used to say when these little boys came to the door, he said there were two clans that used to stay together all the time. There were these Hoof Rattlers and the Bowstrings. The Bowstring was put on the south side .... And when these little boys come to the door – See, my father was the Doorkeeper – him and another man. And they're supposed to be very courteous .... They talk to them and say, "You come to join us?" And these two Doorkeepers, when they're along with their own clan, they sit side by side of the door. So when the other Hoof Rattlers are with them – see, they have two Doorkeepers too – they have to sit on one side. The Bowstrings are on one side and the Hoof Rattlers on this other side. And when the little boys come, naturally those Hoof Rattlers want those little boys for members, and same way with the Bowstrings.

"All right, boys. You come to join us?" Both sides – these men at the door – would be trying to draw them to their side. They said, "Come on in. Come in. Come on and take your place! Here we are right here! Look us over," they tell these little boys. "Which are the best-looking men that you want to join?" They tease them, you know. "See, we're all nice looking over here and look at that other side – they're nothing but old hard-of-hearing men!" They just fuss like that before these little boys. These little boys would just laugh. They'd kind of look back and forth. But they already know which side they're going to join. See, their parents tells them that – "You join the Hoof Rattlers." Or, "You join the Bowstrings." The little boys just stand there. Finally some of them will speak up. "I'm going to join the Bowstring Clan." Or, "I'm going to join the Hoof Rattlers." And the men would say,"Oh, you're welcome. You're our little brothers." They set them over there.

There are three levels of membership in the military societies – ordinary members, little chiefs, and big chiefs. In the past, members who distinguished themselves in warfare were selected as little chiefs for a four-year term. Sometimes there are special emblems or symbols or songs which go with these offices, and the little chiefs are expected to be exemplary in their conduct. In pre-reservation times, they were expected to lead the warriors into battle. More serious were the obligations laid on the big chiefs, likewise elected for a four-year term from among those little chiefs who had especially distinguished themselves. In pre-reservation times, the big chief was flatly "selected to die." That is, he was supposed to be so fearless and aggressive in battle that he would not survive his term of office. Typically, a warrior "selected to die" would give away most or all of his possessions, and might give up buffalo hunting and social activities to devote himself entirely to war medicines, prayer, and fasting. During this time he would be supported by family members and society members, who would bring him and his family food, clothing, and other necessities. Men who took "the war road," that is, men who aspired to be war leaders, frequently eschewed marriage and family and became loners, living with a parent, brother, sister, or friend. They were treated with great respect.

Military societies waxed and waned in accordance with the bravery and reputation of their members, especially the big war chiefs. If members of a society suffered great casualties, it was said that their medicine was bad, and young men were reluctant to join the society. Conversely, if a society distinguished itself in battle, young men flocked to join. Although a man could not quit one society and join another, members of one society could join a war expedition led and organized by a different society.

It has frequently happened that a society "goes down" in membership for various reasons, and at some point everyone begins to take an interest in revitalizing the society, simply to preserve it. This happened most recently to the Elks or Hoof Rattlers in Oklahoma, which had only a handful of older members in the 1970s. To preserve the society, warriors of all societies began to encourage young men with Hoof Rattler ancestors to join the society and bring it back toward its full size. This was done and the society soon recovered to a membership of 20–40. In 1984 I was pleased to provide the Northern Crazy Dogs with everything I could find published or in archives about the society, so that they could reconstruct some practices and ceremonies that had been lost, and rejuvenate the society.

In the 19th century, likewise, we see memberships in the major societies growing and diminishing. When the big chief of the Dog Soldiers committed a murder in 1838, the Dog Soldiers were exiled to live by themselves and had difficulty attracting new members. But when some of the Dog Soldiers distinguished themselves in the Battle of Wolf Creek and reorganized themselves as the militant, raiding faction of the tribe, young men flocked to join them. Membership of the Bowstrings went similarly up and down in the 19th century. After 42 Bowstrings were surrounded and killed by Kiowas, it was said that their medicine was bad and young men avoided them. But Yellow Wolf solved this problem by reorganizing the society around new medicines and emblems. During the warfare of 1864–74, the Bowstrings distinguished themselves in battles against the US Army, and once again rose to prominence.

After reservation life began for the Cheyennes, in the period 1869–78, there was no opportunity for men to participate in warfare and thus gain war honors. Without such participation, a young man could not join a military society, and so the societies became smaller, and the members older, in the years 1878–1918. A few Cheyennes participated in World War I, however, and the issue was raised whether this kind of individual participation was equivalent to participating in traditional warfare, where a whole group of Cheyenne warriors fought together. The old warriors of that period also considered the issue of whether counting coup was absolutely essential for membership in a military society, and they tried to understand the American system of war honors, which they initially considered to be rather peculiar.

For one thing, they did not understand why an American soldier should get a medal for being wounded. In Cheyenne tradition, a wound meant that there was something wrong with your medicine. It was a matter of embarrassment, not honor. The medals for bravery, however, were easier for Cheyennes to understand, and were quickly brought into the native system of war honors. The societies limped along between World Wars I and II, then burst into life with the return of World War II veterans in the late 1940s. After the Vietnam War, however, another tricky issue arose at a meeting of the Bowstrings which I was privileged to attend in 1977. This was the question of why a person should be honored who had allowed himself to be captured. By Cheyenne standards, this was a mark of cowardice. As an Anglo-American and US Army veteran, I was asked to explain this practice to the Bowstrings. I explained that, in this case, the men were being honored for their bravery in enduring the hardships of captivity and, in some cases, brutality, and torture. The Bowstrings were not impressed, but fortunately the man being discussed was not a Cheyenne. He was a white airman, imprisoned in Hanoi, who had asked to be made an honorary member of the society. He was politely refused.

In addition to taking a leading role in warfare, the military societies have also been historically charged with policing the tribe and keeping order during communal buffalo hunts and tribal gatherings. During the great hunts of the 19th century, the appointed military society had to make sure that no one hunted prematurely, thereby frightening the buffaloes so that they escaped, and that everyone approached the herd in an orderly fashion. At the major ceremonies – Arrow Renewal, Sun Dance, and Hat Ceremony – a society was appointed to make sure that the great camp was quiet and orderly, that visitors were greeted, and that the ceremonies proceeded on time.

After reservation times began, the societies continued in the role of peacekeeper. At one point, the Indian agent in Oklahoma Territory, despairing of using the US Cavalry in such a role, since they tended to provoke the Cheyennes instead of quieting them down, hired the Dog Soldiers to keep order on the reservation, which they did. Until modern times, the sponsors of large tribal gatherings have usually appointed one of the societies as temporary police. Recently, such gatherings have included not only ceremonies, but large pow-wows, fairs, and rodeos. Especially, the societies take a prominent role in sponsoring the annual ceremonies. They not only police the gathering but, beginning months in advance, collect food, money, and other resources so that their members can participate as pledgers or dancers or in some other significant role in the ceremonies.

War Mothers

Traditionally, the mothers of slain Cheyenne warriors had certain privileges and duties. They were entitled to war booty and received gifts from men in the same military society as their son. To these ideas, after World War I, was added the Anglo-American idea of the "Gold Star Mother," who had lost a son in the war. What emerged from this, during World War II, was the institution known as the Cheyenne War Mothers.

Organized on a community basis, war mothers in World War II included all women with sons in the military. They took responsibility for honoring their sons as they left for war and when they returned. They sponsored pow-wows to raise money for travel and gifts for soldiers, and they made special shawls for themselves with the name of their community war mothers' group and often the name, rank, and military decorations of their sons.

At the special events they sponsored, the war mothers danced as a group counter-clockwise, the opposite way from other dancers. At victory or coming-home dances, they danced clockwise with their sons. The war mothers' groups had diminished in membership after World War II, but were reorganized during the Korean and Vietnam Wars, but not during the Persian Gulf War. "It happened too quick," one war mother told me.

Military Tactics and Strategy

The difference between strategy and tactics is that the former involves long-range considerations of political goals and geographical objectives, while the latter concerns the weapons and methods necessary to win a battle. In the previous chapter I have explained that the overall military strategy of the Cheyennes in the 18th and 19th centuries was to dominate trade in the central plains and to push aside the tribes who had previously dominated that trade. Another strategic objective was to control the areas of high buffalo density, especially as buffaloes became more scarce toward the middle of the 19th century.

These strategic goals were acted upon during the serious, seasonal warfare of the spring and early summer. After the Cheyenne Nation had gathered for ceremonies, after the horses had gained strength on new grass, and after some food had been put away, a military campaign was decided upon in tribal council. The scale of the campaign could be anything from a war expedition led by a military society, which might involve several hundred warriors, to a full-scale "moving of the arrows" against an enemy, which involved the participation of every Cheyenne. The idealized battle described by John Greany is the result of an offensive expedition led by a warrior society, or several warrior societies acting in concert. The purpose was to defeat and intimidate an enemy nation and to increase Cheyenne territory at their expense.

The arrows were moved against enemy nations on at least six occasions. The least successful was the move against the Pawnees in 1830, which resulted in the capture of the sacred arrows by the Pawnees. Perhaps the most successful was the move against the Kiowas in 1838 at the celebrated Battle of Wolf Creek. As with all such major strategic movements of the tribe, the rationale for this attack was revenge, in this case revenge for the death of 42 Bowstring Soldiers killed by the Kiowas the previous year.

Logistically, it was difficult to manage a move of the arrows, since the whole tribe had to go along, from weak and perhaps bed-ridden elders to little babies, and the soldier chiefs had to prevent the warriors from attacking until the whole tribe had come up to the battleground. For the Battle of Wolf Creek, the Cheyennes moved south-east from their last camp on Beaver River in what is now the Oklahoma panhandle, leaving their tipis behind and traveling all night to reach the site of the Kiowa camp on Wolf Creek. Accompanying the Cheyennes were their Arapaho allies, and camped with the Kiowas were some of their Comanche and Apache allies. There were altogether perhaps two thousand warriors on each side, along with the entire population of Cheyennes, about 3,500 people including warriors, and the main camps of the Kiowas and Comanches, with about the same number of people. The Cheyennes attacked to the south in three columns, the Dog Soldiers on the right, the rest of the Cheyenne warriors in the center, and the Arapahoes on the left. The central column was closely followed by the Cheyenne elders, women, and children.

In council with the Arapahoes, the Cheyennes had already decided that this was to be a war of extermination against their enemies, specifically the Kiowas. Among the first Kiowas killed were 12 women who were digging roots north of the village. More than 20 Kiowa women were killed in the battle, some of them by groups of Cheyenne women on foot and armed with knives. As the battle proceeded across the Kiowa village, the Cheyenne women took an increasingly larger role as they ran up to join the fighting.

The Kiowas were completely surprised, and most of the battle consisted of Kiowas and Comanches trying to organize themselves into small groups to defend themselves and mount a counter-attack. At one point, the Kiowa women dug breastworks near the village to defend themselves, and at another point, a group of Cheyenne warriors pretended to flee, thus drawing out the Kiowa and Comanche warriors into an ambush. Gradually during the day, the Kiowas collected themselves into defensible positions, and after a hard day of fighting the Cheyennes and Arapahoes withdrew. During the course of the battle, hundreds of Kiowa and Comanche men and women were killed, while both the Cheyennes and Arapahoes suffered serious casualties. Several of the Cheyenne big warrior chiefs were killed, and many prominent warriors. It was this battle which convinced both sides that further fighting would simply weaken them all for the coming confrontation with white people, and ultimately led to the great alliance of 1840.

When warfare developed with the United States Army, it was of a different sort.[5] The Army did not operate from movable villages, as the Indians did, but from permanent forts. The soldiers were not men who had to periodically return to their families and domestic obligations, but full-time professional fighters, on call night and day. The Cheyennes, like other Plains Indians, discovered that the best tactic to use against the US Army was to confront the soldiers when they were far from the fort, in small groups, and therefore more vulnerable.

The trick of mounted warfare is to catch the enemy when his horses are tired and your own horses are fresh (Cooke 1862). All the maneuvering and most of the tactics of mounted warfare on the plains were dedicated to that end. One basic maneuver, used in Indian–Indian warfare but developed to perfection against the US soldiers, was to set out a small group of warriors as "bait." They would ride down a trail to meet an Army column or cross a trail in front of them, stop their horses suddenly, and pretend to be surprised at seeing the Army troops for the first time. Then they would pretend to run in terror, far enough to tire out the Army horses, perhaps two or three miles at a gallop, and far enough away to prevent relief from the main body of the troops. Typically, the Army would send out only enough cavalry to defeat the forces which they had observed. The trap was sprung when a large body of Cheyenne warriors emerged from concealment, on fresh horses, to attack a smaller contingent of cavalry whose horses were exhausted from the chase. This was the tactic used to bring about the Fetterman Massacre of 81 US soldiers in Wyoming in 1866.

It is often said that the battles of a new war are fought at first with the tactics of the previous war, and so it was that the US Army, in its first engagements after the Civil War, used tactics against Plains Indians that had been successful against the Confederate Army, but which proved to be inappropriate in a new context. The mounted forces used on the plains consisted of both mounted infantry and cavalry, supplied by wagon trains. On the roadless part of the prairie, and even on the few improved roads when it was wet and muddy, the wagons were very slow and they impeded the daily march of the soldiers to a rate of about 10–15 miles a day. If they carried all their supplies in wagons, the maximum time that a patrol or larger expedition of mounted soldiers could be in the field was about 20 days, perhaps 12 days out and eight days back. Slow and conspicuous, the Army columns were easily spotted by Cheyenne scouts who could then lay traps and ambushes.

The alternative to the wagon-supplied patrol was to organize a group of soldiers who carried their own supplies on horseback, and to load bedrolls and a few days' rations on the horse of each trooper and send them out to chase Indians. The problem with this tactic was that the loaded Army horses, usually tired and lame after a few days on the trail, could not catch the Indian warriors, who carried very little equipment and had several spare horses. The more mobile Indian warriors thus had the opportunity to select a point of ambush where the soldiers were at a disadvantage and their own horses were rested. We should bear in mind that, when attacking, the Cheyenne warriors left their spare horses and equipment in the hands of women and young men who were concealed nearby. When the warriors attacked and dispersed, they were careful not to lead the soldiers to the place where their spare horses were hidden.

The early use of mounted infantry on the plains was even less effective than the tactics used by cavalry (Dept of Indian Territory 1863). Upon contacting the enemy, the mounted infantry were supposed to ride forward, dismount, and deploy themselves as riflemen, perhaps digging foxholes or trenches to form a defensive line laid out on the ground with guidons by the commander. In the Civil War this was a tactic for advancing the battle line into some weak area of the enemy, enabling the regular infantry to come forward and link up with the mounted infantry. But on the open plains this tactic made no sense. The response of the Cheyenne warriors was to bypass the entrenched deployment of riflemen and attack the horseholders, who comprised only one fourth of the total number of infantry in the unit and were usually sent back about one hundred yards to the rear, supposedly out of the combat zone. The bonus of this kind of attack was not only to overwhelm an inferior force of horseholders, but to run off the horses, leaving all the soldiers on foot.

After a few years of fighting Indians on the plains, Army planners realized that they could not continue to use their current tactics to defeat the Plains Indians in mobile conflict – in fact they could not even catch the Indian warriors – and that some other tactics were called for. The basic unit of the new tactics would be the stripped-down and speeded-up cavalry squadron, armed only with sabers and pistols, and carrying no extra equipment or rations. The squadron would rendezvous periodically with its supply wagons, which would be defended by mounted or dismounted infantry. Instead of following along behind the cavalry and slowing them down, the wagons would make their own separate way during the day and meet the cavalry squadron at some pre-arranged place. Meanwhile the cavalry was free to loop around on a longer route and conduct reconnaissance at a walk or quick trot, responding quickly to any Indian attack. Rested and with no extra equipment, the new American "light cavalry" was a match for the Indian forces in speed, and more than a match in firepower. Following the example of the Indians, the Army units began to buy extra horses for their troops and herd them along with the wagons, ironically purchasing some Indian mounts from ranchers and traders on the frontier.

Strategically, there were also some changes. More forts were needed since the lightly-supplied cavalry could not travel very far from the fort. In addition, "cantonments" were built, which were merely supply dumps strategically located so that an Army unit did not have to return to the fort to resupply itself. The cantonments did not have enough troops to initiate an action against the Indians, but only to defend their supplies.

The total number of US soldiers on the plains was also built up. By 1868 there were more than 5,000 soldiers in the field. The overall strategy of the Army was to concentrate the soldiers first in the southern plains to defeat the southern alliance of Cheyennes, Arapahoes, Kiowas, Comanches, and Apaches, and then to move most of the troops to the north to defeat the Lakota alliance. To this end, Indian troops and scouts were recruited who had been the enemies of the allied groups, especially the Pawnees and Crows. These Indian soldiers took a leading role in the battles which ultimately crushed the Cheyennes and their allies both in the south and the north.

One strategy which turned out to be decisive was to attack Indian villages in the winter when the Indian horses were thin and weak. To keep their own horses in the field during winter, the Army imported tons of grain to the plains, which was stashed in selected forts and cantonments. Because their horses were thin from poor winter grazing and they had no grain, the Indians could not move their villages very easily in the winter months, and so they were easier to attack once they had been located. The most disastrous defeats of Cheyenne villages in this condition were at the Battle of the Washita in 1868, and in Montana and the Dakotas in the winter following the Custer battle of 1876.

In response to this new American strategy of building up supplies and attacking villages, the Cheyennes first realized that they had to oppose the building of forts, and they did what they could to harass the surveyors, builders, wagons, pony express, telegraph lines, and even railroad trains sent out from eastern Kansas and Nebraska. After the Sand Creek Massacre, they succeeded in closing the Platte River Road, isolating Denver, and they closed both the Bozeman Trail and the Smoky Hill Road. But in the late 1860s, they gradually succumbed to the strategy of forts, and to the increasing weight of numbers brought to bear by the US Army.

Tactically, to protect their villages in defensive warfare, the Cheyennes returned to a technique which had served them well in a famous battle fought before the Civil War, the Battle of Solomon Fork in 1857 (Chalfont 1989). This tactic involved sending out their warriors to form a long skirmish line to slow down the attackers, thereby allowing the women enough time to take down the tipis, load the travois and pack animals, and disperse in a hundred directions. The women didn't need much time – only an hour or two to pack everything and be out of sight.

The skirmish line defense was most effective when it was used in some constrained area where the attackers could not outflank the Cheyennes and charge the village. During the Battle of Solomon Fork (see map 5.1), the main village of Cheyennes (off the map to the south) was defended by about 4–800 Cheyenne warriors against the 600 men of the US First Cavalry. The battle was precocious in many ways, largely because of the intelligence of the American commander, Colonel Edwin Sumner, who streamlined his expedition in a manner which would be imitated a decade later, after the Civil War. To make his column more maneuverable, Sumner exchanged most of his supply wagons for pack mules, and on the day of the battle he left his four artillery pieces, his infantry, and supplies behind for the sake of speed in maneuver.

The Cheyennes had been watching the progress of the expedition for many months, as portions of the expedition wound around Cheyenne territory along the Platte and the Arkansas Rivers, finally joining together in a camp on the Platte River. In July, the Cheyennes decided to lure the combined Sumner force, which was traveling south, into the valley of the Solomon Fork, in what is now central Kansas, where the river valley narrows to about a half mile in width. They set their village south from this location, out of sight, and sent a large number of scouts north to observe the soldiers and to be seen by them. The task of the scouts was to move slowly and visibly back toward the Solomon, to make sure that the soldiers entered the valley by a route which passed by the constriction where the Cheyennes wanted to fight.

Seeing the scouts, Sumner speeded up his cavalry for the last several miles, so that the horses were already tired by the time they turned the corner into the valley and saw the main body of Cheyenne warriors, drawn up five deep in a loose skirmish line at the east end. At this point the Cheyennes made a tactical mistake. Instead of attacking immediately, they gave Sumner's cavalry time to dismount and tighten their girths, then remount and advance toward the Cheyennes in closely-drawn battle lines "at a trot march." Then the Cheyennes advanced, timing their own charge so that they would meet the cavalry at the neck of the constriction. Several hundred yards further into the valley, the soldiers responded to a bugle call and speeded up to a "gallop march," and the Cheyennes likewise speeded up. The Cheyennes

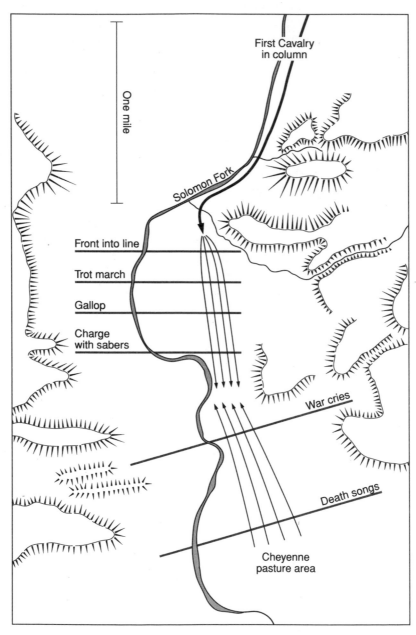

Map 5.1   Battle of Solomon Fork (redrawn from Chalfant 1989)

began shouting ferociously and singing their death songs. And then something entirely unexpected happened.

Suffering a disadvantage in the number of firearms, the Cheyennes had prepared themselves emotionally and religiously for charging fearlessly into the concentrated pistol fire of the cavalry. Their leading medicine men, Ice and Dark, had prepared special war medicines to deflect bullets and protect the Cheyenne warriors. But at the decisive moment of the battle, the soldiers did not draw their pistols as the Cheyennes expected, but rather, at the command of Colonel Sumner and the call of the bugler, they drew their long sabers and held them high overhead. At the command to "Charge!" the soldiers lowered the tips of their sabers, let out a great roaring yell, and galloped down the valley at top speed toward the Cheyenne warriors, who were now within a hundred yards. The Cheyennes, equipped with "anti-bullet" but not "anti-saber" medicines, were confused and reined their horses to a sudden stop. Unsure of what to do next, and with no time to talk it over, they simply fired off a volley of arrows and bullets, and then turned and dispersed into the surrounding hills.

The Cheyennes did not flee from the field of battle, however; rather they engaged the soldiers in small groups around the Solomon for several hours. This enabled the rest of the Cheyenne population to escape, as well as wearing out the horses of the cavalry, preventing immediate pursuit. Although the Cheyennes did not inflict heavy casualties on the soldiers – only two were killed and nine wounded – they essentially ended the expedition, which followed the Cheyennes for a few days and then, with horses and soldiers exhausted, went into camp on the Arkansas River. Nine Cheyennes were killed according to Army reports, four according to Cheyenne sources.

For the next decade, the typical fight between Cheyennes and US soldiers was a small affair between a party of Indian raiders and a cavalry patrol. But toward the end of the Indian Wars, the Cheyennes began forming themselves into large, year-round camps, supplied by raids as well as by hunting. They defended these camps with the same tactics used at the Battle of Solomon Fork. Here the goal was not to try to defeat a superior enemy, but to injure them and keep them in check long enough for the non-combatants to escape. According to Indian accounts, the Cheyennes were surprised to find, at the Battle of the Little Big

Horn, that their defensive skirmish line, sent out hastily to defend the village, had outflanked Custer's command on both sides and surrounded them. With Custer's escape cut off, the Cheyennes and their Lakota allies killed every soldier.

6

Bands and Tribal Structure

Two opposite demographic forces began to operate on the Cheyenne population after they took to the plains in the 17th and 18th centuries. On the one hand, the greater amount of food and the higher protein level obtained from a larger supply of buffalo meat created generally better all-around nutrition, less illness, and hence a higher fertility rate for the population. Although the Cheyennes, like other Indian peoples, were aware of various methods of birth control, in their new environment there was no good reason to control the birth rate – the more children the better. There was plenty of food and plenty of work to be done. On the other hand, acting on the population in an opposite direction, the new European diseases were spreading around the continent in recurrent epidemics, diseases for which the immune systems of Native Americans were not fully prepared, and for which they had no standard cultural response.[1]

It is an exaggeration to say that Indian people had "no defense" against European diseases, for the human body has a number of generalized immunological defenses, even against diseases which it has not experienced before. In addition, the native North Americans had only been separated from Old World populations for about 20,000 years, and so they still carried with them the immune responses of their common ancestors with Europeans, of about that date. And while some of the diseases faced by Indian populations in the 17th and 18th centuries were mutations unknown in the Americas, they were closely related, in many cases, to New World diseases against which Indian people did have some resistance.

Equally as important as the nature of these new diseases which afflicted Indian people were the nutritional and sanitary conditions in which they found themselves when the diseases struck. For sedentary, riverine groups like the Mandans, Hidatsas, and Arikaras, the advent of new diseases found them relatively undernourished compared to the nomadic groups, because they were poor in horses and surrounded by hostile tribes, and consequently did not have easy access to the buffalo herds. Also, sanitary practices among the sedentary groups were bad and human waste tended to build up in nearby areas which were used as toilets, providing a reservoir of human disease which could be carried to the villages through the water supply or by means of disease vectors such as flies and rodents. In addition, because many of the riverine people lived in houses built close together inside palisades, contagious diseases were quickly passed around the village population. By the time a disease had been through its latent period of incubation and had broken out in visible form, large numbers of people had already been infected.

Nomadic groups like the Cheyennes contrasted strongly with the riverine groups in their demographic and epidemiological condition when European diseases first came. For one thing, since the Cheyennes moved camp regularly, they periodically left behind all the garbage and human waste which provided habitat for the flies and other pests which served as carriers of disease. Each time the Cheyennes moved, they also left behind a water supply which might have become contaminated by disease, and exchanged it for a new source which was fresh. The Cheyennes were quite aware of the benefits of good sanitation, and they customarily camped where a spring entered a river, and used the spring for their own water, allowing the horses to drink from the river. Bathing was done in front of the village, and the stock was watered downstream. Toilet areas were also downstream, and jokes prevailed among many plains tribes about which tribes and bands were "downstream people" and hence forced to live next to rivers polluted by the sewage of the "upstream people."

As epidemic diseases such as cholera and smallpox began to decimate the sedentary peoples, the Cheyennes discovered that their best defense against these fearful scourges was to break camp and disperse, just as if they were fleeing from some powerful military force. When a band split into family groups, if they did not already harbor the disease in the family they could

Table 6.1   *Cheyenne population from earliest times*

Year	Population
1985	10,771
1980	9,918
1970	6,872
1930	2,695
1910	3,055
1900	3,446
1890	3,654
1880	3,767
1878	3,298
1780	3,500

Source: Moore 1987: 325; Thornton 1987: 120

not catch it, unless visited by infected people. After the disease had run its course in a few weeks the various family groups could once again gather together. The band as a whole consequently suffered a lower rate of infection than if they had all stayed together during an epidemic, since some family groups would escape the disease altogether.

At the beginning of the 19th century, there were about ten Cheyenne bands comprising about 300 people each, although much larger was the Omisis or "Eater" Band which ultimately became the core of the Northern Cheyennes when they separated from the southerners. In that century the Cheyennes, like the Lakotas and other nomadic groups, generally increased in population, although some bands suffered episodes of epidemic disease and massacre. One episode of disease is important, since it not only shows why the effects of disease were occasionally very serious, but also why the Cheyenne defense of dispersion was most often effective. In 1849 a large band of Cheyennes, the Masikota, was traveling to a huge inter-tribal gathering when cholera appeared in the band. Rather than dispersing as usual, the band stayed together since they were very anxious to attend the gathering, to dance and exchange gifts with their allies. Consequently they suffered high mortalities nearing 50 per cent. The size of the Cheyenne population from earliest times is shown in table 6.1.

Bands – a Brief History

The Cheyenne bands were different from one another in their sizes and histories. Although no one knows for sure which of the groups known archaeologically or from oral accounts turned into which well-known bands of the historical period, some of the southern bands are good candidates to be the descendants of people from the Biesterfeldt site in North Dakota, who moved from there onto the Grand River and the Cheyenne River in South Dakota, and later to a position between the forks of the Platte in Wyoming at the end of the 18th century. The other major Cheyenne village known ethnohistorically, located at one time downstream from the Biesterfeldt group on the Grand River, was probably the parent of the Northern Cheyenne bands, some of which remained in the area of the Black Hills after the Southern Cheyenne bands had moved south to Colorado.

The southern group, known to the Lakota as "Chianeton" in the 17th century, probably called themselves either Heviksnipa-his, usually translated as Aorta People, or Tsistsistas, the tribal name still used but which resists linguistic analysis. Guesses about the meaning of the word range from "the people" to "the sand people" to "the original people." The other, northern group of Cheyennes was known as the Eaters, or in the Cheyenne language as Omisis and in Cheyennized Lakota as Wotapio. Both of these became band names after the term Tsistsistas was settled upon as the tribal name of the new nation, probably in the early 18th century. The historical relationships among the various Cheyenne bands are very complex, and I have written an entire book on the subject (1987): I will not try to recapitulate that book here, except to show the locations of these bands as of 1845 on map 6.1.

Two foreign groups were accepted into the Cheyenne Nation as it was being formed. One was the Sutaio group of four bands, some of whom associated themselves with the Hisiometanio Band in the south, and the rest of whom joined the Omisis in the north, taking with them their sacred buffalo hat. (The Southern Cheyennes had the sacred arrows.) The other group joining the new nation was the Masikota, originally a hybrid

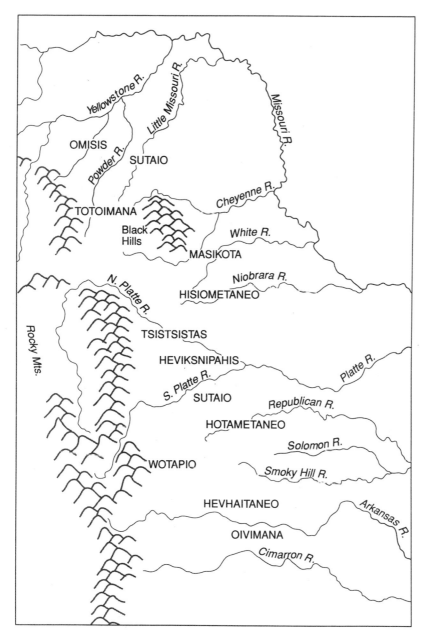

Map 6.1 Usual locations of Cheyenne bands, about 1845 (from Moore 1987: 216)

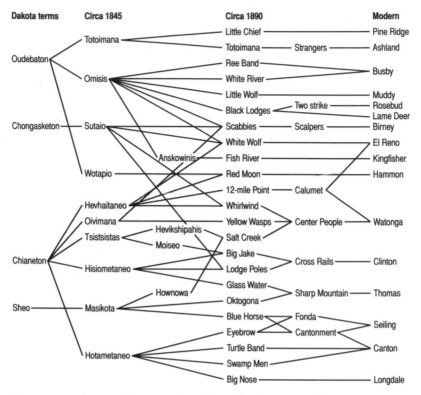

Figure 6.1 How Cheyenne bands evolved into modern communities (Moore 1987: 249)

Sioux-Cheyenne group associated with the Lakota, where they were known as the Sheo.

Figure 6.1 shows the evolution of traditional, nomadic Cheyenne bands into reservation bands, and thence into modern settled reservation communities. On the left are shown the names of the bands as they were known by the Dakotas, and by the early French travelers who transcribed the names. In the center are the names of the reservation bands as they became settled in Oklahoma and Montana, and on the right are the current names of Cheyenne communities on both reservations. Map 6.2 shows the locations of the important Southern Cheyenne communities in Oklahoma, and map 6.3 provides the same information for the Northern Cheyenne communities in Montana. The two divisions of the Cheyenne Nation still feel very close to one

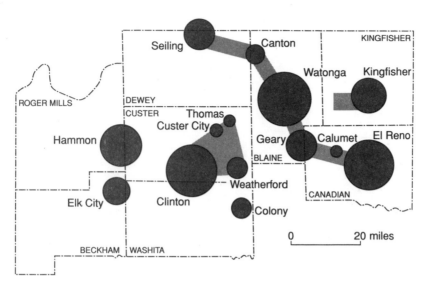

Map 6.2 The Southern Cheyenne Reservation in Oklahoma; the shaded areas joining the communities are rural areas in which there is a high density of Indian homes

another because of their shared history, they constantly visit one another for pow-wows and ceremonies, and there is a great deal of intermarriage. Many modern Cheyennes have the option of enrolling either on the Montana reservation or in Oklahoma, because they have ancestors enrolled on both reservations.

Marriage and Intermarriage

In the 19th century, Cheyenne bands were highly intermarried both among themselves and with foreigners, as evidenced by oral history, the pattern of personal names, and the responses listed in the 1900 US Special Census of Indians.[2] There were positive and negative motivations for someone to marry a spouse from a band located perhaps hundreds of miles away. On the positive side, there were advantages to be gained by creating reciprocal social and economic relationships with distant bands as a hedge

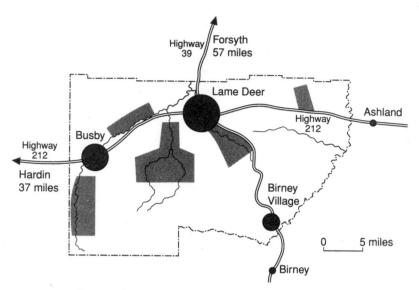

Map 6.3   The Northern Cheyenne Reservation in Montana

against hard times. If a band was hungry, or had lost its horses or tipis to raiders, they could take refuge among their relatives in another band. And since a marriage ceremony required an elaborate exchange of gifts, families from both bands profited by exchanging items which were plentiful in their band for items which were precious to them but more plentiful in other bands, especially guns, horses, kettles and knives.

The bands were specialized economically in the mid 19th century. The southern bands were horse-catchers and horse-raiders, the central bands specialized in making buffalo robes, and the northern bands were rich in guns, knives, and kettles, because of their trade on the Missouri River. Each time a marriage was arranged between distant bands, there was a redistribution and leveling of wealth between the bands. Marriages with foreign tribes brought even more economic and political advantages. Prominent chiefs of plains tribes oftentimes publicly exchanged their sons and daughters as spouses, lavishing gifts on one another in huge public giveaways and cementing alliances for years to come.

Cheyennes were not only pulled into marrying spouses from distant bands for positive reasons, they were also pushed by negative reasons, such as the necessity of avoiding incest. To

Cheyennes, it was incestuous to marry any known relative including any cousin, no matter how distant, a group which usually included most of the people in one's own band, who collectively tended to be the descendants of some historically-known chief and his multiple wives. Neighboring bands might also be taboo for supplying spouses if there had been marriage with that band in previous generations. And so young Cheyenne men and women and their parents were forced to look far and wide for appropriate spouses. Fortunately, the annual tribal gathering in the spring and inter-band visits through the summer and fall provided an opportunity to "shop around" for a spouse. In fact, one of the motivations for visiting among bands was not only to trade and talk, but also to look for available spouses.

Marriages among the Cheyennes were largely arranged by parents until the 20th century, although the potential bride and groom had some say in the matter. Girls were thought to reach a marriageable age at about 16–20 years, men somewhat later, perhaps 20–25. A potential groom usually picked a girl he liked and visited with her publicly or talked to her through her tipi wall at night. A girl could discourage a suitor either by her manner or by telling her parents that she didn't like him. Before anything definite or final was arranged, an older woman from the boy's family, or a chief, would approach the girl's family and ask what they thought about a particular match. If the match was agreeable, then a time would be set for a ceremonial exchange of gifts, which might require several months to prepare. In the meantime, a prospective groom would leave buffalo meat or horses captured in a raid at the girl's tipi, as gifts for the family. Sometimes the girl's family would reciprocate by leaving gifts for the boy's family. All of this symbolized the reciprocal relationship which would be created by the marriage.

To prepare for the wedding ceremony, the bride's mother and female relatives made a new tipi with complete furnishings, which would be set up near the tipi of the bride's family on the wedding day. When everything was in order, the bride dressed up in her best clothing and mounted a horse led by the person who had arranged the marriage. She was followed by her mother and female relatives, all of whom walked behind leading other horses as gifts for the groom's family.

When they arrived at the groom's tipi, the bride was carried inside the tipi by his family. If the male relatives carried the bride, it was done by sitting her on a blanket and carrying the blanket into the tipi. Or the new mother-in-law could carry the bride into the tipi on her back, assisted by her women relatives, symbolizing their love and affection for the groom's chosen bride. Then the bride was dressed in beautiful new clothing made by the groom's family. This was followed by a meal in the tipi, prepared by the groom's mother, where the bride and groom ate together for the first time. Following the meal, there was an elaborate exchange of gifts between all members of the bride's and groom's extended families, whereupon the bride's family loaded the gifts they had received onto their new horses and walked back to the new tipi which had been prepared for the couple, near the tipi of the bride's parents.

The symbolic meaning of the marriage ceremony is very clear – it is not merely the bride and groom who are being joined, but their entire families. In many cases, the marriage of an older daughter to the groom would be followed by the marriage of her younger sisters to the same man, or a sister of the bride to the brother of the groom. Together, the four parents of the couple or couples might become grandparents of perhaps ten or twenty children, enough to start a new band.

Kinship

The kinship system of the Cheyennes has evolved dramatically over the past two hundred years, and there have been variants of the system during each historical period. The system to be emphasized here is that of the prominent chiefs who were, in the middle of the 19th century, traders and political leaders – the so-called "peace chiefs." Discussions of kinship can be very technical, but this particular system can be reduced to a very few central principles which are easily understood. The first principle is that a cohort of sisters and a cohort of brothers are considered in the system as groups, not as individuals. For example, a little baby girl learns to regard as "mother" not only the woman who bore her and nursed her, but also that person's sisters. They are all called "mother" in Cheyenne, *nako*. Similarly, a little girl uses the term "father", *niho*, not only for her biological father, but also for her father's brothers. All her father's sisters are called *nahan*, translated as "aunt", and her mother's brothers are called *nxan*, translated as "uncle". The Cheyenne terms for people whom Anglo-Americans call "uncles" and "aunts," then, are different, and, unlike English kin terms, they tell you immediately whether the person is on the father's or the mother's side of the family. Traditional Cheyennes find it peculiar that Anglo-Americans use the same terms, "aunt" and "uncle", whether they are referring to their mother's or father's relatives.

Because of the dangers faced by Cheyenne adults from warfare, disease, and buffalo hunting in the pre-reservation period, people with children frequently died before their children were grown. In these cases, the brothers and sisters of the dead parents quickly stepped forward as replacement parents. Cheyenne tradition required that a man marry his brother's widow, even if he was already married, and that a woman marry her dead sister's husband, if she were not already married. Otherwise she brought her sister's children into her own household. The terms used in the kinship system anticipated that these adoptions or replacements might be necessary, since children already called their father's brothers "father" and their mother's sisters "mother." In most cases, these replacement mothers and fathers already lived in the same camp or extended family, and so the adoptions, when necessary, were not very traumatic.

For many children, the number of potential replacement fathers and mothers was even larger than the camp or band, because it included their father's male first cousins if they were related through male lines, and their mother's female first cousins if they were related through female lines. The former group, in technical kinship parlance, is called "agnatic kin" and the latter group "uterine kin." In the Cheyenne language, such a group was called a *nisson*, meaning "my sisters and female cousins," female speaking, or "my brothers and male cousins," male speaking. Another way of looking at the structure of a nisson is that an agnatic nisson consists of a group of brothers and their sons, and a uterine nisson consists of a group of sisters and their daughters.

These nisson groups were very important for the continuation of a band, and each band chief tried to attract young men to come and marry the young women of his band, thereby adding to the size and importance of the band. Such marriages, where the groom comes to live in the bride's band, are called "matrilocal." An even better arrangement, when it could be arranged by two band chiefs, was for each to send his sons to the other chief's band as grooms for the other chief's daughters.

For various reasons, relationships between husband and wife were different among Cheyennes than among modern Anglo-Americans. The ideal relationship among proponents of "romantic love" in the Western tradition is that the husband and wife are constant companions, best friends, confidants, and constant lovers to one another. By contrast, the narratives of Cheyenne women reveal a much less intense relationship, largely domestic in nature.[3] A woman's best friends were her sisters, mother, and mother's sisters, not her husband, who was usually a stranger from another band whom she saw only in the evenings, and not every evening if he was gone to war, to hunt, or to trade. Adult women commonly report that they originally felt some passion for their husband, but that they didn't feel any real affection until they had spent many years together.

The traditional, respected characteristics of a "good woman," or a "good wife," are still presented explicitly by Cheyenne people in their competitions for pow-wow "princess." Women who win such competitions are not necessarily the most beautiful, physically, the most personable, or the most articulate. There is no "swim suit" competition as in the Miss America pageant! Instead, other kinds of characteristics, other social and cultural values which are honored in traditional Cheyenne society, are upheld and respected in the competitions for princess. First of all, a woman must compete wearing elaborate traditional clothing, usually made by herself, her sisters, her mother, and her mother's sisters (see plate 6.1). There is a great deal of conversation during the competition about who made what items, and how much work is represented, for example, in a beaded buckskin dress with boots and shawl. In her formal interview before the judges and the audience, the contestant does not talk about herself and her opinions, as a Miss America candidate might, but about her family, her grandmother, her deceased ancestors. She is asked to speak her native language and is likely to win the contest if she is fluent. She is asked questions about her culture and Cheyenne history and is expected to be modest about herself and about her knowledge of traditional matters. An appropriate answer might be: "My grandmother told me about the Sand

Plate 6.1   Katie Flynn, left, and Ricque Richardson, two Indian princesses from Oklahoma (photos by Darrell Rice of the Watonga Republican)

Creek Massacre. Other people say different things, but this is what I know because I listened to my grandmother." Any candidate who brags or shows off or is otherwise immodest does not win the contest. Women from large, respectable, influential families tend to win, reflecting the judges' opinion not only of the candidate, but of her extended family. Potential princess candidates with relatives in disrepute or in jail don't bother to enter such contests no matter what their personal qualifications might be. This is all by way of explaining that Cheyenne people, although they are surrounded and constantly buffeted by the values and attitudes of the dominant Anglo-American society, truly live in a different world.

Historically, these have been the virtues of good Cheyenne women and good wives – modest, hard-working people who have close relations with their sisters and other female kin. These groups of women, which anthropologists call "minimal matrilineages," have been the essential building blocks of Cheyenne society for a long time. In their horticultural days in Minnesota and the Dakotas, it was women in minimal matrilineages who tilled the soil, collected the crops, and prepared the food. In their buffalo hunting days, these were the women who dressed the buffaloes and prepared the robes for trade. In reservation and modern times, these are the women who manage the households, keep a job, and organize the food and gifts for pow-wows, giveaways, and the major ceremonies.

By contrast, the relationships among Cheyenne men have historically been more loose and negotiable, and have extended beyond the boundaries of kinship. Although men customarily joined the military society of their father, so that fathers and brothers tended to be in the same society, each society also included many men who were not related to one another. During the years of warfare against the US Army, some military societies reorganized themselves like domestic bands, and forced their wives to live with them in camps which did not necessarily include the women's mothers and sisters. This kind of social organization required some radical revisions in the kinship system, which I have described in some technical articles (1988; 1991a). When reservation life began in the period 1868–78, Cheyenne families reorganized themselves yet again, some reverting to the "peace chief" type of organization, some hanging onto the military type of organization, and some adopting new types of family and community structures which reflected their experiences with Anglo-Americans.

Over the past two hundred years, the extended family, consisting of a group of siblings, their parents, and their children, has remained the fundamental unit of Cheyenne society. At different times, the family was recruited differently, perhaps through female lines, perhaps male lines, perhaps both. But no matter how the extended family was recruited, certain principles of personal address, kinship and respect have been consistently honored. A child learned to call all the men present in his extended family "father," whatever the biological relationship, if they were of his father's age, and to call women "mother" if they lived in the same band as the child and were of the same generation as the child's mother. Older relatives in the extended family, whether they were parents, aunts or uncles of parents, or unrelated, were and are called "grandmother" (*niscehem*) or "grandfather" (*namcem*). In fact, these terms are used to show respect for any Cheyenne elder, related or not.

A child's own siblings, however, were carefully ranked by the kinship system to differentiate older children from younger children. Especially important was the eldest girl in each cohort of children, or sibship, for she would have the responsibility of assigning personal names to all her brothers' children. The children so named would use a special kin term for her, *naun* or "namesake," and she would call them by the same term. Each child would also use kin terms which indicated whether the sibling was older or younger than them: *namhan* for elder sister, *naniha* for elder brother, and *nasima* for younger sibling, whether male or female.

One principle which permeates Cheyenne kinship, as well as many other aspects of culture, is the notion of respect. In the context of kinship, special respect is shown by avoiding contact with certain categories of kin, even to the point of not speaking to them directly. In the case of a man's older sister, this respect develops slowly through the years, beginning with the mere acknowledgement that one of his playmates is *namhan*. As his older sister approaches puberty, however, a boy is encouraged not to talk to her very much, and especially not to tease her. In a respectable, traditional family, even now, an adult man does not speak to his older sister, but must communicate with her through a third person, such is his respect for her and her status as the name-giver for his children.

Concerning mothers-in-law, a respectable Cheyenne man must show even more deference to her than to his older sister, to the point of leaving a house if his mother-in-law enters, and not entering her house except for emergencies. My old friend Sam Buffalo used to tell the story of unexpectedly meeting his mother-in-law at a four-way traffic stop in Seiling, Oklahoma, each in their separate cars. Noticing his mother-in-law stopped to his right, Sam quickly looked away. She did the same. They both sat for long moments, each afraid to look at the other to see if they were pulling their cars into the intersection. Sam finally broke the impasse by getting out of his car and raising his hood as if he had engine trouble. Then his mother-in-law pulled away without looking at him.

Cheyenne people usually structure their activities so that an outsider would not notice that there are avoidance and respect relationships all around. In my own fieldwork, about 1972, I first noticed something unusual when I was taking a group of

Cheyenne people home from a pow-wow in my van. In typical Anglo fashion, I soon turned around and asked, "Well, who's first?" I was directed to the far south-western edge of Clinton, Oklahoma, where we let off an elderly woman. "Next," I asked, and was directed to the north side of town where we left off two sisters. Two more stops and we had let off a middle-aged man only two blocks from where the elderly woman lived, and another man a short distance from where the sisters had got out. Finally, with one person left in the car, I had the courage to ask what was going on, and was told you couldn't leave two people on the same seat in the car at the same time who had avoidance relationships, nor could you let them out at the same stop. So we drove about fifteen miles all over town, doubling back several times, in recognition of the formal respect which Cheyenne people must exhibit for one another.

Another special kin relationship among Cheyennes is something known in anthropological writing as a "joking relationship." In Cheyenne society this relationship exists especially between women and their brothers-in-law, men and their sisters-in-law. Oddly, although a man cannot speak at all to his wife's mother, he can make constant, sometimes bawdy jokes at the expense of his wife's sister. Although multiple wives are illegal in modern times (they are not unknown), much of the teasing has to do with this practice, called polygyny. For example, a woman might tell her sister's husband that if she were his number two wife, she wouldn't let him get away with all his misbehavior. And everyone laughs. Or a man might joke that his wife's sister should be ready, he'll be over to visit after dark.

At an outside dinner which preceded a giveaway in about 1978, the guests were forced to stand in the sun as they waited in line to eat. Somebody said that they needed a canvas or a sheet to make a shade. A man whose sister-in-law was of generous proportions volunteered to get her shirt, saying that it was "big enough to shade everybody." She "got him back" by pouring a cup of fruit drink down his neck when he wasn't looking. All of this teasing was quite within cultural boundaries and was appreciated by everyone, and the anecdote was told over and over in the following weeks. People kept asking the man if he liked fruit drink.

Band Organization

The ideal life for many traditional Cheyenne men has been to enter old age as the head of a large extended family, or even a band. In the days of buffalo hunting, the peace chiefs tried to create a large band by marrying several wives, preferably sisters, and encouraging their own brothers to do the same and remain in the same band, so that two or three brothers (ideally four) with their wives and children could serve as the nucleus of a large, cooperative residence group. Then they would try to attract young men to join their group by offering their daughters and grand-daughters as wives. This strategy of band-building was successful many times, and it is reported that many of the most prominent bands – Oivimana, Wotapio, and Hisiometanio – were started in this way (see Moore 1987).

To encourage other, more distantly related families to join a band, the chief could offer to loan horses. If a family had few, poor, or no horses, they might make an arrangement with a chief to supply a portion of buffalo meat, skins, or other goods in exchange for the loan of good horses. Since chiefs often maintained herds of scores or hundreds of horses, they could make some horses available to build up their bands in this manner.

Another strategy of collecting band members, already mentioned, was used by soldier chiefs in the period of warfare with the US Army. This was to use war comrades as a nucleus of a band, encouraging them to bring their wives with them to form a new kind of band. This, of course, disrupted the traditional hunting and trading bands of the peace chiefs, and was part of the reason for the hostility between peace chiefs and war chiefs in the middle of the 19th century (explained in Moore 1987).

In early reservation times and on into the 20th century, Cheyenne men have built bands by having large numbers of children, by recruiting the spouses of their children and all their offspring to come live in the extended family, and by organizing them together as a cooperative work group, with some members working for wages, some taking care of children, and others undertaking domestic work both for themselves and for those who work for wages. The leaders of these modern bands are usually active in the traditional religion and knowledgeable about dealing with the various bureaucracies with which Cheyennes are in daily contact – the Bureau of Indian Affairs, the Indian Health Service, the public schools, and a host of social service agencies. The members of a band, or "bunch" as modern Cheyennes say, usually live in neighboring houses clustered in some rural area or along the same street in town.

The organization and division of labor in a traditional pre-reservation band was different from now, of course, and fortunately some of the details of organization have been preserved in a unique document, the 1880 US Census. One of the questions asked of Cheyennes at that time was about their "vocation," and many tried to cooperate by explaining that they were herders, or midwives, or arrow makers, or gave other traditional occupations. These responses allow us to reconstruct the kind of work done in a traditional band in the buffalo hunting period, the kinds of special skills required, and how people with these skills were distributed in the Cheyenne nation. According to the evidence of the 1880 Census, a band of about 300 people would comprise the following kinds and numbers of full-time specialized workers, beginning with the most senior people:

2	Sun Dance or arrow priests
3	Doctors
3	Apprentice doctors
1	Pipe maker
5	Arrow makers
5	Root-diggers (women who knew about wild plants)
4	Midwives
2	Butchers (men who taught and supervised butchering of animals)
70	Hunters/warriors
80	Housekeepers
25	Wood choppers (older girls)
10	Wood carriers (girls)
65	Herders (boys)
25	Water carriers (young girls)

Chiefs and the Chief's Council

It is interesting that no one reported himself as a "chief" in the 1880 Census, but the reason for that is Cheyenne modesty. Even now, real traditional chiefs do not say that they are, relying on someone else to tell you their status. And one can be sure that any man telling a stranger or casual visitor that he is a chief, is not.

Any man who became leader of a residence group, who decided when the band would move and where it would go, was a *manawa*, now translated as a "family head." This is an informal title simply indicating the senior status and authority of a man in his extended family. There is presently some confusion in English between this term, "family head," and the term "headsman," used for the leader of a soldier society. Being a chief, however, is a very different matter. This title means that a man has been selected for membership of the Chiefs' Council, also called the Council of Forty-Four, a membership which is very ceremonial, and very serious.

The origin of the Chiefs' Council, or Chiefs' Society, is very much in dispute among Cheyennes, as is much concerning the authority and status which chiefs should have. Some say that the council was originally organized by the prophet Sweet Medicine; others say that a Cheyenne woman who was captured by the Assiniboins and escaped showed the Cheyennes how the Assiniboins organized their council. Those saying that the council was organized by Sweet Medicine also tend to regard the council as a group set above the soldier societies in Cheyenne politics, while those accepting a more lowly origin for the council say that it is an organization of about the same status as a military society. The latter refer to it in English as the Chiefs' Society, not the Chiefs' Council.

There is also some dispute about who is eligible to be a chief. Some say that membership is handed from father to son, or at least that one must have an ancestor, in the male line, who previously served as a chief, to be considered for membership in the council. Other people say that the membership of the council is by band, and that each band is entitled to a certain proportional representation. These are not merely recent arguments among Cheyennes; they go back to the earliest recorded documents, covering events in the early and mid 19th century. But these arguments arise anew each time someone wants to convene the council to induct new members.

There is general agreement, however, about how the council is supposed to operate, and about what the ideal behavior of a council chief should be. The standards of behavior for a chief are rigorous and demanding. Ideally, they are supposed to be impossible to anger, and generous to the point of giving away all their possessions. They are supposed to be humble, modest, and constantly in service to the people.

The very best council chief that I have known personally, the one who best exemplified the ideal role, was John Black Owl. When I first saw John, in about 1975, he was picking up trash around the tribal complex at Concho, Oklahoma. I thought perhaps he was the custodian, employed by the tribe. But I also noticed that nearly everyone entering the building stopped and shook his hand and spoke to him. He was a small, gentle, kindly man who had a pleasant smile and a nice sense of humor.

When I first attended a chiefs' meeting, I noticed that John was there and that, although he didn't say anything, everyone deferred to him. Once he came to a meeting at the last minute, and about five grown men leaped from their chairs to give him a seat. No seat was good enough, and I have never seen people so fussy about finding just the right chair and putting him in it. Often, in driving around Cheyenne country, I would see John's car parked at an Indian cemetery, and sometimes I would see John cleaning the graves, straightening up the plastic flowers that had been left the previous memorial day, cutting the grass, fixing the fence.

John and his wife Susie lived in a small house near the North Canadian River east of El Reno, with old furniture and two refrigerators. Visiting with John, one saw a constant parade of people from all over, bringing food to him, taking food from the refrigerator, giving him money, asking him for money, depositing and picking up clothing and furniture from the carport. John kept nothing for himself, and was always shabbily dressed, despite the best efforts of his family and friends. He was always giving away his hats and belt buckles. But still, I didn't know the whole story about John until he died.

I arrived on time at the funeral in El Reno, and the chapel of the funeral home was already packed full, the parking lot was full of people for whom outside loudspeakers had been erected, the street was full and had been cordoned off with local police in attendance, and I had to stand on an embankment across the street from the funeral home, after depositing a blanket and shawl near the casket. The pile of blankets and shawls was so

Plate 6.2   John Black Owl (photo by author)

high you could scarcely see the elevated casket and the podium where speakers of all sorts praised John for several hours. Such was the love and respect that people felt for this kind and gentle man, the ideal chief (plate 6.2). John's nickname among the people was Super Chief, a name taken from the special Santa Fe passenger train which formerly passed through El Reno.

John represented the extreme of the ideal Cheyenne chief, but other chiefs try to represent the same moral characteristics. They are constantly called upon for help in the form of money, food, a ride, or a long-distance phone call (although most chiefs don't have phones because they can't pay their phone bills). In temperament, council chiefs are very different from the soldier chiefs described previously, who are supposed to be mean and fierce, barking orders to their subordinates on the field of battle, or telling a war story at a pow-wow or naming ceremony.

Because of the heavy obligations imposed on council chiefs, they are supposed to be reluctant, and frequently are reluctant, to accept the invitation to join the council. The council frequently meets during the course of the annual ceremonies, but also can meet at other times, particularly if some political issue has come up regarding treaties or government policies.

An elaborate etiquette must be observed at chiefs' meetings. The procedures are based on tipi etiquette, but must also be observed if the meeting is indoors, in which case one of the entrances to a room is designated the tipi door and is the only one used. The meeting begins when all are assembled outside the room or tipi, and all the participants line up in strict order of rank and precedence. The north doorkeeper enters first and walks to the left around the room or tipi, followed by about five people of decreasing rank and age, then of increased rank are the senior chiefs and the arrow keeper (hat keeper in Montana), who sit at the back of the tipi, followed by honored guests, some more ordinary chiefs, increasing again in rank and age to the south doorkeeper, who enters last.

After everyone is seated there is a prayer, and perhaps the chiefs' pipe or another pipe is passed around to bless the proceedings. Then a knowledgeable person presents the business to be discussed. After a polite silence, the most junior members present begin to speak. Ideally, each person speaks only once, and sometimes must give a gift to the arrow keeper or a senior chief for the privilege of speaking. The general rule is that one may not speak after a person of higher rank has spoken, although there is often some ambiguity about relative rank. This means, of course, that after the most senior chief or the arrow keeper has spoken, the meeting is over, although there still might be a smoke to acknowledge agreement on the consensus of the meeting, and a final prayer.

On several occasions I have seen men arriving late who, it was felt, had to be included in the meeting. To accommodate them, the meeting was adjourned formally, everyone filed out clockwise, lined up again to include the late arrival, and marched back into the tipi. The senior chiefs or doorkeepers line up the participants, and assign rank based on age, reputation, participation in the ceremonies, and other factors. Sometimes men are offended at the rank they have been assigned and leave the meeting.

The most senior and respected men, as well as speaking last, actually speak very little at the meetings. They do not try to be great orators, and they often apologize for their inability to speak persuasively, as modesty requires them to say. But they inevitably get their way. On one occasion, a meeting had been called to discuss a pipe ceremony requested by Southern Arapaho chiefs, to commemorate their long historical relationship. Some Cheyenne men, especially those married to Arapaho women, spoke eloquently and at length about the history of the alliance and its importance, and pleaded with their fellows to sponsor the ceremony. After several hours of mostly positive discussion, everyone had spoken except John Black Owl and the arrow keeper. Everyone glanced at John expectantly, and he smiled and spoke one sentence: "I ain't smoking no pipe with no Arapaho." End of speeches. End of meeting. The arrow keeper had nothing to say. A pipe was passed, a prayer was said, and everyone filed out of the tipi and went home. There was no pipe ceremony with the Arapahoes, and the anthropologist (myself) was left puzzling over why this quiet, gentle man who tended graves, gave away hats, and picked up trash around the tribal complex could have so much influence at the highest political level.

It takes a certain temperament to be a Cheyenne chief. Walter Hamilton, a Cheyenne chief who spent a lot of time solving other people's problems, told me that his job was "to pour oil over troubled waters." Another chief, Laird Cometsevah, told me that the most essential equipment for being a chief was a coffee pot and plenty of coffee. So the job of chief is different from that of a family head. The family head is the leader of a family of relatives who look to him for his wisdom and judgement about what the family should do in various circumstances. A chief is a tribally-recognized officer who solves problems for many people, not just his own family, and whose selection and service are highlighted periodically by ritual and ceremony. For example, at pow-wows and giveaways chiefs are often called out for special gifts, they are asked to lead prayers, and they are asked to attend naming ceremonies or to speak for people who want to get married or who wish to make a request of another person.

Not all chiefs fit the ideal picture. Those who are reluctant to share their car, money or food are often met with shrill demands: "You're supposed to be a chief, so why won't you help me?" Those who are not generous on repeated occasions cease to be regarded as chiefs: people say that their election was not legitimate, or that their chiefship is no longer valid.

The circumstances under which modern chiefs are elected leave a lot of room for debate, discussion, and misunderstanding about legitimacy. Ideally, chiefs should be elected at the annual ceremonies, when all current chiefs are present to discuss the candidates. But in fact many modern chiefs have been elected at special meetings at other times of the year, with perhaps only a few chiefs in attendance. If new chiefs are elected at such a meeting, chiefs not present may or may not honor the results of the deliberations. It is said of one modern chief, of dubious generosity and reputation, that while he was present at the meeting, he was not elected; others have said that there were not enough chiefs present to have an election. In fact, there are certain families and communities who recognize only certain chiefs and not others. Periodically, when there is a full meeting of the chiefs with appropriate ceremonies, not only are the newly-elected chiefs considered to be legitimate, but the acceptance into the tipi of other chiefs elected at small meetings tends to confirm their legitimacy also.

Chiefs are selected for life, but can choose to retire at any time. When they do, another chief can be elected to the council, up to a maximum of 40. In addition to the regular chiefs, there are four senior chiefs, "Big Chiefs" or "Old Man Chiefs" elected from among those chiefs who are older, have taken their office seriously, and have been generous and gained respect. This makes a total of 44. Since 1895, when the Northern Cheyennes decided that their separation from the southerners was permanent, there have been two Chiefs' Councils, one in Oklahoma and one in Montana. While each can have a maximum membership of 44, in fact there have not been more than 20 or 30 chiefs in each place at any one time during the last 25 years.

The elaborate rituals for electing chiefs have been described several times (see Dorsey 1905). Largely they involve the erection of a special tipi at the annual ceremonies and the manipulation of 44 sticks which represent the membership and are kept in a special "chiefs' bundle." As the new chiefs are assembled, a stick is put in place around a circle in the center of the tipi and the name of the chief is assigned to the stick. Prayers are said, sacred objects are displayed, and the new chiefs are instructed about their responsibilities.

In about 1903, the anthropologist George Dorsey had the opportunity to record the traditional "charge to chiefs" according to two of the leading men of the time, De Forest Antelope and Bushy Head. The charge and admonition were as follows:

Now, listen to me! When the old chiefs wore out, they appointed you to carry on their leadership. We, who are here representing the sacred magicians of old and the sacred arrows and the sacred sun, earth and animals, have this day advised you and placed every man, woman, and child of the Cheyenne tribe in your care. When it is necessary you will help not only your own tribe, but all other Indians. You have been appointed on account of your bravery, character, and courage. In the future you will cause no disturbance or help to cause a disturbance among your own people. If another member of the tribe kills your own brother, take your pipe and smoke it to the Great Medicine, and you will prevent disturbance. Do not notice your brother's murderer. If your young men look despairing and lonely, take your pipe and pledge yourself to perform the great Medicine-Arrow ceremony, in order that the Great Medicine will bless you and your people, because of your remembrance of him. (Dorsey 1905: 14)

The Leadership of Women

Legally, women could not be council chiefs, nor could they be soldier chiefs. Although the soldier societies have selected certain young women as "sisters" or "mascots" (similar to modern pow-wow princesses), they have had no authority in the society. And while women could and did participate in warfare, they did not become members of the soldier societies on that account. In modern times, even though certain women have served with distinction in the military, they are not asked to join the soldier societies or other veterans' organizations sponsored by the Cheyenne people. But women do have at least three leadership roles which they can earn by their seniority and personal characteristics. Of these, the most frequent is that of female family head – although a woman is not called a family head, she is simply referred to as the grandmother of the family.

In modern times, there are many female family heads largely because women are living longer than men. As family heads, they take on many of the attributes of a chief, although they frequently act through the auspices of a son or nephew, the nominal family head. They exercise authority over who will live where in the houses occupied by the extended family, who will work for wages and who will stay home to do domestic chores and child care, who can pledge ceremonies or participate in giveaways, and what candidates will be supported in tribal elections. In sum, nothing of any importance is done within the extended family or by extended family members without consulting with "grandmother." Even something seemingly as minor as participating in school sports or visiting a clinic must be referred to grandmother to get her acknowledgement and approval in traditional extended families.

Formerly the status of grandmother or "woman chief," as some say, was more surrounded by ritual and public display. In the traditional mode, a woman past menopause could ask one of the four official Cheyenne "criers" to announce at the annual ceremonies that she intended to seek the status of a "woman chief." To do so, she had to put her entire life and reputation up for scrutiny. At the appropriate time, the crier would circle the ceremonial camp and announce the name of the woman intending to be a woman chief. He would declare that, if anyone could criticize her for being unfaithful to her husband, or if anyone had ever left her house hungry or thirsty, or had ever been refused any request by her, they should report to the crier. If the announcement was made four times without response, then the crier declared that the woman had taken up a walking stick and tobacco pipe in recognition of her new status. Frequently, this new status also involved retiring as the active cook and house-keeper of a household, and spending more time in beadwork, story-telling and other activities more appropriate for an elder.

A woman can also be the leader of what have been called "craft guilds." Like many other skills in Cheyenne society, beadwork and the making of tipis and buffalo robes has been under the control of certain experienced people. To learn to do beadwork, for example, a young woman in modern times must apprentice herself to an older woman who knows how to do it, and who has made many pairs of moccasins (plate 6.3). Becoming an apprentice gives a young woman access to certain patterns and techniques which belong to her mistress, and which can be used only with her permission. The young and middle-aged women who have been the apprentices of a certain woman are considered to be members of her "guild." Rank within the guild is based on how many pairs of moccasins or other objects have been completed. Women who are members of the same guild are frequently related to one another, usually through female lines.

Plate 6.3   Aurelia (Littlebird) Blackbear working on moccasins (photo by Eugene Blackbear, Jr.)

In addition to beadwork guilds, there are presently also guilds for making canvas tipis, buck-skin dresses, Indian dolls and toys, and tipi liners. While the most traditional sector of Cheyenne society still respects the proprietary interest of certain women in certain designs, there is nowadays some "poaching" of designs and skills. Some women, often criticized by their peers, even take their designs from books and museum specimens. But more properly, a woman should present gifts to her mistress in respect of the skills she is being taught. Earlier in the century, there were celebrations sponsored by guilds when a woman had completed, for example, her fourth tipi or her sixteenth pair of moccasins. There were also titles and symbols maintained by the guilds which were and are semi-secret, or at least private to the members of the group.

Names and Name-Changes

Changes in status in Cheyenne society, becoming a chief or being acknowledged as a veteran or respected elder, are usually marked by taking a new personal name, which gives us the opportunity of considering the totality of this interesting and colorful aspect of Cheyenne culture.[4] First of all, unlike many other plains societies, Cheyenne men and women have names which are mostly gender-specific. That is, there are two different sets of names that are used for men and women, and very few names that can be used for either sex. Cheyenne personal names are mostly of two kinds – those selected from the natural world and those reflecting personal appearance or behavior. But the frequency of names taken by men and women indicate that there are male and female aspects of the natural world which must be respected in selecting names. Men most often take names from cosmic and meteorological events, or predatory birds and animals, while women are named after animals and natural entities more closely bound to the earth.

A lot of silly names have been invented for Cheyennes by literary writers, names which have no significance at all for Cheyennes. For example, here are some names from Karen Bale's "bodice-ripping" romantic novel, *Little Flower's Desire*. The Cheyenne men are named Stalking Horse, Old Man Bear, Horn, and Laughing Bird. Women's names include Little Flower, Sun Dancer, Little Fox, and Nahkohe. Of the men's names, only Old Man Bear is possibly legitimate, except that "old man" in Cheyenne means a chief or priest, so that the name would translate as Bear Chief, which is a legitimate name. Of the women's names, Nahkohe is supposed to mean "bear", but it is applied to a woman and has a male ending, so that the girl in the story is literally named Bear Man. Little Fox is not legitimate because the name is reserved for the Fox Soldier society and cannot be used for personal names, and Sun Dancer is downright sacrilegious as a woman's name, since women are not allowed to dance at the Sun Dance. For the male names, a stalking horse is used to flush game in European hunting practices, and has nothing at all to do with Cheyenne or American Indian tradition. Horn cannot be used as a name without a modifier, like Elk or

Bull, and the word "Laughing" does not occur among Cheyenne name modifiers. "Bird" cannot be used as a personal name unless the kind of bird is specified, in the same way as, in English, a girl can be named Pearl, Opal, or Ruby, but not Gemstone, and a boy can be named Lance, but not Weapon. Most of the names used by Bale, and others who write fiction about the Cheyennes, sound ridiculous to native speakers of the language.

I have compiled a dictionary of Cheyenne names appearing on the 1880, 1892, and 1900 Cheyenne Censuses (Moore 1984). About half the men's names and about a third of the women's names come from the natural world, with frequencies shown in table 6.2 for the 1880 Census. The table is arranged with the more celestial entities at the top and the more terrestrial at the bottom, and we can note that men dominate among names from predatory birds and animals, while women dominate among buffalo names and names relating to the earth. (It is also worth noting here that Cheyenne tradition alleges that buffaloes live in caves.) Most of the balance of Cheyenne names were originally nicknames given to children. Some of them have to do with behavioral traits that perhaps amused or irritated their parents, like Howling All Night, Dripping with Spit, Crawling Fast, Little Runny Nose, and Long Sleeper. Other childhood nicknames are derived from body peculiarities, such as Crooked Foot, Flat Nose, Stiff Neck, Short Face, or Lump Shoulder. In modern times, only the most traditional families still inaugurate these kinds of nicknames for little children.

When a boy reaches puberty, he gets a more serious name, bestowed by his father's eldest sister. In aboriginal times, this name was received after his first participation in a war party, but in modern times it is given when a young man graduates from high school, or in preparation for his first participation in the annual ceremonies. Even the less traditional families bestow traditional names and have naming ceremonies; it is the most persistent of traditional customs. Boys' names are either from the natural world, or childhood nicknames previously carried by some ancestor on the father's side who was a famous chief, warrior, or religious leader. It sometimes happened that a young man did something meritorious before he had an adult name, in which case the nickname he carried became venerated and carried on in the family. For example, the nickname Roman Nose (literally "arched nose") is one of the most respected of

Table 6.2 *Frequencies of Cheyenne personal names*
(also see figures 8.1 and 8.2)

Cosmological location	Root of name	Meaning	Number of men bearing name	Number of women bearing name
OTATAVOOM	*esehe*	sun, moon	2	2
	nonoma	thunder	1	4
	hoeta	lightning	1	9
	hohona	mountain	7	1
	Maheonevekseo	holy birds	5	5
SETOVOOM	*Nizeo*	eagles	7	–
	aeno	hawk	11	–
	aenohes	sparrow hawk	16	–
	maevecess	cardinal	10	–
TAXTAVOOM	*Vekseohes*	small birds	13	7
	Mahpevekseo	water birds	2	5
	Hoevekseo	game birds	7	3
VOTOSTOOM	*honehe*	wolf	20	3
	hokom	coyote	8	–
	nako	bear	35	16
	voae	antelope	3	1
	moehe	elk	12	14
	vaoseva	deer	3	–
	hotoa	bull	23	6
	mehe, esey	cow	4	6
	moksa	calf	10	8
	Veshovan	small animals	3	10
	Hestohestan	foreigners	11	8
	Xamaehestan	Indians	21	26
NSTHOAMAN	*Zeamevoneso*	crawling things	5	5
	Zeevasomaoeva	underwater things	6	4
	Hoxzz	trees	3	9
	Moez	plants	4	7
	navo	root, dig	5	10
	hoe, hesek	soil	–	9

Source: Moore 1984: 300

modern adult male names, because it was a nickname carried by several famous chiefs and warriors.

A girl frequently gets her adult name at birth, and carries it through her life. Sometimes she has to wait until puberty for an adult name, which is bestowed by her father's sister, who thereby becomes the girl's special friend. Often, the eldest sister receives at puberty the personal name of her "namesake." Otherwise, she receives the name of some honored and respected woman in her father's ancestry.

Like men, women can change their names later in life if they think their name is unlucky, or if they undertake some significant enterprise. For example, a woman elected to tribal office might take a new name, having it announced by a chief or crier publicly at a dinner or pow-wow. Men frequently change their name to celebrate the fulfillment of a ceremonial vow, or in remembrance of a long-dead ancestor. Cheyenne people respect the tradition of not mentioning the personal name of someone who has just died until at least a year has passed. Until then, the person is referred to indirectly as the mother, father, sister, or brother of someone who is still living.

Another class of men's names derive from war experiences or religious quests. A man who killed a Crow warrior might take the name Crow Man. A man who broke his lance in killing an enemy might take the name Broken Lance. Religious names have to do with a vision experience acquired on a personal quest or at the annual ceremonies. Names like Cloud Coming, Star Man, or Wolf Medicine are of this sort. Most often, the vision experience is alluded to obliquely, rather than stated explicitly.

When men change their names, they tend to move up the cosmological ladder as illustrated in table 6.2. That is, a boy might start with a name of minor significance, perhaps a bear name, but later he might exchange that name for one higher on the cosmology – a hawk or an eagle – or a name previously carried by a famous person. Only an extremely successful, respectable, and popular man would venture to take a name like Sun Man or Mountain, taken from the highest cosmological entities, or Dull Knife or Black Kettle, the names of famous chiefs. The names taken by older women, too, reflect their respect for female ancestors who were well known, or for the religious significance of the earth and soil.

Among Cheyennes, traditional names are regarded as personal

property, and a person willing to give up a name must receive a gift from the recipient. Some people have more than one name, and names can be loaned out for special purposes. Especially the name Lightning Woman is loaned to young girls if they are sick, and the name returns to the owner, usually a grandparent or medicine person, when the girl is better.

Cheyennes sometimes give obscene or insulting names to people they dislike, such as officials of the Bureau of Indian Affairs (BIA), missionaries, or anthropologists! The wife of a former superintendent of the Northern Cheyenne Reservation once proudly told me that her Indian name was Moxachesta ("Diseased Vagina"), which she translated as "Pretty Deer." A lawyer from Hardin, Montana, well known for selling out Indians in court cases, was named "Bald Eagle," not the majestic white-headed bird which serves as an emblem of the United States, which would be Voaxa, but an ordinary eagle whose head feathers had fallen out, Okasniz. Two fundamentalist missionaries in Oklahoma are known among Cheyennes as Pimples and Big Butt, and a well-known writer on Cheyenne subjects is known as "No Legs," because of his short stature. Cheyennes who criticize me call me Mista, or "Spook," because I once admitted to handling Indian bones as part of an anthropology course.

Traditional Cheyenne personal names are not secret, but they are private. They are only supposed to be used under certain circumstances and in certain environments. It is considered rude to ask a Cheyenne person their personal name unless you know them very well. For ordinary discourse, Cheyenne people fall back on their "office names," English names with a surname inherited through the male line and kept on file by the BIA bureaucracy and the tribal enrollment office. Among themselves, Cheyenne people use nicknames in English and Cheyenne, or kin terms. For many traditional children, their first use of an office name is when they attend public schools. In about 1982 I was asked to intercede when a Cheyenne boy, on his way to the first day of class in the first grade, had just been told by his mother what his office name was. By the time he got to school, he had forgotten his name and when the roll was called he didn't respond. The teacher thought he was being a "smart aleck" and sent him to the principal's office for discipline. The boy's older sister found out that he had been sent to the office and directed some insults at the principal and teacher, and the situation worsened. Even after the problem was sorted out, it was said around the school that there was an Indian kid who was "so stupid he didn't know his own name." Such are the realities of racism and misunderstanding which Cheyenne people have to face every day.

Literature and Values

Cheyenne stories are often presented as if they were transparent or self-explanatory – needing no cultural context or historical framework to be clearly understood. And certainly it is true that these stories have an inherent mystery and charm which are not dependent on the listener knowing very much about the Cheyenne people. They possess a certain literary value merely on the basis of the clever characterizations of the stories and the marvelous accomplishments of the heroes.

But I would argue that the stories are more meaningful if one knows about Cheyenne society and history, and especially about the moral, ethical, religious, and aesthetic values which have been important to the Cheyenne people. The same is true of Anglo-American traditions. One can't truly understand our stories – presented in books, television programs, and movies – unless one understands the totality of Anglo-American culture. My generation, for example, was raised on movies like *Bambi* and *Robin Hood*, and the Saturday afternoon cowboy movies. Films of this sort, meaningful in Anglo-American culture, tend to puzzle Cheyenne traditionalists. The personalities of the animals in *Bambi*, for example, and the attitude expressed toward hunting, are wrong-headed by Cheyenne standards. *Robin Hood* they like better, especially the part about egalitarianism and sharing with the poor, but the idea of political submission and bowing even to a "Good King" they find problematic. The glib individualism and arrogance of the Saturday afternoon gunfighters like Lash La Rue and Hopalong Cassidy they find downright disgusting, not to mention Indian "sidekicks" like Tonto and Little Beaver and the recurrent dramatization of warfare against the "red savages."

Cheyennes tend to like some of the movies about Indians made since the early 1970s. I have been fortunate to attend such films with Indian people, to our mutual amusement. My Cheyenne friends liked *Little Big Man* because it showed the horrors of the Sand Creek Massacre and portrayed the authentic supernaturalism of the character played by Chief Dan George. And then there was *A Man Called Horse*, which I saw with a mixed group of Cheyennes and Lakotas in Lawrence, Kansas, when we were nearly thrown out of the theater. The first trouble developed when two characters in the movie, speaking in Lakota, were supposed to be discussing the fate of their new captive, played by Richard Harris. According to our Lakota friends, the translated dialog was something like this:

"Damn, brother, are we going to get a break or not?"
"I don't know, they said break at ten, but it's nearly noon."
"What's for lunch, anyway?"
"I think it's some kind of fish. I'm not going to eat any. I asked them to find me some baloney. After lunch we're going to play some cards at Tony's trailer."
"Sounds good to me. Well, I guess we talked long enough. The guy's waving at me."
"Yep, that's it. See you later."

The Lakotas in the theater, some of whom were related to the actors, were completely broken up by the dialog, and fell over each other laughing, to the point that the usher had to come down and ask us to be quiet. We had just recovered our sobriety when the Sun Dance came on the screen.

In real Sun Dances, the atmosphere is very calm, joyful, and light-hearted. Even when flesh offerings are made from the arms, or when someone's chest or back is pierced in the traditional manner, the participants are not supposed to make a fuss. It is a sacrifice, not an ordeal. Potential pledgers are told, "If you think it's going to hurt, don't do it." Men being pierced and their piercers say encouraging, calming things like, "I'm going to tickle you a little, now," or "Oh, that feels good." But in *A Man Called Horse*, Richard Harris groans and writhes around in agony for many long minutes as he is pierced and strung up to the centerpole. But that wasn't the worst of it.

According to one of the Lakotas with us in the movie theater, the singers and drummers hired to provide music for the film were from different reservations and didn't know many of the same songs. So they decided to sing a song that they all knew, a children's counting song that the director liked. The net effect, as one of the Lakota men told me later, was like witnessing a very serious high mass in a Catholic church, except that in the background a group of men were drumming and singing, "One potato, two potato, three potato, four . . ."

Cheyenne people had a similar experience watching the movie *Windwalker*, in which most of the dialog was in Cheyenne, with English sub-titles. The main characters, however, were not Cheyennes, but said to be Hawaiians and Mexicans, and they had to learn their Cheyenne by rote. Their pronunciation was pretty good, according to the Cheyennes who watched the movie with me, but they tended to mix and match sentences so that very often actors in the same scene were discussing entirely different matters. A sentence like, "I fear the Crows will attack at dawn" would be met with the response, "The old man wants to jerk the buffalo meat, and save the skin." The dialogue was confounded even further late in the movie when two characters had face-to-face conversations in which one was speaking Cheyenne and the other was speaking Crow. They each pretended not to notice, hoping that the audience wouldn't either, as they were assumed to be reading the English sub-titles. But Cheyennes in the audience were puzzled, both by the fact that the sub-titles had little to do with what was being said, and because they couldn't understand Crow. But they did appreciate that the producers of the movie had at least tried to use Cheyenne actors in minor roles, and let them speak their native language.

By far the best and most authentic movie about Cheyennes is *Pow-Wow Highway*, made in 1989. It is a completely realistic movie about modern reservation life, and I have never heard a Cheyenne say a word against it. It is also funny and entertaining.

In relating these anecdotes, I want to make the point that all stories we hear are filtered through our own cultural experiences, and these stories are interpreted differently according to the culture and language of the listener. Before narrating here some old stories which are important to the Cheyenne people, I think it is important to discuss briefly certain cultural and moral values and commitments which are traditionally significant to Cheyennes, which serve as their cultural filter. Unless we understand the importance of these values, we are likely to be as puzzled in reading Cheyenne stories as they are in trying to understand *Bambi*, a cowboy movie, or a modern TV drama. After presenting an overview of Cheyenne moral values, I will tell a few short stories which illustrate some, but not all, of these most important values.

Traditional Values

Two of the most important Cheyenne values – personal bravery and familism – have already been discussed in different contexts. But here are some others which have not yet been properly emphasized.

Sharing

Among Cheyenne people there have historically been two distinct types of sharing – within the extended family and with other families. The first kind is done casually and automatically. Within the family, the sharing of personal property is continual, and involves not only food but items such as tools, jewelry, and vehicles, which are not held as tightly by a person as they often are in Anglo-American families. In this regard, an Indian woman once told me how amused she was to witness events at an Anglo-American daycare center. "White people are funny," she said, "they spend half their time telling kids which toys are theirs, and the other half trying to get them to share."

Among unrelated extended families, sharing is more serious and sometimes more stressful. But the obligation to share with any other Cheyenne is absolute and cannot be ignored. If a person asks for something you don't have, you must give that person something of value – a few coins, even a drink of water. The most denigrating word that can be used against another Cheyenne person, worse than any obscenity, is to say that they are "selfish." When encouraging young people to share with people outside the extended family, parents say, "They are your relatives. You must live with them. You must share with your brothers and sisters." Sharing within the extended family is used as a model for all kinds of sharing.

Respect for elders

Unlike many Anglo-Americans, Cheyennes look forward to getting old. They anxiously anticipate becoming a parent, and then a grandparent, both of which are taken to be emblematic of attaining senior status, something that is more important than chronological age. Elders receive a deference within the extended family which is generally much greater than in Anglo-American families. Ideally, a person honors and respects all Cheyenne elders, not just those who are relatives. These elders are honored with the kin terms "grandmother" and "grandfather," no matter what the actual kin relationship. Cheyennes are reluctant to describe elders as "senile," and they do not attribute bad memory to old age, but rather expect elders to have a better and deeper memory than younger people.

In discussing elders, there is not much talk among Cheyennes about the physical disabilities of old age. Rather, Cheyennes like to talk about how healthy and strong their elders are, and how good they look. Illness and infirmity, as we shall see in the next chapter, are attributed to other factors, and are not held to be an inevitable part of getting old. In Cheyenne stories, then, one expects characters who are elders to be knowledgeable and to be treated respectfully, and one expects younger people to be treated casually. We are then surprised when the opposite is the case.

Medicine

Cheyenne people use the English word "medicine" not just to mean an herb or an amulet, but the whole body of special knowledge which it symbolizes. Everyday, casual tasks that everyone knows how to perform – cooking, getting dressed, cleaning the house, fixing a tool – do not require special knowledge, but many skills require a knowledgeable person, usually an elder, to teach the skill. For women, this includes such tasks as beadwork, tipi making, and midwifery. For men, the tasks are mostly religious and ceremonial, but also include creating war medicines, making pipes, and training horses. In every case, etiquette requires that the potential student must approach a potential teacher respectfully, and present an appropriate gift to begin the instruction and receive the medicine.

Roads

The English terms "road" and "path" are used by Cheyennes to indicate that a person is following a particular design or recipe for living. Religious people who have received medicine from a coyote, for example, are said to follow the "coyote's road." A person who has decided to become a professional military man is following the "soldier's road." A student who decides to get a college degree and a well-paid job has followed "the white man's road."

Each road has certain obligations and certain medicines. Cheyennes think that it is important to follow only one road at a time, and thereby avoid "mixing medicines." The term "mixing medicines" is also used in warning young people not to follow the traditions of other tribes, whose ideas might not be compatible with Cheyenne ideas.

Personal modesty

Individuals are part of a family, and so they are supposed to subordinate their own abilities and achievements to the status of the family. This modesty also extends to how one treats members of other families, creating enormous problems when Cheyenne children go to public school. Most often, they will not raise their hand if they know the answer to a question, and they will not answer a question even if asked directly, because they do not want to embarrass other Cheyenne children in the classroom, especially family members.

Modesty also requires that Cheyenne people of good character must assent to every direct question. To dissent or disagree shows disrespect to the questioner, and so every direct question is answered in the affirmative. When Cheyennes are asked by non-Indians if they will come to a meeting, they always say "yes," creating consternation when they don't appear. Among themselves, Cheyenne people try to avoid a direct request unless it is truly important.

Modesty extends to "being first." No one volunteers to be first in line for dinner, or to receive any kind of recognition: to do so is arrogant and selfish. And so Cheyennes invite visitors to go first, or elderly chiefs whose status is generally accepted. No one wants to dance first, or enter a meeting first, or do anything to attract attention to him- or herself: to do so invites criticism.

Hospitality

Any respectable person invited into a Cheyenne house for the first time is treated like royalty. Gifts are made and the visitor is expected to eat and drink with the family. Because of the requirements of hospitality, invitations into a house or tipi are not made without careful thought and discussion. And concomitantly, accepting an invitation to visit carries with it some obligations of friendship and reciprocity. The idea of "dropping by" an acquaintance's house is not part of Cheyenne social practice, and in fact a stranger or unexpected visitor might be treated in a manner which Anglo-Americans would find rude or abrupt.

In Cheyenne stories, therefore, the kind of reception accorded visitors is very significant. When a stranger in a story is invited in straightaway, this strikes Cheyenne listeners as being very unusual and meaningful.

Respect for the natural order

The natural order of the earth is presented, as we have seen, in the ranking from top to bottom of the entities used to make personal names, as in table 6.2 (page 172). In this ranked cosmology from earth to sky, all material entities are said to be alive, even stones and air, and each has a specific place in the whole structure which is referred to as *xamaetoz*, "the natural order."

In the traditional stories, the natural order is communicated to the listener by the peace and calm which exists when everything is in its appropriate place – eagles in the sky, buffaloes in caves, and water in the springs and streams. But a disordered universe can also be created in a story, either for comedy or to show what befalls a person who does not respect the natural order. The problem for non-Cheyennes, in understanding these stories, is that the natural order for Cheyennes is different from the natural order as seen by members of other cultures. For example, when birds emerge from snakes and horses spend the night underwater, this is perfectly normal for the Cheyenne universe. And, in fact, it is by means of these stories that the nature of this orderly universe is first communicated to children.

Empowerment

As we shall see at greater length in the next chapter, Cheyennes believe that the power to sustain life, in all its manifestations, is obtained from above, by the actions of God and good spirits on the weather, on birds and animals, and on sacred people. Consequently, the major problem facing a traditional Cheyenne person is how to obtain this power in some legitimate manner. To seek power, the characters in stories, just like real traditional Cheyennes, seek the intercession of spirits or appeal to the manifestations of spirits in birds, animals, natural phenomena, and sacred people.

Proper behaviour

Traditional Cheyenne people, even today, spend most of their time with their families, some time with other Cheyennes, and very little time with outsiders. Consequently, their inventory of personal behavior includes very little small talk. For example, there is no word for "hello," and Cheyennes normally approach each other and begin immediately to describe the nature of their business, rather than spending a few minutes in small talk about the weather, what you're wearing, and who you're with, as is customary with Anglo-Americans. Visiting in a Cheyenne house, people come and go without being introduced, and in fact the notion of "introduction" is based on living in a society where one meets new people every day. That is not necessarily the case with traditional Cheyenne people. They mostly know the people they see every day, and no introductions or small talk are necessary. So we can expect to find the same pattern of interactions in Cheyenne stories.

It is ironic that the Cheyenne people, despite living historically on such a vast expanse of prairies, in fact were such intensely social people. They moved about in tight family groups, and seldom ventured out on the prairie alone. This is why the Cheyenne culture heroes, alone on the prairie or venturing alone into secret places, seem so marvelous to Cheyennes. And that is why the vision quest, which is undertaken alone, is held to be so significant, because it contrasts so strikingly with normal, social, collective Cheyenne behavior, in which one is seldom out of sight of parents or siblings.

Writers like Thomas Mails (*The Mystic Warriors of the Plains*) and Ruth Beebe Hill (*Hanta Yo*) have got it all wrong about Plains Indian individualism. Instead of authentically describing Plains Indian values and behavior, which are familistic and collective, they have taken traditional Anglo values and projected them into stories and anecdotes which have Plains Indians as characters. In so doing, they have made it more difficult for non-Indians to understand the realities of Indian culture.

Stories for Children

This class of stories is intended to present cultural values in a positive way, to encourage boys and girls to behave properly. They are usually told by elders to a group of children at night. In modern times, an elder from outside the family, usually a woman, is invited for supper and presented with a gift for telling the stories. The moral values of the story are deeply imbedded in fascinating tales of monsters and heroes, and the wonderful supernatural powers the heroes and heroines must use to kill monsters, find food, and otherwise bring blessings to their people. In my opinion, the two groups of stories which are by far the most interesting and exciting focus on the magnificent adventures of two heroes named Star Drops and Little Calf.[1]

Star Drops

A Cheyenne girl once followed a remarkable red porcupine up a tree, and through a hole in the sky, where the porcupine revealed himself as the Red Star. They were married. Red Star and his bride lived happily together for many moons.

Every day the young woman went into the sky fields and picked prairie turnips for her husband. "Always pick the short-topped turnips," he warned her. "Never touch those with the long tops. They are bad medicine." She did as she was told, but she often wondered why Red Star had forbidden her to pick the turnips with the long tops.

A baby boy was born to Red Star and his Cheyenne wife, and they were very happy in their tipi in the sky. But sometimes a strange loneliness overtook the young woman, as she thought about her home on the earth below.

Each day she would pick turnips with her baby son fastened in a cradleboard on her back. One day she became intensely curious about the long-topped turnips. So she picked one, which was very long, and when she had pulled it out of the ground she looked in the hole and saw that she had made a hole in the sky, and down below she could see her Cheyenne camp. She became very sad and homesick and lay down beside the hole and wept.

After she had cried for a long time, she got up and began to braid a rope from long grass. When it was time to go home, she hid the rope and gathered a few turnips to take back to the tipi she shared with Red Star. "I was tired and took a long rest," she told him when he noticed she had but a few turnips. Each of the following days she went to pick turnips with her baby boy and looked through the hole in the sky. Each day she made the grass rope longer, and at the end of the day covered the hole with grass and took a few turnips home. After four days she thought the rope was long enough, and she laid her digging stick across the hole and tied her grass rope around the stick. Then, with her baby on her back, she lowered herself down the rope. "Now," she thought, "my boy will see his mother's people and live in the lodges of the Cheyennes."

As she climbed down the rope, she was getting very tired and when she reached the bottom of the rope, she was alarmed to see that the earth was still far away. She was too tired to climb back up the rope, but she held on as long as she could before finally slipping off and falling down and down, with her baby on her back. When she hit the earth, she landed face down and was killed. Her baby was saved because he was cushioned by his mother's body.

A meadowlark had been building a nest nearby and had hatched five eggs. The mother bird saw the baby lying on his mother's back and took pity on him. "I will build my nest a little larger and take that boy to raise with my own children," she said. So she made her nest larger. A great heron was flying by and saw the child. He stopped and gave it some water he had been carrying in his bill. Then he untied the straps which held the baby, and gently rolled the little boy into the meadowlark's nest. The mother bird moved her young around and helped the heron place the child among them. Then she spread her wings over the six little ones in her nest.

Because he was the son of a star, the little boy grew quickly in the next few months on a diet of grasshoppers and worms, and berries and water brought by the heron. By the time the baby larks could fly a little, the boy could walk. When the larks were fully grown, the young man could run and play with them across the prairies.

Autumn came, and it was time for the larks to fly south. But the mother lark said to the young man, "You must go north, into the Black Hills. There you will find the camp of your mother's people, the Cheyennes. You must find your grandmother. She is very sad because her daughter went to live in the sky." The lark told him where to find a deserted Cheyenne camp, where he could get skins and rawhide for clothing. In the camp he also found some dried meat, which he ate before setting out to follow the tracks of the people to their next camp.

Coming to the top of a hill, he saw spread out before him a large Indian camp. He walked straight to a tipi where an old woman was wailing and weeping. She looked like his mother, except she was old and gray. "Old woman," he said, "will you give me something to eat?" "We have no food," she replied, "We have no wood to burn, so we cannot cook. Everyone here is hungry. Every time anyone goes into the forest to gather sticks a monster catches him and throws him into his ear. No one dares to try and get fuel."

The boy picked up a stone axe that was lying in the tipi. "I will get some wood for you," he said. He went into the forest and cut some short pieces of wood. While he was chopping, the monster appeared. The boy paid no attention to the hideous creature. Suddenly he felt a huge hand seize him and thrust him into the beast's ear. In the ear was a room filled with people. They were sitting on the ground with their robes drawn over their heads, weeping and singing sad songs. "Why don't you do something?" the boy asked. "Why do you sit around and let this go on? Why don't you kill this monster?" No one answered his questions. All were frightened and sad.

When he was thrust into the monster's ear the boy had clung to the axe. Now he looked around the room. In one corner he saw the side of some large bones which he knew to be part of the giant's spine. He swung the stone axe over his head and drove it with all his strength into one of them. The creature fell dead, spilling the people onto the ground.

Then he hacked off the monster's head and returned to the tipi of the old woman with some wood for her fire. "Now tell all the people that it is safe to get wood," he said. "I have killed the monster. Tell them that I am Star Drops – your grandson."

Little Calf

Little Calf decided to leave his parents' tipi to look for adventure. His father and mother were heartbroken at the thought of their only son leaving, but they realized that he wanted to go, so they wrapped some dried meat with his extra moccasins and stuffed them into the quiver that held his arrows. "Perhaps our son will become a great warrior," his father said, "He may be the one chosen to slay the monster elk that burrows in the sands along the river to the south."

Little Calf walked a long distance before he became tired and climbed to the top of a high peak to rest. From there he could watch the approach of wild beasts. After making sure he was safe, he slept. While he was asleep, an old man came to him and said: "I live under this peak. I am without food and am getting hungry." Little Calf knew at once that this was one of the good spirits that help people, so he promised to aid the old man. He hunted for the old man, and the old man ate his fill.

"Go to the south," he said, "A great elk that no one has been able to kill lives there. I will give you much strength for the journey if you will slay this beast. The underground beings will help you on your way."

Little Calf no longer sought high places on which to rest. He slept all night on the ground, close to the homes of the underground beings. At sunset on the first day of his journey a weasel came to Little Calf and led him to his home, where the two rested and feasted. Before the youth departed, his host gave him a sharp-pointed arrow. "This arrow is faster than any other," the weasel said. The second night Little Calf found himself in a prairie-dog town. The chief of these tiny creatures led him into a tunnel-like tipi. There the boy saw many fat children. Before he started on his journey the next morning, his new friend gave him an agate-headed arrow.

On the third night Little Calf stopped at the camp of the badgers. There he rested. As he was about to leave the lodge to continue his journey, the chief gave him an arrow with a cactus thorn for a point. "That arrow won't last long," Little Calf said. "Oh yes, it will," the badger chief answered. "You can pound it, and it will not break. You are going to a dangerous place, and I don't believe that you can kill that elk. I will help you, though, and am giving you this wonderful arrow in hopes that it will bring you good fortune."

On the fourth evening, Little Calf came to the village of the gophers. He was led into a large underground tipi, where he saw many tiny warriors seated in a circle. "Where are you going?" the chief asked. "I came here for help," Little Calf said. "I know you are a powerful animal. My grandfather has sent me to kill the great elk." The gopher chief gave him a special arrow. "It will break into tiny bits and kill whatever it strikes. Save it for last."

When Little Calf awoke next morning, the gopher chief led him through a long tunnel to the riverbank. They peeked outside and could see the monster elk sitting under a tree by the riverbank. "Now shoot your arrows," said the gopher chief, "then turn and run as fast as you can to my tipi." Little Calf first took the arrow the weasel had given him and shot the monster elk in the leg, pinning him to the ground. Then he quickly shot the prairie-dog arrow, pinning the elk's body to the ground. Next he shot the cactus-point arrow, hitting him in the nose and pinning his head down. The elk could not move.

Little Calf turned and fled down the tunnel as fast as he could, his tiny friend close behind. When they reached the gopher's tipi, he shouted, "Follow me; don't look back." With that, the gopher and his family began to dig through the ground. They dug so fast that the youth could barely keep up, even though he ran as fast as he could. At last they emerged from the ground at the top of a high hill. When Little Calf looked back, he could see the monster elk's mate, tearing up the ground as she destroyed the tunnel almost as fast as the gophers had dug it. "Take your last arrow," said the gopher, "and shoot it when I tell you." When the elk was right upon them, the gopher gave the signal and Little Calf loosed the arrow, killing the mate of the monster elk.

"Leave this elk for us," the gopher said, "take the other one for yourself." Little Calf returned to the riverbank and found that the monster elk was dead. Dressing the elk, he saw that there was much fat meat. Cutting the meat from the carcass, he loaded it on two long poles, which he balanced on his shoulders. On his way to the home of the old man who lived in the mountain, he stopped with the badger, the prairie dogs and the weasels and shared his meat. When he reached the mountain, the old man cut up the meat and dried it. Then he hung up the head and horns, which were powerful medicine. The two lived together for many days, feasting on the fat elk meat.

These two stories are loaded with symbolism and moral instruction, as well as being very entertaining. The listeners learn respect for elders and animals. They learn that brave and good behavior is rewarded. And they learn to share. Beyond that, they learn the proper place of animals in the natural world, both positively and negatively. The weasels, prairie dogs, badgers, and gophers live naturally in the ground, but an elk who burrows in the ground is a monster. Other stories teach the listeners lessons of this same kind, but the most prominent is the story of "The Great Race," which explains how it is that some animals eat other animals, while yet other animals eat berries or grass (Randolph 1937).

The Great Race

There was a time long ago when animals hunted, killed, and ate people. That is, in those days, human hunters did not set out every day in search of buffaloes, antelopes, deer, and elk, but rather these animals would form themselves into hunting parties every day and look for humans to kill and eat. Because of this, the Cheyennes of that time were always fearful of their lives, since they were in constant danger of being attacked.

At last the humans were able to arrange a great council to discuss the situation, and see if a plan could not be worked out to decide forever which animals would be the hunters and which would be the hunted. There was at that time among the buffaloes a young female who was a swift runner. She could outrun any antelope or bird or any other creature of the plains. For that reason, the buffaloes and their allies proposed that there would be a great race between two teams of animals, each team consisting of the fastest runners from each species. They would race all the way around the Black Hills to determine the winner, whose team would become the hunters. The other team would become the hunted and would thereafter be killed and eaten by the winning team. The buffaloes and their allies were confident they would win. Surprisingly, the humans and their allies agreed to the plan.

The allies of the humans were the birds and animals who liked to associate with them – the magpie, the crow, the hawk, the coyote, and several others. On the other side were the buffaloes, the antelopes, the deer, the elks, and all the other kinds of birds and animals. On the day of the race, all the birds and animals, and all the tribes of Indians, gathered at Bear Butte, on the eastern side of the Black Hills, to begin the race.

When the race started, the young female buffalo sprang into the lead, running easily. She looked behind and decided to show them just how fast she could run, but she speeded up so fast that blood began to flow from her mouth, and she fell dead, staining the ground. Seeing her fall, the hawk, an ally of humans, sprang into the lead until she, too, broke her heart and fell to the earth, bleeding. One by one, all the birds and animals saw their chance to lead the race but, one by one, they were straining themselves and dying of the effort.

But the magpie had started far behind and, being a slow flyer, she did not expect to lead the race. But as the day progressed, she could see the other birds and animals falling to the ground in front of her. Finally, she was the only creature left in the race, and she crossed the finish line all by herself. And since that time, the magpie, the hawk, the coyote, and human beings have had the right to hunt and kill the other birds and animals. In celebration, they painted themselves in bright colors, while the members of the losing team had to paint themselves in brown and black, so that the hunters would have difficulty in seeing them.

From the hero stories, and from the animal stories, Cheyenne children learn the names of all the birds, animals, and plants in the Cheyenne world, and the locations of the important geographical places on the plains. They learn that it is good to help others, but that to do so requires discipline and supernatural assistance from elders and from the creatures of the natural world. They learn that the ultimate goal of heroic action is to help other people. They learn the importance of kin and family relationships, and how to show respect to their elders and to people with knowledge that they wish to receive.

Another set of stories are also teaching stories, but they are enjoyed by adults as well as by children. They are essentially parodies of the heroic stories, in which the hero tries to do something marvelous, gets it wrong, and suffers hilarious consequences. We have equivalent stories and dramas in Anglo-American culture. Wile E. Coyote in the Roadrunner cartoons fancies himself a technological genius, but somehow can never get his contraptions to work. Characters like the Three Stooges, Laurel and Hardy, or Beavis and Butthead would dearly like to engage in collective enterprises like everyone else, but somehow can never overcome their personal problems and animosities sufficiently to accomplish their objectives.

The character who gets it all wrong in Cheyenne stories is the Trickster, known in the Cheyenne language as Veho, the same word as is used for spiders and white people. The underlying theme for all these creatures is that they construct elaborate schemes to ensnare other creatures, but they fall victim to their own avarice and pretentions. Spiders are eaten by their mates, white people kill themselves with elaborate weapons, pollution, and horrible diseases, while the Trickster – well, the Trickster would like to enlist powerful supernatural forces for his own personal benefit, if he could just remember what they told him. The first story, entitled "The Elk Skull," is a parody of the story of Little Calf.[2]

The Elk Skull

Once Veho was walking along when suddenly he heard singing. He looked around but he didn't see anyone. So he listened and began hunting for the singers. He soon found that the singing was coming from an old elk skull that was laying on the prairie. He got down on his knees and looked inside.

The little mice were having a dance in the elk skull. A white tepee stood inside and food was being cooked for a feast.

When Veho saw this, he wanted to join them. "Oh, little brothers," he said to the mice, "let me come in. I want to dance too."

"No," said the mice. "You'll have to stay outside. There isn't room for you in there."

Veho begged them to let him come in. But again they told him "no." So Veho decided he'd go in anyhow. He made himself small so he could go in through the hole at the back of the elk skull. Then he twisted and turned until he got his head in. This frightened the mice and they all ran away.

When Veho saw that the mice had gone, he tried to get his head out of the hole. He pulled and pulled, but he couldn't get his head from the hole. It was stuck fast.

Finally, he started home. It was hard walking with the elk skull over his head. He couldn't see where he was going. He cried as he went, for he kept tripping over stones and stumbling over buffalo bones and falling into gullies. At last he reached the river and followed it towards his camp.

Veho's children were swimming near the camp. When they saw him coming with the elk skull over his head, they didn't know just what he was. They became frightened and ran crying into camp. Then Veho's wife came out of their lodge to see what had frightened her children.

She saw Veho and didn't know what to think. Then she heard him crying and talking to himself and knew at once who it was. She became very angry and got an axe.

When Veho stumbled into camp, she ran up and hit him on the head with the axe and tried to break the elk skull. She knocked Veho down. He got to his feet and she hit him once more and knocked him down. She kept hitting him and knocking him down until, finally, she broke the elk skull and set him free.

The Lost Eyes

One time Veho was walking along when he saw a man up ahead. The man was lying on his back on the prairie. Veho wondered what he was doing so he hid in the brush and watched.

The man said something, then his eyes flew out of his head. They hung in the top branches of a nearby tree. The man spoke again and his eyes flew back down into his head. The man did this four times.

Veho watched, then he went over to the man. "Oh, brother," he cried, "I want to learn how to do that!"

"All right," said the man. "I'll tell you how, but you must only do it four times. Otherwise, something bad will happen." Then the man gave Veho his power and went on his way.

Veho couldn't wait to make his eyes fly out of his head. "Eyes, fly up to that high treetop," he said. And they did. Then he called them back. "That time was just for practice," said Veho. "It didn't count." He did it again and again. Each time his eyes flew to the treetop. He did it four times, but he told himself it was only three.

The next time he tried it, his eyes flew to the treetop just as before. But, when he called them back, they didn't come. They stayed in the treetop. After a while some magpies flew over and ate them. Veho couldn't see at all. He began crying for his lost eyes.

After a time, he started crawling across the prairie. He crawled until he became tired. Then he lay down to rest. Suddenly he felt something running across his chest. He reached up quickly and caught it. It was a little mouse. Veho was lying across a mouse's road.

"Oh, mouse," said Veho, "lend me your eyes so I can see where I'm going."

"Well," said the mouse, "I can't lend you both my eyes. I wouldn't be able to see then. But I will lend you one eye." Then he gave Veho one of his eyes. Veho put it in one of his eye-sockets. It was very small, but it was better than having no eyes at all.

Veho had to walk slowly and feel his way, for he couldn't see very much with the mouse's eye. Before long he saw a buffalo bull and went over to him.

"Brother," said Veho, "I am almost blind. Lend me one of your eyes so I can see where I'm going." Then the bull lent Veho one of his eyes. He put it in his empty eye-socket and went on his way.

Now Veho had a tiny mouse's eye and a great buffalo's eye. When he reached camp and his wife saw him, she became very angry.

"What did you do with your eyes?" she asked.

"I traded one to a little mouse so I can see at night," he told her. "And I traded the other to a buffalo so I can see far and wide."

The Sacred Stories

Although the following Sweet Medicine story is of the same form and structure as the hero stories, it is taken much more seriously by Cheyenne people. Only qualified priests are allowed to tell the story, and only under certain conditions. Ideally, the story is told on four consecutive nights, sometimes during the annual ceremonies. This narration provides an introduction to the next chapter, on Cheyenne ceremonies, since a large portion of the serious ceremonies is built around a ritual version of the saga of Sweet Medicine.

The whole Sweet Medicine saga is very long, and it has many versions which sometimes contradict one another. But just as devout Christians are not troubled by any logical flaws or historical contradictions in their Holy Bible, neither are traditional Cheyennes troubled by the fact that different elders will tell different versions of the Sweet Medicine story which are not consistent with one another. The abridged version presented below has been edited to make it internally consistent, and contains most of the central episodes which are important for understanding the beliefs and ceremonies presented in the next chapter.[3]

Once, a long time ago, a baby boy was born. The parents wrapped it in its covering, and used to leave it in the lodge. Sometimes at night, when they went to bed, the baby was gone. Only its wrapping would be there. In the morning, when they arose, the baby was there again. The boy's father and mother died while he was little. A poor old woman took care of him as best she could, and reared him. He had strange ways about sleeping. Sometimes he would lie down to sleep anywhere, and, if people tried to wake him, they found they could not. It would seem that he were dead.

In this old time the people used to come together and dance. One day the boy asked his grandmother if he might not dance too. "No," said his grandmother, "you had better wait. This dance is a religious one. You cannot go to it; you are too small." The boy kept nagging to go. He nagged and nagged, and at last he cried and said he wanted to go. "Well," said his grandmother, "you can go. How do you want to be dressed and painted?" He said to his grandmother, "I want my body to be painted yellow, in stripes, and my robe to be painted white. I want the feather I wear on my head yellow, and the bowstring that I shall wear about my neck also yellow."

The old woman asked, "Why do you want to wear a bowstring about your neck?" The boy said, "I want it so that I can take my head off my body." "Can this be true?" said the grandmother. "Yes," the boy said, "and after my head is off my body, I want you to place the head close to the body, and lay the head toward the rising sun, and cover me with my calf-robe."

There was a great crowd about the dancing lodge, and when they entered, the medicine man who had charge of the dance said, "Why, here is Mutsiuv come to dance! Come over here and sit down by me." The dance went on, but from time to time they stopped and rested and talked. At the last part of the dance, just before they would eat, the boy arose and began to dance. Suddenly, he pulled the bowstring tight and it cut off his head, which fell to the ground, but his body continued to dance. When they all stopped dancing, the body fell down, and the old woman walked over and put the body and the head together, and placed the bowstring by the boy's side, and put the robe over the body, and let it lie there for a little time. Then she took the robe off and shook it four times, and put it back over Mutsiuv. When she had done this, Mutsiuv rose with a smile on his face. He did this to show the people what he was, so that all the people might know what he could do.

One day the people had surrounded buffaloes and had killed many, and the wonderful young man had killed a fat two-year-old bull, with a robe as black as charcoal. He skinned the bull, and left the head, legs, and even the hooves on the hide. A great chief came up, "Ha, that is just the kind of a robe I need. I will take it." Mutsiuv said, "No, I need the robe, but you can have the meat." The chief grew angry and drew his knife and cut the hide into small pieces. Then the young man was angry, and he caught up the bone of the buffalo's hind-leg and struck the chief on the head with the hoof, and killed him. Then he went back to camp.

By the time Mutsiuv reached his lodge, everyone knew he had killed the chief. The soldiers ran to his lodge and surrounded it. His grandmother said, "Run, run, the soldiers are coming." Mutsiuv shouted to the soldiers outside, "Go away, you trouble me." When the soldiers entered the lodge, Mutsiuv spilled water onto the fire, and he rose up out of the smoke hole with the steam and ashes. The soldiers all looked for him but could not find him. Then they saw him sitting on a hill nearby, but when they got there he had disappeared.

In the next few days, four times the people surrounded Mutsiuv in the bushes near the camp. The first time he turned himself into a coyote and ran away. The next time he turned himself into a magpie, and then a crow, and then an owl. The people could not catch him.

A few days later, Mutsiuv appeared at the edge of camp dressed with crow feathers on his head, carrying a rattle and a dog rope.

This was the dress of the Dog Soldiers, but it was the first time the people had seen it. The people chased him and he seemed exhausted when they got close, but when he was out of sight he ran far away. Next he appeared to the people wearing a bonnet of buffalo-hide, and a belt strung with buffalo tails, rattles on his moccasins, and he carried a lance which he used as a cane. This was the dress of the Red Shields. They chased him as before. Then he appeared with a crooked lance and a war bonnet, like an Elk Soldier, and they chased him. Then he appeared painted black all over with a lance like those of the Fox Society. On the fifth day he appeared with an owl head-dress and bull-hide moccasins, like a contrary warrior, and the next day he came as a chief, carrying a pipe and tobacco sack.[4]

The next day they heard thunder approaching and looked to see a giant buffalo running toward the camp. Then it turned into an elk and then into other animals, and then it turned into Mutsiuv playing the wheel game. The people were afraid and did not chase him, and he turned away and they did not see him for a long time. During this time, the buffaloes and all other game disappeared, and the people were hungry. They could find nothing to eat but mushrooms and the bark of trees.

One day seven little boys were following behind the camp as it moved; they were thin and starving and stopped to eat some mushrooms. As they sat along the trail a handsome mysterious man appeared. He told them to throw away their mushrooms, and to collect some old buffalo chips, which he placed on his robe. When he folded and unfolded the robe, there was meat and fat for them to eat. Then he told the little boys to eat, and take the rest of the food to their camp. They should tell the people to stop and set up their lodges in a circle, with an opening toward the rising sun.

In the morning, Mutsiuv's grandmother noticed that someone was sleeping in her lodge; it was Mutsiuv. The chiefs came to talk to him. Mutsiuv said, "Put up a big double lodge facing the sun, and level off the ground all around." When the lodge had been put up, Mutsiuv went inside and said, "Bring me an old buffalo skull, and put it in the opening of the circle." Then he taught them a song to sing, and when they sang it, the skull came to life. They put it in the double lodge. Mutsiuv told them all to sing, and after they had sung for three days, they heard buffalo approaching. Mutsiuv told them to kill the buffalo and eat all they wanted.

After everyone had eaten, Mutsiuv told them that he had been traveling all around the world, and had found a sacred mountain within which sacred people lived. He said he was going back there, with a woman chosen to be his wife. A great chief gave his daughter to Mutsiuv for a wife, and they went together to the sacred mountain, carrying their belongings on a travois pulled by a dog.

When Mutsiuv returned with his wife to the sacred mountain, the people living inside it said, "Ah, here is our grandson come back again. Come in, and sit at the back of the lodge." The people who lived in this lodge in the mountain were all the things and beings that belong to this earth. There were persons and buffalo and antelope; all animals and birds, rocks, trees, bushes, and grass; all things that grow or exist upon the earth. There were also four handsome men of different colors and appearance. The chief of the lodge said to Mutsiuv, "Choose one of these men that you would like to look like." Mutsiuv chose the brown man at the left of the door. The chief frowned, "If you had chosen one of the other men, you would live forever, for they are stones. But now, although you will be very handsome, you will die some day."

At this point, one man from the lodge said, "This man is a fool," and he stalked out of the lodge. The chief said to Mutsiuv, "Follow that man, for he has great powers." Mutsiuv did, and after following him all around the earth and back to the sacred mountain, the sacred people gave Mutsiuv four sacred arrows. The chief said, "Take these arrows with you, and guard them carefully. They will be a great help to you for a long time; but you will keep them until they will cease to be a help, and will be of no more use to you."

When they left the sacred lodge, the girl carried the arrows, wrapped in a coyote skin, on her back, and they led the dog. When they returned to the camp, Mutsiuv told the people to camp in a circle, with his lodge in the center. He went into his lodge, and hung the arrows over the door. Next morning he unrolled the arrow bundle and took out the four medicine arrows. He showed the arrows to the men. "Two of these arrows," he said, "are for killing buffaloes. Make your buffalo arrows like this. And two of these arrows are for war. Make your war arrows like these." Then he rolled up the arrows in the cover and hung them in his lodge.

Mutsiuv lived with the people for four generations. Every spring he would appear to them as a child, then in summer as a young man, in the fall as a mature man, and in the winter as an old man. During this time he told them a prophecy:

"I shall not be with you long now. I chose the wrong person: I wanted to be too good-looking. Now I am getting to be old. Now my people, you must not forget what I am telling you. After I am dead, you must come together often, and when you do, call my name. A time is coming when you will meet other people, and you will fight with them, and will kill each other. Each tribe will want the land of the other, and you will be fighting always.

"Far away in the south is a strange animal, with long hair hanging down from its neck, and a tail that drags on the ground. This animal you shall ride on, and pack. The buffalo will disappear, and when the buffalo have gone, the next animal you have to eat will be spotted. When you get toward the end, your people will begin to gray very young, and you will come to marry even your own relatives. You will reach a point where you will be ashamed of nothing, and you will act as if you were crazy.

"You will soon find among you a people who have hair all over their faces, and whose skin is white, and when that time comes, you will be controlled by them. The white people will be all over the land, and at last you will disappear."

Mutsiuv died in the summer, when he was a young man.

Cosmology and Ceremonies

The religion of the Cheyenne people is so colorful and interesting, and the ceremonies so spectacular, that a great deal has been
written and published about their religious beliefs and practices.
Unfortunately, some of the most prominent and most available
literature is severely distorted, and has been disavowed or
criticized by Cheyenne religionists for several decades. Perhaps
the most popular book which was allegedly about Cheyenne
religion is *Seven Arrows* by Hyemeyohsts Storm, still in print
and prominently displayed in bookstores. Immediately after its
publication in 1972, Cheyenne priests and chiefs made a huge
public protest, forcing the author and publisher to revise the text
and advertising claims.

Originally touted as a description of esoteric Cheyenne beliefs
and practices, the book contained very little which was familiar
to the Cheyenne priests I was working with in Montana and
Oklahoma when the book was published. In fact, Hyemeyohsts
Storm was completely unknown to them. More bothersome,
however, were allegations about strange religious customs which
included sexual intercourse between a man and his mother at
puberty! Writing on behalf of Cheyenne priests and chiefs on
February 22, 1974, Chief Laird Cometsevah of the Southern
Cheyennes described the book as follows:

The book *Seven Arrows* is a farce, and a parody of traditional
Cheyenne beliefs. It is nonsense from cover to cover, a dressed-up
concoction sold to the naive public as authentic Cheyenne lore. What
has enraged us most, however, is the scene on pp. 144–149 where a
young Cheyenne man fornicates with his mother, and where the text
describes this act as a rather natural thing to do.

In response to pressure from Chief Cometsevah, from Joe Little Coyote of the Northern Cheyennes, and from Rupert Costo, editor of the Indian newspaper *Wassaja*, publisher Douglas Latimer of Harper and Row wrote a long letter to the Cheyennes dated July 22, 1975, making the following promises for subsequent editions of the book:

1 "We have removed the sentence saying that 'Storm's first teachers were the elders of his tribe'."

2 "All references to Storm having been 'trained as a Shield Maker' have been deleted."

3 "The main description of *Sevens Arrows* now says 'it is a teaching story, using symbolism and allegory to express a philosophy based upon the equality and brotherhood of all living beings, and the great balancing harmony of the universe' .... Note that the reference is made simply to teaching 'a philosophy.' It does not say a Cheyenne philosophy, or for that matter even an Indian philosophy. Similarly, the symbol of the Medicine Wheel has come down from many cultures over the world, including parts of Europe, China, Tibet, Russia and even Africa."

4 " ... nowhere in the publicity is there any reference to the Cheyennes, other than the one clearly stating that Cheyenne traditional leaders have criticized *Seven Arrows* as heretical. This should make it abundantly clear to all readers that *Seven Arrows* is not about the Cheyennes; that it is *not* sanctioned or endorsed in any way by the Cheyennes, but rather the reverse; and that it is a *novel*, not a factual description of either history or religion."

In the same letter, by way of atonement, or as Latimer put it, "further expression of our concern about the past difficulties," he offered to send to the Cheyennes "all profits presently accrued to *Seven Arrows*, as well as all future profits earned by it." In fact, a check for $7,500 was received by the Southern Cheyennes, and I understand a similar amount was received by the northerners. I doubt, however, that this was or is the full extent of the profits.

Despite this private disavowal, *Seven Arrows* as well as Storm's other books still in print continue to be accepted by the non-Indian reading public as authentic descriptions of Cheyenne or Plains Indian religions. I mention this episode merely to illustrate how difficult it is for the proverbial "intelligent reader" to get a clear conception of Cheyenne religion through the fog of misunderstanding and sometimes outright fraud and chicanery which surround the publication of books about Indian religions. In general, popular books about Indian religions cater to the public's *expectations* about Indian beliefs, rather than reality. In fact, the reality of Indian religions, as can be seen from the stories in the last chapter, is much more difficult to understand than the familiar body of themes we call "Indian lore," which has almost nothing to do with Indians but is largely borrowed from European folklore and witchcraft, with recent additions of Asian, especially Buddhist, themes, and more recently astrology and New Age philosophy.

Another prominent writer about Cheyenne religion is Father Peter Powell, who is certainly neither fraudulent nor deceitful, but is in my experience a very kind and thoughtful person who has devoted many years to Indian welfare through his ministry at Saint Augustine's Center in Chicago. Here the problem is that Father Powell is a convinced and practicing Anglican priest, and tends to have, in my opinion, a perspective on Cheyenne religion which is distorted by his own Christian convictions. He is, to use the vernacular of anthropology, "ethnocentric" in his descriptions of the Cheyennes. He tends to see the Cheyennes as imperfect Anglicans with primitive rituals which anticipate prayer and the Mass as conducted by Anglo-Catholics. In fact, Father Powell uses the vocabulary of Christian theology to describe the practice of Cheyenne religion. He sees Catholic or Anglican ritual as more advanced and more evolved than Cheyenne ritual. He describes Cheyenne religion not from the standpoint of a believer in Cheyenne religion, but as a Christian theologian, and in my opinion does not properly understand just how different Cheyenne religion actually is.

In his writings about Cheyenne history, Father Powell similarly sees events on the plains through Judeo-Christian eyes. His book, *People of the Sacred Mountain*, casts the Cheyennes as primitive Hebrews, migrating about the plains in accordance with theistic instructions and experiencing recurrent miracles along the way. This is not to say that some Cheyennes are not firm believers in prophecy or in miracles, for they are, but only that Powell emphasizes this side of Cheyenne character to the exclusion of their rationality and common sense in entering the plains, reorganizing their culture, and making war against their enemies. He deprives them of their reason and their humanity in making them fit the Christian mold.

Cheyenne priests criticize Father Powell's descriptions as the "sing a song and turn around three times" school of ethnography.[1] That is, while Powell's writings have provided a detailed description of how the ceremonies are performed, there is little explanation of why the participants do what they are doing; the overall motivation and structural framework are missing. There has been some concern among Cheyenne priests that books like Powell's might "put them out of business," enabling anyone at all to refer to the book and conduct Cheyenne ceremonies. So far this has not happened, although Powell's book is popular among Boy Scouts and European hobbyists, all of whom conduct pseudo-Indian ceremonies. In Germany and Hungary there have even been full-blown Cheyenne Sun Dances, based on Powell's description. The Cheyenne people, however, realize that the ceremonies provide blessings only when organized and conducted by qualified priests who have fulfilled a lengthy apprenticeship. And so Cheyenne ceremonial life, in both Oklahoma and Montana, is stronger than ever.

My own research into Cheyenne religious beliefs was conducted in 1969–74, when the Cheyenne priests were angry both with Hyemeyohsts Storm and with Father Powell, and were anxious to set the record straight about their religious beliefs. My original purpose, established with my dissertation committee at New York University, was to try to understand the body paints of the Cheyennes used during the Sun Dance, which had been pictured in scholarly books, but with no accompanying explanation of why these particular symbols were selected – hail, tornadoes, dragonflies and birds.

Both in Oklahoma and in Montana I was welcomed by Cheyenne priests and invited to ask my questions. After asking fragmented questions about this and that and getting fragmented responses, the Southern Cheyenne priests finally decided that they had better start at the beginning, and they authorized Roy Nightwalker to explain to me the formal cosmology which constituted the structural framework in which everything, including the ceremonial activities, was conducted. If I had been raised as a Cheyenne, listening to stories and paying attention to my elders, this kind of formal instruction would not have been necessary. But as it was, since I was an outsider, I needed to learn the fundamentals. I was told that the same kind of instruction was sometimes given to Cheyennes who wanted to participate in ceremonies but had been too much acculturated to Anglo-American society. And so, mostly in one all-night session at the ceremonial grounds in Seiling, Oklahoma, I was instructed in the fundamentals of Cheyenne cosmology. This was then supplemented by interviews with Jim Medicine Elk, who was arrow keeper at the time, and Alex Brady and Albert Tall Bull in Montana, as well as several other priests in both Montana and Oklahoma. This material was presented as my doctoral dissertation in 1974.

In collecting information about religion, I have tried to behave ethically. I have tried not to publish anything which was private or would embarrass the Cheyennes as a people. I have tried not to supply any information which is part of a priest's apprenticeship. The formal cosmology explained below is something like an orientation for outsiders, similar to what one would receive if one asked a Muslim or Jewish religious leader to speak to a Christian forum on comparative religion. It describes the physical, psychological, and cognitive structure of the Cheyenne universe, and sketches in the major characters. It is against this background that Cheyenne stories are told and Cheyenne ceremonies acted out. With this background in mind, both the stories and the ceremonies are much more intelligible.

The Sky-Spaces

Hestanov, the Universe, is divided by the earth's surface into Heamahestanov, the World Above and Àtonoom, the Underworld. Each of these, in turn, is divided into several regions, of which the highest and most important is Otatavoom, the Blue Sky-Space. This region is at the upward limit of the universe and includes as dominant features two "suns," one which is born daily in the east and one which is born monthly in the west. Both of these are called Eëhe in ceremonial language, although Taeëhe, "Night-Sun," is sometimes used to particularly designate the moon. The sun and moon, as celestial phenomena, are merely the most obvious manifestations of two major spirits who are known by priests to be anthropomorphic, or "human-like" in appearance. The traditional names for these spirits are Atovsz (sun) and Ameònito.

Also prominent within the level of the Blue Sky-Space are the stars, especially the Milky Way and the Pleiades. The Milky Way, Seameo, is the road taken by the souls of Cheyennes on their way to the land of the dead, Nãevoom. The souls of those who die by their own hand, or who were exceptionally evil during life, must travel down a particular branch of Seameo which leads to nothingness. The Pleiades, Manohotoxceo (meaning "the bunch of stars"), are prominent in a sacred story involving seven brothers. They are also mentioned in tribal ceremonies, as are the morning and evening stars, meteors (scratching stars), and several constellations which are different from those of scientific astronomy. Some examples of Cheyenne constellations are the Circle of Stars, the Beaver, and the Heart.

The second highest level of the universe is the Nearer Sky-Space, Setovoom, which includes especially the following phenomena: clouds, dust devils, tornadoes, sacred birds, and the tops of hills and mountains. Setovoom mediates between humans and the sacred forces of the Blue Sky-Space, and so it is filled with atmospheric agents which are especially diagnostic of the moods and intentions of the major forces of the universe. Clouds, for example, predict the coming weather and the change of seasons. Birds also predict changes, but relating to good or bad events and the proximity of animals and groups of people. Especially sacred are the magpie and the raven, who live close to people and are able to carry messages to spiritual forces. Other important birds are eagles and hawks, and a bird which is seldom or never seen, the thunderbird. In the 20th century, three sacred birds, residents of Setovoom, have been added to Cheyenne tradition because of the peyote religion:[2] these are the macaw, the Mexican turkey, and the waterbird (*anhinga*), which are known only from their feathers, used in peyote ritual.

The vertical axis of the universe, from zenith to nadir, provides the sexual dimension of Cheyenne cosmology. The zenith is the residence of the principal or high god, who has many names in Cheyenne but is usually referred to as Maheo, translated simply as God, the Creator, or the All-Father. Maheo is entirely spiritual in essence. By contrast, the nadir, at the center of the earth, is the domain of the female principle, Heëstoz, which is entirely material or substantial in nature, and has no spiritual essence.

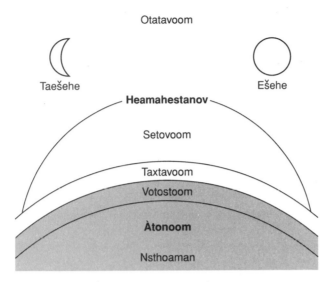

Figure 8.1   Cheyenne cosmology from zenith to nadir

The layers of the Cheyenne universe, then, illustrated in figure 8.1, are successively more male from bottom to top, and more female from top to bottom, with the zenith being entirely male and spiritual, and the nadir being entirely female and material. Each level of the cosmos represents some combination of male spirituality and female materialism. Those elements above the surface of the earth are predominantly male, and those under the surface predominantly female.

The air near the surface of the earth, the space between Setovoom and the surface, is called Taxtavoom, the Atmosphere. It is defined as the region where dust rises from horses and vehicles, where objects can be thrown, where bullets and arrows can be shot, and where small birds and insects fly. Taxtavoom covers the whole surface of the earth, from horizon to horizon. It is considered to be one of the special gifts from God since it causes breathing, entering the lungs of people and animals and keeping them alive and moving, even when asleep.

The surface layer of the earth is called Votostoom, the Surface-Dome, and fills the space between the surface, where people walk, and Nsthoaman, the Deep Earth. The Surface-Dome includes that part of the earth where plants and their roots grow, where insects and animals burrow, and includes the caves where bears, buffaloes, and other animals live. Votostoom also comprises the surface water of lakes, creeks, and rivers, and the fish, turtles, and other aquatic life which lives in the sunlit waters. Rocks, sand, and other geological features of the surface are also considered to be part of the living world encompassed by Votostoom.

Nsthoaman, however, is the deep and sterile part of the earth, where there is no life, only substance. Nsthoaman embodies the essence of Heēstoz, literally "femaleness." Heēstoz, however, is emphatically not a spirit, in so far as "spirit" implies animation and personality. In fact, the essence of the female principle, in striking contrast with "femaleness" in some other cultures, is the idea of spiritual inertness and biophysical sterility.

The Cardinal Directions

Like most people in the world, the Cheyennes recognize four cardinal directions on the horizontal surface of the earth, but the Cheyenne directions are oriented somewhat differently from the cardinal directions of Europeans. East, or *hesen*, is the direction of the rising sun, somewhat south of the European east; *sovon*, or south, is the direction from which warm winds and thunderstorms come in the spring; the west, *onxsovon*, is where the moon rises, and the north, *notam*, is the source of winter weather. Each of these directions is dominated by an anthropomorphic spirit, whose respective names are Hesenota, Sovota, Onxsovota, and Notamota. These spirits are said to live at the horizon, where everything converges and the Blue Sky-Space touches the surface of the earth, and each is associated with particular sacred creatures and other phenomena.

Creatures and objects which are colored red or yellow are said to be associated with the east. These colors are prominent in the sky at sunrise. Red-headed woodpeckers, yellow-shafted flickers, red willows, and the red catlinite used to make pipes for smoking are also associated with the east, as is the human penis. Blood, which contributes the linguistic root for the Cheyenne word for red, "-mae-," is also associated with the east and with Hesenota.

Opposite the east is the domain of Onxsovota, the west, where the sun dies each day and the moon is born each month. Colors associated with the west are the colors of the sunset – purple, violet, dark blue, and black. While Hesenota is associated symbolically with birth and life, Onxsovota is associated with death, darkness, and the fear of death. Dark, deep water where monsters live is a part of this symbolic system. These negative associations are relieved only by the symbolism of the moon, which pierces the night with its glow, and consequently is a symbol of protection from death. The crescent, waxing moon in particular, along with birds and animals who bear this design, are held to be protective from death and darkness. Especially the black neck design of the flicker and the crescent-shaped claws of predators are taken to be moon symbols. In the summer, when the points of the crescent new moon point directly upwards, the moon is said to be emblematic of buffalo horns, and it is at this time that the major ceremonies are supposed to begin.

The other cosmic axis which falls across the earth's surface is between Notamota and Sovota, the spirits of the north and south. These spirits are somewhat equivalent to Hesenota and Onxsovota in that south, like east, is mostly helpful to man, whereas north, like west, is mostly dangerous. South and east bring blessings to mankind because they share a relationship with the sun, Atovsz. The sun, as life-bringer, favors the east each day at sunrise, while it favors south on a seasonal basis.

After the summer solstice, Atovsz is driven further and further south by Notamota, the spirit of the north, manifested as the anthropomorphic Hoimaha, usually translated as Frost or Old Man Winter. By the time of the winter solstice, however, Atovsz has regained his strength and he begins to return northward. This enables Sovota to generate the thunderstorms and south winds which bring summer once again to the earth's surface.

The color symbolism of Sovota cannot be understood except as it is related to the symbolism of the north, Notamota. The material things which are sacred to Sovota are not those which are typically and emphatically of one color, as with east and west, but rather those objects which are capable of showing a regular change from one color to another, in this case from green to white, green representing Sovota, and white Notamota.

The most prominent example of this regular green–white transition is furnished by the earth itself, or more specifically the

surface of the earth, Votostoom. In the words of Roy
Nightwalker,

Everything in the world turns white and green. In summer, even the
rocks turn green and grow [referring to moss and lichens]. Or if you
leave leather or meat or anything on the ground in summer, it turns
green. Everything is green. But in winter, everything is white. The snow
covers everything. The rivers freeze over and they are covered with
snow too. You go out in winter around here, and I bet you can't find
anything which is not white.

The surface of the earth can be understood not only by
reference to the cardinal directions, but also by reference to
specific regions of the surface, defined by their ecology and
consequent utility for human beings. For example, the forested
part of the earth is called Matavoom, while the open prairie is
called Zistoxton. The inhabitable part of the world, where useful
plants and animals are found, is called Noavoom in ceremonial
language, while Votostoom, strictly speaking, means the places
where people actually live.

Spiritual Forces

The anthropomorphic spirits of the universe are ambiguous; they
are capable of transforming themselves into greater or lesser
entities, as when the spirit of the north, Notamota, is manifested
in the fall as Frost, or Hoimaha. Cheyenne theology is not
concerned with describing the nature of these transformations;
they are merely accepted as part of the mystery of the supernatural world. Nonetheless, there is said to be a hierarchical arrangement among the anthropomorphic spirits. Maheo is the highest
and most sacred, manifested in the Sun and Moon and in the
spirits of the cardinal directions, who are in turn represented by
such lesser manifestations as Hoimaha and Nemevota, the rain
spirit.

It is interesting that, in contrast with the classic Greek and
Roman traditions, Cheyenne spiritual entities are not said to
interact very much with each other, but only with humans. While
the classical literature abounds with stories about struggles and
love affairs among the gods, Cheyenne stories are about the

interactions of ambiguous spiritual forces with humans. The most important interactions occur when a spiritual force lends its power to some Cheyenne supplicant, usually a young man in a dangerous situation.

The anthropomorphic spirits can also be manifested as special kinds of birds and animals. These are usually referred to as "chiefs" or "fathers" in English, attempts to translate such Cheyenne terms as *maheonevecess*, "sacred bird," or *honehev-eho*, "wolf chief." Sometimes reference is made in English to "bird-fathers," or "wolf priests." All such names are attempts to represent the personality of a special or spiritual kind of bird or animal which is said to have authority or power over others of its kind. Sometimes these special creatures can take the form of an ordinary human, or they can transform themselves into an anthropomorphic spirit, even a star or meteor. Despite the attempts of humans to understand them, they remain mysterious and ambiguous.

A different kind of spirit, *hematasooma*, inhabits the human body. A normal human has four of these, two mostly good and two mostly bad. A healthy person must have all four of these soul-forces to constitute a natural body, or *xamaemavōxoz*. The good forces are antagonistic to the bad forces and they some-times struggle physically within the body. Each soul-force is capable of leaving the body independently, especially during sleep, and sometimes two or three might be absent at the same time. If all four leave, a person dies. At death, the soul-forces unite and form the immortal soul, Seoto, which must then find the Milky Way, Seameo. Sometimes a soul-force cannot find the others, and so it wanders the earth bothering people, especially relatives.

Animals also have spirits, which must be released ritually when an animal is killed. These spirits are manifestations of even larger spirit-forces, or *maiyun*, which are themselves manifesta-tions of the anthropomorphic spirits. There are complex and mysterious relationships among these entities which are explored by Cheyenne religionists when they participate in ceremonies or undertake a vision quest. Sometimes the spirit of a human may inhabit an animal, and vice versa.[3]

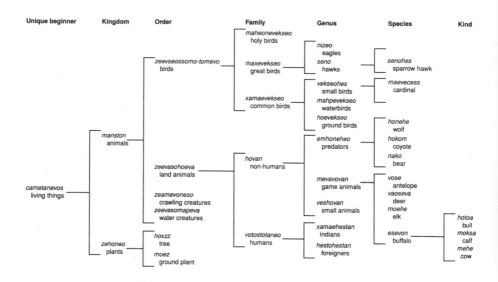

Figure 8.2   Taxonomy of flora and fauna in Cheyenne cosmology

Birds, Animals, and Plants

Living things are considered to be more or less sacred, and more or less important for helping people, depending on their location in the vertical cosmology. The taxonomy of Cheyenne flora and fauna is presented in figure 8.2, and the regions of the cosmos in figure 8.1. From the top, the birds which are capable of penetrating the Blue Sky-Space, the sacred birds, are called *maheonevekseo*. The *maxevekseo*, literally "great birds," are mostly the large predatory birds of the plains, and are said to inhabit the Nearer Sky-Space. The *xamaevekseo*, ordinary or "natural" birds, live in the Atmosphere, Taxtavoom, where they nest in trees or on the ground.

Some creatures considered by Euro-Americans to be "birds"

are not so considered by Cheyennes and, conversely, some Cheyenne birds are not so designated by Euro-Americans. For example, some of the most sacred Cheyenne birds are several kinds of dragonflies and butterflies. On the other hand, all but one species of owl are considered by Cheyennes to be spooks of the night, rather than birds. Only the short-eared owl, which is active in the daytime, is referred to as a bird by Cheyennes. It is also the only bird which lives in the earth, Votostoom, inhabiting the vacated burrows of badgers and prairie dogs.

Most four-footed animals or "land creatures," *zeevasohoeva*, are said to inhabit the surface, except for those who live in caves or burrows. The burrow-dwelling animals especially include badgers and prairie dogs, while the cave-dwellers especially include bears and buffaloes. All the rest – antelopes, elks, deer, wolves, foxes, etc. – have no necessary association with the earth. In aboriginal times, when it was difficult to find buffaloes, they were said to have returned to their caves. In 1981, when a stray buffalo suddenly appeared on a country road in western Oklahoma, it was said by Cheyennes to have come from a cave.

Plants are said to occupy three different cosmological layers. Domesticated plants such as corn, squash and beans, also wild berries, as well as any plant whose fruit or seeds are above the ground and are sought for food, are taken to be part of the surface world. Altogether these are referred to as *zehoneo*, roughly translated as "those which grow on the ground." Plants which primarily reside within the earth, whose roots are eaten, are called *eseohonoz*, while certain sacred plants whose roots reach deep within Nsthoaman are called *maheonezehoneo*. These latter especially include cottonwoods and the "big medicine" plant, whose long, red roots can be seen growing down the steep embankments of plains rivers, where the bank has been washed out by floods.

Energy Theory

All the life-force in the universe originates in Maheo, and is transmitted down the hierarchy of spirits, birds, animals, humans, and plants by means of *exhastoz*, which I translate as "cosmic energy." The present keeper of the sacred arrows, William Red Hat, Jr., refers to *exhastoz* as "Cheyenne electricity," explaining further that it only travels in one direction, downward, from the more sacred entities to the less sacred. Like electricity, he says, Exhastoz can be dangerous, and must be used only by people who know how to channel the energy properly. Most ordinary Cheyennes use the word "blessings" in English to indicate the flow of energy from spiritual forces to humans. Although the use of the word is very similar between Cheyenne tradition and Christianity, the underlying idea is very different. For Cheyennes, "blessings" are not general and ambiguous: they flow from the Creator under rigid laws which human beings must understand and try to observe.

From Maheo, cosmic energy is transmitted to the anthropomorphic spirits, who use the energy to fuel the sun and moon, and to cause seasonal changes. Energy is also transmitted to Nemevota for rain, to Nonoma for thunderstorms. Either directly or through the intercession of anthropomorphic spirits, energy is transmitted to sacred birds and animals, who might then transmit energy to humans. Energy is transmitted directly to the earth by Atovsz, in the form of sunlight which causes plants to grow.

Human beings can plug into the system of cosmic energy at any level and, although there is more energy to be gained by plugging in at higher levels, it is more difficult, and more dangerous. To receive energy directly from the source, one can pray directly to Maheo, or fast on a mountaintop or hilltop, closer to the zenith. Especially, one can fast and pray on the top of the Cheyenne sacred mountain in south-western South Dakota, called Nowahwus in Cheyenne, but known to non-Cheyennes as Bear Butte. The purpose of so-called "vision quests" is to create a relationship with spiritual powers who might provide energy or "blessings" to the human who requests assistance.

Another method of receiving energy is to become a pledger or dancer at one of the major ceremonies, and receive energy by participation. This energy can come either directly or through the person of a man serving as instructor for the pledger or dancer. Special kinds of energy, especially for healing illnesses, can come from doctors who have individual relationships with cosmic entities, especially spirits, animals, and plants. This kind of energy, however, is only for special purposes.

Once a person has received energy by vision quest, participation in ceremonies, or from some other person, they must decide how to use the energy. The amount is finite and if it is used for one purpose it cannot be used for another. For example, the energy can be used to obtain food, either by hunting, gardening, collecting, or, in modern times, working for wages. The food gained by this work sustains not only the person who has solicited blessings, but also the family. By this means, the family prospers by the work and prayer of the solicitor.

Intimate contact, such as sexual intercourse between spouses, or hugs, touches, and kisses in the family, also serve to distribute cosmic energy. Even being in the presence of an elder or priest, or shaking hands with one, is a way of collecting energy, "a blessing." And so if an elder or religious person chooses to distribute blessings in this way, it is regarded as a generous act.

Because cosmic energy is finite, it runs out and must be renewed every year. It is believed that all cosmic energy comes to a standstill at the end of winter, when the earth dies, and all sources of energy must therefore be renewed. Cheyenne people note the number of deaths which occur in late winter, and attribute it to the weakness of spiritual forces at this season. Consequently, they have always looked forward to the ceremonial season, when all kinds of energy, from all sources, can be renewed.

The following descriptions of Cheyenne ceremonies are necessarily incomplete, because the ceremonies are so long and complex. One reason they are so long is that nearly everything is done in fours. That is, each ceremonial action, such as handing sage to an assistant or opening a bag of herbs, is accomplished only on the fourth attempt, and songs are sung in groups of fours, or four groups of four each. Even if each action were done only once, there are still hundreds if not thousands of ritual acts required by each major ceremony. Consequently, the published descriptions of Cheyenne ceremonies comprise hundreds of pages, as well as hundreds of photographs. Rather than provide detailed and necessarily incomplete descriptions of the ceremonies, I will try to capture here the spirit of the ceremonies, and their significance for the people. In general, Cheyennes say that the Arrow Ceremony is to purify the people, the Sun Dance is to

renew the people and the earth, and the Massaum and Peyote
Ceremonies are for healing and doctoring.

The Arrow Ceremony

The mechanics of the Arrow Ceremony have been well described
by Father Powell, who witnessed and photographed the entire
proceedings in 1960.[4] The ceremony is built around the four
sacred arrows, *mahuts*, which were given to the Prophet Sweet
Medicine in the great cave inside Bear Butte long ago. The
arrows are kept in a special medicine bundle, hanging inside
their own tipi, under the care of an arrow keeper, who holds the
highest religious office in the Cheyenne Nation. The arrows
represent the nation, and the fundamental purpose of the
ceremony is to purify the arrows, and thence the nation, so that
they are worthy of receiving the blessings of Maheo during the
Sun Dance.

For the Arrow Ceremony, or Arrow Renewal or Arrow
Worship or Arrow Doings, as it is sometimes called, the families
of the participants come to a pre-arranged location at a set time,
usually in June or July during a new moon, and pitch their tents
and tipis in a great circle with an opening in the direction of Bear
Butte. Originally, and in the description of the 1903 ceremony
provided by Dorsey, all Cheyennes were supposed to be present
before the Arrow Ceremony could begin. In modern times, it is
usually only the families directly involved in the ceremony who
camp while the rituals are being conducted. The rest of the
traditional community usually arrives and camps after the Arrow
Ceremony is completed, which is when preparations for the Sun
Dance can begin. For the Arrow Ceremony, the sacred arrows
are carried from the arrow tipi to a special large double tipi
where the rituals will take place.

I should explain my own participation, or lack of it, in the
ceremonies. Although I have attended the Southern Cheyenne
ceremonies and slept at the campground most years between
1970 and 1987, it was largely for social purposes, to see my
friends and further my research in demography and kinship
studies. In my interactions with Cheyenne people, I have not felt

that it was proper for me to participate too intimately in Cheyenne rituals and ceremonies. Nevertheless, on three occasions I have entered the arrow tipi, although not during the ceremonies. Once I was asked to come with my son, Jeremy, by a man who wanted to bless his own grandson but did not have the resources to make a proper gift to the arrow keeper. So I provided the gift and smoked the pipe with the arrow keeper, Ed Red Hat, my son, my friend, and his grandson. On two other occasions I was invited into the arrow tipi to smoke on promises made in connection with research I was conducting. I have declined several other invitations when the issues did not concern me directly, explaining that I did not want to intrude on Cheyenne business, and I have also declined invitations to view the sacred arrows when they were exposed as part of the ceremonies. Fundamentally, I have done this because I am ashamed of the treatment of Cheyennes by my own ancestors and their countrymen, and I feel that the participation of any white person in Cheyenne ceremonies essentially pollutes the proceedings. Because I have been present at the ceremonial site, however, I have learned a lot about the organization and logistics of the ceremonies, which are very complex. Since I frequently have stayed in the tents and tipis of priests at the ceremonial grounds, I have heard much discussion and debate about the conduct of the ceremonies.

For the Arrow Ceremony, enormous practical and psychological burdens are borne by the pledger, who is often a chief, priest, or apprentice priest, and the instructor, usually an older and more experienced priest who will lead the pledger through the ceremonies. As with the Sun Dance pledger, to be described later, the pledger of the Arrow Ceremony must make sure that the tipi and the arrow priests are available and that all supplies necessary to the ceremony are gathered together at the appointed place, and must feed everyone who helps and present them with gifts. To do this, he needs the support of the women of his extended family. In addition, the pledger must participate in some very serious and demanding rituals, and learn how to conduct them. The role of pledger therefore requires a man of great organizational and intellectual abilities.

The sacred arrows were empowered originally when they were received by Sweet Medicine, the prophet. As stated in the stories, two of the arrows are for causing buffaloes to become confused and vulnerable, and two for causing the same effects on enemies of the Cheyennes. The first two are called "buffalo arrows" and the last two, "man arrows." All four arrows were seized by the Pawnees from the Cheyennes in a battle in 1830, but the two buffalo arrows were returned a few years later. At that time, Cheyenne priests made replacement arrows for the man arrows, and these are now in the bundle, along with the original buffalo arrows. The two original man arrows remain with the Pawnees.

A description of the sacred arrows, from Dorsey (1905), follows:

These sacred arrows are somewhat different from ordinary Cheyenne arrows. They are about thirty-six inches long, one-half an inch in diameter, round, very straight, with flintstone points. The points are tied in at the end, and over each of the four arrow points is tied a covering of white, downy eagle feathers. At the other end are whole wing feathers of the eagle, split in two, and tied on each side of the arrows. The shafts are also partly covered with the white, downy feathers of an eagle. All the feathers are painted red. On each of the four arrows are painted figures of the world, the blue paint meaning blue heavens, the sun, moon, stars, the red paint meaning the earth. Buffalo and other animals are also painted. So these sacred arrows are held symbolic of the Great Medicine, who made the sun, moon, and the stars, and the earth. When the great Prophet, the real Prophet, who brought these four sacred arrows, returned to his people, he did what the Great Medicine taught him while inside of the earth, and to this day the whole medicine-arrow ceremony is performed exactly as the Prophet taught them in the beginning.

I am sad to report that replicas of the sacred arrows, based on the descriptions of Dorsey and Father Powell, are now available commercially in shops selling Indian curios, to the dismay of Cheyenne religionists. But Cheyennes comfort themselves that these replicas, although embarrassing, have no religious power since they have been manufactured by people with no religious knowledge. It is only the real arrows and the real ceremony which can bring benefits to the Cheyenne people.

The Arrow Ceremony is ideally conducted over four days, and it has the following component rituals, not necessarily performed in this order:

1   The Arrows are examined for any blotches or damage caused by murders or other crimes committed among the Cheyennes. The arrows are cleaned and repaired if necessary.

2   Food is distributed from the arrow lodge to bless all the people assembled.
3   Prayers are sung to the four directions and other spirits, and to the bird and animal spirits.
4   Prayers are said to bless the soldier societies.
5   Sweet grass incense is burned and pipes are smoked to carry prayers and supplications, in the form of smoke, from priests to Maheo.
6   The sacred arrows are tied to a stake and exposed for Cheyenne men to view.
7   The journey of Sweet Medicine to the Sacred Mountain is recounted by reference to sacred objects contained within the arrow bundle, including a lock of hair from Sweet Medicine's head. A buffalo skull represents how Sweet Medicine magically brought meat to the Cheyenne camp when he first returned.
8   The prophecies of Sweet Medicine are recited.
9   Collateral to the ceremonies inside the arrow tipi, all Cheyennes perform the rituals which renew their personal and family sacred objects.
10 Small ceremonial sticks are manipulated inside the ceremonial tipi, and sweet grass burned, to represent the purification of all Cheyenne families.
11 Unity with the Sutai band is expressed by reference to the buffalo skull and to the "Sutai earth" sculpted on the ground inside the ceremonial tipi.

Although I have not witnessed events inside the ceremonial tipi, I have heard a great deal of discussion in the family camps about how the ceremony has been conducted in different years. It should be noted that the Arrow Ceremony is never the same, year to year, for various reasons. Sometimes a ritual object or a person with special knowledge is not present at the ceremonial camp. Sometimes the order of the rituals is rearranged to accommodate a priest who cannot be present for the entire ceremony. The most usual modification, however, is to omit some of the rituals so as to shorten the ceremony so that it can be performed in a weekend, from Friday to Sunday, rather than being spread across four days, which is the ideal length of time for the ceremony.

The cosmological framework of the Cheyenne universe is recognized and respected during the Arrow Ceremony in several ways. First, there is constant reference to Maheo at the zenith, to whom prayers of incense and tobacco smoke are addressed.

Second, when birds and animals are mentioned, they are addressed as groups, resident in the sky-spaces, rather than as species or individual creatures. And third, the spirits of the four directions are invoked whenever water is drunk, by tracing a cross in the bucket of water with an eagle feather, and naming the four spirits and Maheo in the center.

Energy theory is also respected by the physical arrangement of the camp and the ritual paraphernalia. The circle of tents and tipis is open to accommodate the transfer of energy from the sacred mountain to the arrows, which are laid on a framework in the tipi pointing toward Bear Butte. Contrary to some descriptions, the transfer of energy is not from the arrows to the mountain, but from the mountain to the arrows. People are not allowed to walk across the opening in the camp circle when the arrows are pointing in that direction. Also, the arrows are never pointed toward people, but either upwards, downwards, or toward the opening in the circle.

By participating in the ceremony, the pledger and priests increase their control of energy, which they receive directly from Maheo through prayers and smoking. They transfer much of this energy to the assembled families by burning incense in their behalf and sharing sacred food with them. In addition, some ceremonial items used in the ceremony are distributed to supporters of the pledger, to bless them and their families. The health and well-being of individuals, families, and the whole tribe are therefore renewed by the Arrow Ceremony, and they are made ready for their participation in the Sun Dance.

For Northern Cheyennes, their sacred hat or *issiwun* is somewhat equivalent to the sacred arrows as a symbol of their existence. The hat has its origin among the Sutai people, although the Northern Cheyennes also comprise the Omisis Band and fragments of other bands which are not Sutai. To be keeper of the hat, one must be of Sutai ancestry. There is a renewal ceremony for the hat, but it is much simpler than the Arrow Ceremony, and is not performed annually. (Plate 8.1 shows the sacred tipi with its cover removed revealing items used in the Arrow Ceremony.)

Plate 8.1   Some Arrow Ceremony paraphernalia left inside after the cover has been removed from the sacred tipi (Stovall Museum Collection, Western History Collections, University of Oklahoma)

The Sun Dance

Unlike the Arrow Ceremony, which is unique to the Cheyennes, the Sun Dance in some form is shared among nearly all Indian nations of the Great Plains. Nearly all tribes celebrating the Sun Dance exhibit three standard practices: (1) they require the attendance of the whole tribe, (2) they have a central arbor for the performance of the ceremony, and (3) they incorporate the dancing of painted, fasting supplicants. Beyond that, however, there are many profound differences among the tribes. If there is an underlying agenda for all groups, I believe it is the celebration of tribal unity and cultural continuity. This is just as important now, in facing the threat of acculturation by the dominant society, as it was in the early 19th century, when the various tribes were mobilizing their forces and facing off against one another to make war.

There are at least three versions of the Cheyenne Sun Dance, one northern version performed in Montana and two southern versions performed in Oklahoma. These versions are maintained by different communities of priests, are slightly different from one and another, and represent, I believe, modifications to the ceremony inaugurated when the northerners split off from the southerners, and when the so-called Dog Soldiers split off from the other Southern Cheyennes and held their own Sun Dances. Father Powell (1969) has described the Northern Cheyenne version, as he observed it between 1956 and 1964, while one of the Southern Cheyenne versions was described by George Dorsey (1905). Dorsey commented on some variations in the ceremony which were called to his attention.

The Cheyennes do not call their ceremony a Sun Dance, except when speaking to white people. Among themselves it is referred to as the Oxheheom in Cheyenne, and the New Life Lodge, or more precisely Life Generator Lodge, in English. As with the Arrow Ceremony, there is a main pledger who, with the help of his extended family and his military society, is responsible for gathering all the paraphernalia, feeding the priests and other participants, and presenting gifts to the priests and their helpers. Although the pledger of the Arrow Ceremony is usually a priest or chief, the pledger of the Sun Dance can be anyone. The Sun Dance pledger is ordinarily someone who has had illness or other misfortune in his family during the past year. In times of distress, a person will vow to serve as pledger for the ceremony, to secure the blessings of Maheo for the life and health not only of his family, but of everyone. A woman can pledge the ceremony, but she must find a male surrogate to actually perform the pledger's rituals.

The following written instructions, from Eugene Black Bear, Sr., are distributed by him to the pledgers he instructs for the Sun Dance:

1   The day you make vow you are a holy person, you have restrictions, you can't do too much of anything. You can select your instructor anytime and he can start helping you right away by giving you all the list of things you will need, or ask a Sundance Priest but it would be nice to give him a gift for the information.
2   You can not sleep with your spouse until you are through with your vow.
3   You can not go to dances or Pow-wows unless you are invited. At

that time you have to wear a white sheet [sash] and carry your
pipe.

4   You're not to get your own water and food.
5   You are supposed to be calm at all times. You are never supposed
    to get mad or mean.
6   You can help sick people by putting your hand on their head and
    praying for them, if they come and ask you. This is the only
    ceremonial you can perform. You can not perform any kind of
    ceremonial during your vow. After vow is complete you can resume
    your self.

Under the supervision of his instructor, then, the pledger
undertakes to collect all the paraphernalia he will need for the
ceremony. There are essentially two parts to the Sun Dance. The
first part is conducted by the priests, the pledger, and his wife,
the "sacred woman," mostly inside the lone tipi erected on the
ceremonial grounds. Working together, they recapitulate the
creation of the universe by constructing mounds of earth on the
floor of the tipi. They also engage in various pipe rituals to
ensure the success of the ceremonies, and they prepare, or help
to prepare, the various items which will be incorporated into the
Sun Dance altar. Many of their activities anticipate in miniature
the major activities which will take place later in and around the
Sun Dance arbor. The creation of mounds of earth in the lone
tipi, like the building of the Sun Dance arbor, recapitulates the
creation of the earth. The small, simple altar in the lone tipi
anticipates the large altar which will be built in the Sun Dance
arbor, containing most of the important religious and cosmological symbols of the Cheyenne people.

In addition to the main pledger, there are men who have
vowed to fast and dance during the second part of the ceremony,
after the arbor is built. While there is usually only one main
pledger, any number of men can pledge to dance, as long as
there is room in the arbor to accommodate them. Each dancer
must have an instructor, someone who has danced at least four
times and is therefore qualified to instruct. In most years there
are 15–30 dancers, but a smaller number of instructors, since
some instructors accommodate more than one dancer.

Like the Arrow Ceremony, the Sun Dance is an attempt to
secure health and well-being by tapping into the energy network
created by Maheo. In Oklahoma, the Sun Dance is usually
performed on the same site as the just-completed Arrow

Ceremony, and the tents and tipis are thus already in a proper alignment, although sometimes the opening of the circle is changed so that it is toward the rising sun, depending on who the instructor is. In the center of the camp circle, the special ceremonial arbor is constructed, usually referred to as the Sun Dance arbor, or new life arbor. Inside the arbor is the elaborate altar centered about a decorated buffalo skull.

Nearly every important social and moral theme in Cheyenne society is presented symbolically during the Sun Dance. The center pole is a phallic symbol, and during the ceremony sod is cut away in rectangles to expose the deep earth and the embodied female principle, Heëstoz. The 12 other vertical poles around the Sun Dance arbor, clockwise from the door, represent a person's progression through life from child to elder, and the progression of the seasons, which for the prophet Sweet Medicine were the same thing. The fork of the center pole is the thunderbird's nest, or "all birds' nest," and the important plants and animals of Cheyenne tradition are symbolized in the objects incorporated into the altar, into the songs and prayers, and into the special paints worn by the dancers.

The tree which will serve as the center pole of the arbor, a live cottonwood, is selected by a chief or other highly-respected male elder. A coup is counted on the tree and it is felled and taken to the ceremonial site. There it is trimmed so that it has a fork in the top, and a "thunderbird's nest," made of dogwood branches, is placed in the crotch, along with prayer cloths and other small offerings from various families.

While the center pole is being prepared, the four soldier societies seek four upright posts to help support the circumference of the arbor. These poles will represent not only the societies, but also the four cardinal directions. As with the center pole, each society chief finds an appropriate cottonwood and counts coup on it. Then the tree is felled and trimmed to support a framework of horizontal crosspieces, as shown in plate 8.2. In addition to these four uprights, eight more are cut to complete the circumferential structure. As a special honor, other chiefs, headsmen, and elders are selected by the pledger and instructor to find the other eight trees and cut them. When the peripheral poles are all set in holes in the ground, and when crosspieces have been laid in them, the center pole is raised with accompanying rituals. When all the poles are set in the ground, the arbor

Plate 8.2   Framework of the Sun Dance or, more properly, New Life Lodge, in the early 20th century (Hugh Scott Collection, Smithsonian Institution National Anthropological Archives)

structure is shaped approximately as pictured in figure 8.3. The figure also shows where the pledger and instructor will sit during the ceremonies, where the fire will be, where the dancers will stand, and where the singers will sit around the drum.

Ritual smoking is very much a part of the ceremony. Not only are there many smokes among the pledger and priests, but after the Sun Dance arbor is complete, and just before the center pole is raised, all the families approach the priests with their family pipes and ask that prayers be offered for them. Food and other gifts are also exchanged. After the center pole is raised and just before the dancing begins, other gifts of food are exchanged between the dancers' families and their instructors' families, and each dancer smokes with his "grandfather," or instructor.

The dancing itself is not very complicated and, in the beginning, does not seem to be very demanding. At the appointed times, the painted and costumed dancers merely line up and bend their legs in time to the drumming, blowing rhythmically on their eagle-bone whistles (plates 8.3 and 8.4). While they do not expend much energy dancing, we should bear in mind that they

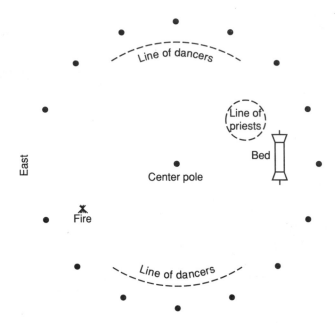

Figure 8.3   Interior of Sun Dance lodge

are dancing while abstaining from food and water, and by the end of the ceremony, after several days, the dancers can barely manage to stand up from their seats on the ground and assume a dancing position. Nearly every year, some dancers faint from fatigue or the heat, and must be removed from the arbor. While dancing, each dancer is assisted by his instructor and a "runner," usually a younger man or boy who runs errands for him. To participate, each dancer must have a supply of paint, an eagle-bone whistle, a small forked stick to hang his whistle on, a blanket or cushion to sit on, and special objects which are tied to his limbs when he assumes the various paints. These objects, such as deer tails, sage, and eagle feathers, represent the four *matasooma* of the body as well as the four directions.

During the ceremony, which like the Arrow Ceremony is ideally supposed to last four days but is in fact usually shortened to one weekend, the dancers assume four colorful body paints which are called "green hail," "white hail," "green whirlwinds," and "white whirlwinds." There are some preliminary paints which are variable among the different versions of the ceremony,

Plate 8.3   Dancers with hail paint, about 1925 (Grinnell Collection, Museum of the American Indian)

and a few dancers have paints which they assume instead of the hail and whirlwind paints, but these four paints are the symbolic heart of the ceremony. Each paint is worn while dancing to a repetition of sacred Sun Dance songs, then it is washed off outside the arbor and a new paint is applied.

To understand this hail and whirlwind symbolism properly, a person should actually see one of the giant thunderstorms which march across the great plains during two seasons of the year, in spring and fall. On the open plains, one can see the full structure of the storm, with a high billowing thunderhead leading the storm, often in the shape of a bird, animal, or mysterious creature. This is followed by the dark body of the storm, continuously lit up with lightning and reverberating with thunder. The body of the storm deposits enormous quantities of rain over the prairie, and is often trailed by tornadoes dragging along the ground behind the storm and accompanied by the deposition of large, wet, green hailstones. For Cheyennes, the tornadoes trailing behind a storm are symbolic of the human penis, and the

Plate 8.4   Men watching sun dancers, 1927 (Smithsonian Institution National Anthropological Archives)

hailstones are symbolic of semen. Altogether, a spring thunderstorm is seen as an enormous fertility structure parading across the plains, bringing them to life with the vitality of its tornadoes and hailstones.

Green hail, then, both symbolizes seasonal change by its color and actually provides the seeds for the renewal of the earth in the spring. The energy of the storm, its lightning and thunder, are manifestations of the struggle between the winter forces, Notamota and Hoimaha, with the summer forces, Sovota and Atovsz. White hail, which is the sleet associated with thunderstorms in the fall, represents the same struggle but with the warm forces of the south losing out to the forces of winter. Summer storms move from south to north, but fall and winter storms move from north to south. White hail freezes and kills the earth just as green hail animates it and brings it to life.

In Cheyenne, the word *vovetas*, usually translated as "whirlwind," means both tornadoes and what white people call "dragonflies." The association between the two symbols is provided by two characteristics of one kind of dragonfly, the green darner. First of all, the green darner turns white over the summer, exuding a white waxy substance from its shell, and it also hunts communally, forming tornado-shaped columns around streams where small insects can be found. And so the Cheyennes have two hail paints and two whirlwind paints, both symbolizing the seasonal change in different ways. Some painters use dragonfly symbols for whirlwinds; others draw small spiral tornadoes.

In addition to the sexual symbolism of thunderstorms, other efforts are made during the Sun Dance to show the connection between the annual renewal of the earth's fertility and the fertility of people. At one point in the ceremony, rawhide cutouts of humans with exaggerated genitals are attached to the centerpole. Certain items in the altar, such as red willows and tightly-bound sage bundles, are also explained as phallic symbols. And most years, sexual intercourse between the instructor and the sacred woman is part of the ceremony. Children conceived at that time are considered to be especially blessed and, throughout their lives, people want to touch them and shake their hands.

The Cheyennes are sexy people, but sexiness is not the same as immorality or sexual promiscuity. In fact, early visitors to the Cheyennes commented on their high moral character, the chastity of their unmarried women, and the singular devotion of older spouses to one another. But as intellectuals and religious seekers, the Cheyennes have always been interested in publicly and symbolically explaining their own sexuality by reference to sexual symbols from nature – birds, animals, trees – and to the dualistic male–female structure of their cosmology. Without embarrassment, they have over the years explicitly acted out their notions of sexuality at ceremonies even under the scrutiny of missionaries and other Americans with quite different notions of sexuality and sexual propriety. Ironically, the Cheyennes have persisted with their notions of sexual symbolism into an age when such notions have become quite acceptable to the mainstream of the dominant society.

The altar inside the Sun Dance arbor, in addition to containing some sexual symbols, also contains representations of the natural phenomena which are important to Cheyennes for other reasons. The central and most visible feature of the altar is a painted buffalo skull, with plugs inserted in its eyes and nose, dug into the earth and surrounded by five pieces of sod. Sun and moon symbols are painted on the skull, and red paint represents the earth. The stars are represented by white sand. Boughs of trees important to Cheyennes – fruit trees, dogwood, and cottonwood – are arranged all around the altar, and a rainbow of four arching painted sticks is placed in front, symbolizing the calm after a storm. The altar also contains eagle feathers, representing all birds, while grass is present in the eye and nose plugs of the skull, and in braids and bundles around the altar. Herbs for healing are represented by sage and sweetgrass.

When all the songs have been sung the required number of times, and all the dances done, the ceremony is over. At this point the altar is dismantled, and the arbor taken apart. The pledger and his family, and the dancers and their families, give away the paraphernalia they have used, to bless the recipients with health and long life. Along with the sacred food and the prayers offered through numerous pipes, the blessings of Maheo are secured for another year. The earth is made new again.

Massaum Ceremony

Although the Massaum Ceremony has not been performed since 1927, it has been masterfully reconstructed by anthropologist Karl Schlesier, using available photographic and written descriptions, and information supplied by Cheyenne elders who actually witnessed and participated in the ceremony (Schlesier 1987). Essentially, the ceremony recapitulated a story about how the Cheyennes had originally gained control of the animals of the plains, to use them for food and other purposes. The ceremony required the main participants to assume the roles of certain humans, mysterious persons, animals, and animal-spirits, and illustrated the relationships they created long ago according to the story of Ehyophstah, the Yellow-Haired Girl (plate 8.5).

The story begins with two men on a quest to find food for the people, who are starving. One of the men is a shaman, the other is younger. Attacked by an underwater monster, they are saved by two mysterious people, a Wolf Man and an Old Woman, who take pity on them and give them their beautiful yellow-

Plate 8.5 Buffalo women dressed for Massaum Ceremony, 1925 (Smithsonian Institution National Anthropological Archives)

haired daughter, Ehyophstah, to bring animals to the people for their benefit. The younger man marries Ehyophstah. They return to the tribe followed by all kinds of plains animals who have come from their caves in the mountains, attracted by the power of the yellow-haired woman.

The Massaum Ceremony essentially acted out this story. The

five main characters were Ehyophstah, her parents, and the two men who found her. Other characters were the two wolves who were masters of the plains, a red wolf and his wife, a white wolf, and seven characters known as the "young wolves." Unlike the other two major ceremonies recounted above, the Massaum required the main pledger to be a Cheyenne woman, who took the part of Ehyophstah. Women also participated as the seven young wolves and among the mass of animals called forth by Ehyophstah.

The Massaum Ceremony was held just after the Sun Dance each year, and utilized the same camp circle as the Arrow Ceremony and Sun Dance. For the first part of the ceremony, a double-sized tipi was erected in the center of the circle around a young cottonwood tree whose branches stuck out the top. Like the other two major ceremonies, the Massaum required lengthy preparations inside the tipi, including body painting, prayers and songs, and a decorated buffalo skull. It also included a re-enactment of the creation of the universe, very much like the one incorporated into the preliminary rituals of the Sun Dance.

The most spectacular event of the ceremony, however, was the emergence of the animals. On the fourth day, brush lodges were erected inside the great circle of lodges, and the representatives of all the kinds of animals gathered, each kind in its own lodge. All the people who represented animals wore masks, skins, and paint which transformed them into their patron animals. At dawn on the fifth day, in response to the calling of Ehyophstah, all the animals emerged from their lodges, which represented their caves, and followed her around the camp circle. At this time, anyone who was ill or wanted some blessing from the animals would follow them to their den and touch them, or be touched by them, or receive some medicine or amulet. Then Ehyophstah called again, and the animals set out around the camp, this time followed by ritual hunters, who simulated the killing of these animals. A ritual impoundment with wings, of the sort used prehistorically to hunt antelopes and buffaloes, was built inside the tribal circle and incorporated into the ceremony. After a ritual slaughter of real animals, bits of meat were distributed from the central tipi to all the Cheyenne families. To end the ceremony, all the animals set out through the opening in the camp circle across the plains. Finding water, they drank it, and returned to the camp as normal people.

Symbolically, the Massaum had a different emphasis from either the Arrow Ceremony or the Sun Dance. First of all, it exhibited the transformations of anthropomorphic spirits into *maiyun* and animals in a much more explicit and elaborate manner. Also, while the Sun Dance emphasizes birds with its "all birds' nest" on the center pole, the Massaum emphasizes animals. The Massaum, as described by Schlesier, is also much more concerned with stars and astronomy than the other ceremonies. During the course of the ceremony, explicit transformations were noted between the spirits of the sun, moon, and stars, and with *maiyun* and other mysterious spirits and personages of Cheyenne tradition. Schlesier traces similarities between the Cheyenne Massaum and the ceremonies of other Algonquian peoples in North America, and even shows similarities between these ceremonies and those of modern circumpolar peoples in general, including those in Siberia.

Fasting at Bear Butte

This ritual is developing into a standard form, although there are still many variants. The basic idea is to go to Nowahwus (Bear Butte) and pray and fast on the summit or slopes, seeking a vision. Twenty years ago, this was done informally by a vision seeker and his instructor, and how it was done depended on the instructor and his particular medicine. Now these individual quests are being replaced by a standard form in which a man pledges the ritual and, to fulfill it, recapitulates the journey of Sweet Medicine and his wife. Frequently, a group of Cheyenne men travel together from Oklahoma or Montana, along with their families, and spend several days camping at the state park which is on the site.

As with other Cheyenne ceremonies, the pledger requires an instructor who has himself completed the pilgrimage four times. After a day of fasting in camp, the pledger is taken up the mountain late in the afternoon to sit on a blanket or cushion, and is given another blanket to place around his shoulders. He has a pipe and tobacco, and is instructed how to smoke it. He also might have other medicines or amulets, depending on his own and his instructor's experience and training. Left by himself, the pledger usually has a fitful night, periodically smoking and drifting off to sleep.

In the morning, the instructor visits the pledger and asks if he has had a vision. If not, the pledger must stay another night and is left alone. If he has had a vision, the instructor interprets it for him, and if possible tells him who the sacred spirits were that visited him. If the vision was incomplete, the pledger will be asked to stay another night. As a result of a successful vision experience, a man usually creates a relationship with a spiritual entity, gathers some medicine or makes an amulet to represent that relationship, and includes his new medicine in a medicine bundle. Often, a pledger is inspired by a vision to take a new personal name, or he learns a song.

The nature of vision songs is widely misunderstood by non-Indians. As a highly educated Cheyenne traditionalist, a successful vision seeker once told me, "It's not like Walt Disney, with some little rabbit saying, 'Follow the bouncing ball and sing along with me.' It's more like a suggestion of a song in the pitch and rhythm of the wind or the howling of a coyote. The spirit only gives you the general idea; you have to work out the words and the meaning with your priest, based on his knowledge and experience. That's why you can't do it by yourself. You might get it wrong and do yourself some damage."

The Peyote Religion

The peyote religion, officially known as the Native American Church, is not part of the great tribal gatherings, but comprises ceremonies held in single tipis throughout the year.[5] Each tipi is under the control of a leader, called peyote chief or "road man," who decides where and when to meet, and conducts the ceremonies. A ceremony is "put up," as they say in English, by someone desiring help with a personal illness or other problem, either for him- or herself or for someone in the family. The person putting up the tipi makes sure that everything needed is assembled, presents a gift to the road man and other helpers, and feeds all participants after the all-night ceremony.

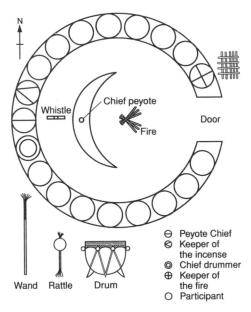

Figure 8.4   Interior of tipi used for peyote meeting (Goggin 1938: 28)

The ceremonies themselves are different in the different tipis, depending on who the road man is and where he learned his version of the ceremony. There is no particular Cheyenne version of the ceremony, but several versions among the ten or so road men who lead ceremonies in Montana and Oklahoma. Each leader usually has his own tipi and paraphernalia, to use if the person putting up the ceremony doesn't have everything necessary.

The Native American Church is a variety of Christianity, and incorporates Christian prayers with the eating of buds from the peyote cactus, which causes hallucinogenic visions. The ceremony begins about dark, when the participants file into the tipi to the left, resulting in the arrangement shown in figure 8.4. Men and women can both participate in the ceremony. A crescent moon built of earth has already been made on the ground by the road man, with a particularly large peyote button (or cactus bud), called the chief peyote, on top. A fire is built as shown, and maintained by the firekeeper, who periodically replenishes it from a woodpile just outside the tipi. The instruments used in the ceremony include a water drum, made of a steel kettle half filled with water, on which a chamois or soft deer-skin drum head is attached with thongs tied around small stones or marbles. Also required is a rattle, which is shaken in accompaniment to songs, a fan of eagle, macaw, anhinga, or other feathers to fan the fire, a wand which is passed around, and a drumstick.

Before the singing begins, the leader asks each participant to say why they are there, particularly what illness or problem they are worried about. Then the peyote is passed around and eaten, and tobacco is smoked, either a pipe or cigarette. After a pause, the leader sings four songs and his wand and rattle are passed all around the tipi, with each person singing in turn. The drum is also passed, and is played by the person to the right of each singer, so that each person first sings and then drums for the person to their left. This continues through the night, except that the participants begin to substitute their own rattles and fans after the first round.

At midnight, the wife of the person putting up the ceremony enters with a bucket of water, which is shared by the participants. At dawn she enters again with food and water. After eating, the cover is taken from the drum and all share in drinking the sacred water. At that point the ceremony is essentially over, and the participants begin to share their dream experiences and take naps until a great feast is served at noon. Then the tipi is taken down, but the moon and ashes are left in place to weather away.

Periodically, the peyote religionists have asked that a peyote button and other paraphernalia be included in the sacred arrow bundle or the chiefs' bundle, which contains the chief sticks and pipe. Sometimes they are accommodated and sometimes not, depending on whether the recent pledgers and instructors of the ceremonies have been peyote men.

The Sweat Lodge

This is another ritual which is not uniquely Cheyenne, and in fact they seem to use it less than other tribes, especially those in the north. Traditionally among the Cheyennes, the Sweat Lodge

Plate 8.6 Sweat Lodge with cover removed, 1935 (Campbell Collection, Western History Collections, University of Oklahoma)

is used collateral to other ceremonies to purify the individuals who either will participate or have participated in some ceremonial role. The modern tendency, however, is to use the ceremony as an event of itself, with people being invited as to a peyote meeting. The ritual is also becoming longer and more standard.

The basic idea of the Sweat Lodge is to sweat and purify one's body, while at the same time praying and purifying one's mind and spirit. A community of Sweat Lodge leaders is currently developing, parallel to the religious leaders of other rituals, and nowadays "putting up a sweat" requires gifts to the leader, who usually has the Sweat Lodge erected on his property.

The Sweat Lodge is a low, hemispherical hut built of bent branches about four or five feet high on the inside, as shown in plates 8.6 and 8.7, and covered with willows, cedar, or sometimes poplar branches. In front of the Sweat Lodge is a fireplace, where the stones used to generate steam will be heated. There is a low door to the lodge, to conserve the steam inside, and pieces of canvas or old blankets are kept nearby to place over the lodge to keep the steam inside.

The participants usually wear bathing suits or underwear, over

Plate 8.7   Joe David Osage, Larry Roman Nose and Freeman White Hawk, Jr., prepare a Sweat Lodge near Watonga, Oklahoma (photo by Darrell Rice of the Watonga Republican)

which they have thrown some loose clothing or a robe. When they are ready to enter, they take off their outer clothing and the leader lines them up so that he sits at the far side with an assistant near the door. The leader then asks each person their reason for being present, as during a peyote meeting. Then he says an introductory prayer, the hot stones are brought in, and the leader pours water from a bucket over the stones. People breathe in the steam and lean toward the stones. The participants usually stay in the sweat for about 30 minutes, or until the stones have cooled off, and then they go outside. If water is available, they wash themselves and then dry themselves with towels or in the air. The more traditional people dry off by rubbing themselves with bundles of sage. Then another prayer is said and they put on fresh clothing, purified and renewed in mind and body.

The Sweat Lodge is becoming very popular, especially among younger Cheyennes, and one advantage of the ritual is that it can be performed in a very small space, even in the yard of a city residence. Another advantage, for urban Indians, is that the ritual does not require much preparation or much time to complete. At present, however, there is a broad spectrum of Sweat Lodge rituals performed by Cheyennes, from the long, traditional version performed collateral to the major ceremonies, to the shorter version more typical of young, urban Cheyenne people. However the performance of the Sweat Lodge seems to be getting longer, more serious, and more religious.

Gourd Dance

Among Cheyennes, the Gourd Dance can be semi-religious, depending on who is doing it. Gourd Dance groups are usually organized at the community level, and each group has its own ideas about propriety and rules for membership. Some groups are nearly secular, with no requirements for membership other than residence in the community and an invitation from existing members. To join other groups, you must be a veteran of the armed services, must learn some special Gourd Dance songs, and are expected to have a serious and religious attitude toward dancing.

Gourd dancers perform at pow-wows, and are usually the first to dance. Their costume is simple, merely a sash, narrow blanket, rattle, and fan. The dancers use two particular styles, either bending at the knees or moving from one foot to another, depending on the music. Some gourd dancers regard their paraphernalia and the drum as sacred, and there are rituals connected with taking them out of a special box or small suitcase, and putting them away.

Cheyenne Doctors

Many traditional doctors received their power through the Massaum Ceremony in aboriginal times, and they were specialists. That is, bear doctors could only treat certain kinds of illnesses, and elk doctors certain other illnesses. The members of each animal lodge were in doctor–apprentice relationships with one another and perpetuated the lodge and its medicines in that manner.

Other Cheyenne doctors received their power from *maiyun* spirits. These doctors were also specialized, so that some of them provided war medicines, some treated gunshot wounds, while others could provide the power to fly or run swiftly. In most cases, the doctor received with his power the responsibility for taking four apprentices, usually former clients or patients, who could become doctors after four years.

In modern times, a few traditional doctors persist in their practice. Nowadays, however, a doctor might have several different kinds of medicine received from different sources. These medicine powers are usually accompanied by a medicine bundle which contains herbs and amulets of various kinds. In a curing ritual, the amulets are manipulated, the patient takes various herbs, and particular songs are sung by the doctor.

Life-Cycle Ceremonies

Until the middle of this century, significant life-cycle rituals were performed at birth, at naming, at puberty for girls, at menopause for women, and at death. Not all of these rituals have survived into modern times, and some have been gradually transformed.

Only the most traditional Cheyenne families still practice a birth ritual, which consists of the prayers of a chief, the wiping of vernix from the body of the baby, and painting a baby boy's penis red. Sometimes the naming ritual is part of this ceremony, where the genealogy of the baby is recited, with special attention to the previous bearers of the name.

Another ceremony fallen into disuse is the ear-piercing which accompanied a Cheyenne girl's first menstrual period. This also required the attention of a chief or male elder, and perhaps the counting of a coup, and the exchange of presents between mother's and father's families.

Traditionally, there was no marriage ceremony beyond the exchange of gifts and escorting of the bride and groom back and forth between their families' lodges as recounted in chapter 6.

After a period of submitting to Christian and civil marriage ceremonies led by ministers and public officials, Cheyennes are now developing marriage ceremonies which incorporate aspects of Cheyenne and European traditions. Especially, they have added to the traditional Cheyenne ceremony the idea of a chief, priest, or elder standing before the bride and groom to make a speech, and the exchange of rings. In addition, there is a giveaway of traditional items, the whole extended family stands by the bride and groom during the ceremony, and the ceremony is frequently conducted outside under a traditional arbor, or in a tipi with the sides rolled up. As with the pilgrimage to Bear Butte and the Sweat Lodge, it may be that a standard marriage ceremony is also developing. At present, there are certain elders in Montana and Oklahoma who are increasingly called upon to conduct marriage ceremonies.

The ritual by which a post-menopausal woman "takes the pipe," described in chapter 6, has not been performed in recent years. But of course death is universal, not optional, and so is the Cheyenne funeral. This ceremony has already evolved into a somewhat standard form incorporating both Christian and traditional elements.

When a person dies, they are returned home, dressed in their best clothing, and placed in an open casket in their living room for a wake. Among Cheyennes, wakes and funerals are very important, and usually hundreds of people come to sit with the family or to attend the burial. In the first day or two, a stream of visitors brings food for the family, and blankets and shawls for the giveaway which will follow. During this period, anyone may by custom come into the house and take what they like of the deceased person's belongings. In practice, few people do this, and usually it is friends reclaiming something they have loaned to the deceased, or something they had been promised.

For the more traditional families, at some point during the wake a Cheyenne priest or chief is asked to address the body of the deceased, warning them not to tarry and bother their family or friends on the way to the spirit world. On the day set for the funeral, some personal belongings of the deceased and some special gifts are placed in the casket. The face is painted in a traditional way for the journey, and the casket is closed. Then there is an enormous giveaway of all the gifts that the visitors have brought, and there is a feast. Before or after the feast, it has become traditional to sing Christian hymns in the Cheyenne language, the most popular being "Amazing Grace." Traditional Cheyennes say that since Christianity is largely a religion which is about death and immortality, it is appropriate to incorporate Christian traditions into funerals.

Following the feast, the family and friends travel to the grave site with the body, where ministers, chiefs, friends, and families are invited to share their feelings about the deceased person. Then the person is buried, following the European tradition of each person in attendance dropping a handful of dirt into the grave.

The Pipe Ceremony

Of all the Cheyenne religious rituals, the Pipe Ceremony is probably the most frequent, and the most important for understanding personal relationships among men. Traditionally, smoking is not a trivial matter, and traditional Cheyennes frequently point out that before the white man came, smoking was more infrequent and taken more seriously. Among traditional people, tobacco, along with the sumac, willow, and other herbs which are included in the mixture, is regarded as medicine, not recreation.

Smoking can be done alone, as prayer, especially in connection with personal medicine bundles. But more often, smoking constitutes a contract, a promise, a sacred vow. "Smoking on it" has the same importance among Cheyennes as signing a contract with witnesses among Anglo-Americans. It is a solemn promise that one person shall do one thing, and another person shall do another. For example, when a young man decides to dance at the Sun Dance, he carries a pipe to his selected instructor, who is obliged to smoke with him. By smoking, the young man promises to fast and dance, and the instructor promises to teach him how to do it properly.

All pipes have histories, and some have names. Generally speaking, the more important events require use of the more important pipes. The promise is no less binding when one uses a less distinguished pipe, but the punishment is more severe if one breaks a promise on a respected pipe, such as those from the chiefs' or sacred arrow bundles. Certain pipes represent extended families, and are inherited among the elders of that family.

Most ceremonial pipes are made of Catlinite, or sometimes slate or soapstone, and have a long, detachable stem. Pipes are kept in decorated pipe bags, along with a tamper and sometimes a bag of tobacco. Opening the bag is a serious matter, and is usually accompanied by ritual and accomplished only at the fourth repetition of the attempt. Each pipe has its own rules of use – the direction in which it must be pointed, usually with the bowl toward the ground, and the way it must be loaded, tamped, and lit.

When smoking on a promise, the participants usually sit on the ground facing one another, preferably in a tipi. Then the owner of the pipe, observing the rules of the pipe, lights it and smokes four puffs. Then he passes it to the left on the fourth try, and the next man smokes. Religious Cheyenne men usually have some customary, individual way of smoking or receiving the pipe. For example, a man might ask that the pipe be passed into his left hand, or at shoulder level, or with some other specification. When passing the pipe to the next man, he too respects the particular preferences of the next smoker, and so on clockwise among the participants, each taking four puffs. In a tipi, the pipe is not passed across the door, but is returned counter-clockwise all around the circle. The pipe is passed around until it is exhausted, whereupon it is passed back to the owner, who undertakes to clean it.

The smoke from the pipe constitutes the promise, sent upwards to Maheo. The ashes from the pipe are also sacred, and are carefully disposed of, usually buried in the earth in front of the pipe owner. It is said that the Custer catastrophe was occasioned by his promise in the arrow tipi after the Battle of the Washita never to attack the Cheyennes again, and the deposition on his boot of the ashes of that promise from the pipe kept with the sacred arrows. And so, in the Cheyenne way of thinking, the Battle of the Little Big Horn was not so much the result of circumstance or bad tactics, but the inevitable result of breaking a promise made on a sacred pipe.

Plate 8.8   Edward Red Hat, Sr., late keeper of the sacred arrows (photo courtesy of Lou White Eagle)

The Role of Arrow Keeper

In recent years, the role of the arrow keeper has been redefined, mostly through the activity of the current arrow keeper, William Red Hat, Jr. Traditionally, the keeper was not supposed to be necessarily a chief, priest, or prominent person, but only "a good man," someone who stayed close to home and respected the values of Cheyenne culture. But beginning with Edward Red Hat (plate 8.8), the current keeper's grandfather, the role began to change.

Edward Red Hat took responsibility for organizing an array of traditional cultural, religious and political activities that went beyond those of his predecessors. At his death in 1982, there was a period of dispute and confusion about who the new arrow keeper should be, resolved when a group of chiefs, priests, and headsmen essentially captured the arrows and brought them to the home of Wayne Red Hat, Edward's son. In this period, the new arrow keeper, in this case encouraged by his son, the present arrow keeper, continued the trend toward politicizing the office of arrow keeper, and began to enforce discipline upon those who wanted access to the arrow tipi and the ceremonies. People were banned from the ceremonial ground by the arrow keeper, who insisted that his approval was necessary for any kind of traditional activity. Some Cheyennes began to complain about a "theocracy."

With the death of Wayne Red Hat in 1993, William Red Hat, Jr., has established himself as one pole of Cheyenne religious, cultural, and political activity, and as the primary antagonist of the tribal government. Some families of traditionalists, however, have objected to this new definition of the arrow keeper's role. But in a traditional manner, they are content to, as they say, "let the arrows decide" who is right and wrong in this dispute, by bringing illness or death to those who have violated traditional rules of conduct. Among the Northern Cheyennes, there have been several attempts to politicize the role of hat keeper and make it more important, culturally, but these attempts have not been generally approved and the sacred hat remains strictly a religious symbol.

Concluding this chapter is figure 8.5, drawn by a Cheyenne priest for educational purposes. It includes most of the symbols important for understanding Cheyenne religion, many of which have been discussed in this chapter. The symbols are identified in the letter-keyed caption under the illustration.

Figure 8.5   The most important objects and symbols used in Cheyenne ceremonies

a, Sweet Medicine's tracks around the world; b, crescent moon; c, blue sky; d, morning star; e, sun and stars; f, red woodpecker's head; g, blue jay's head; h, straight pipe; i, Sweet Medicine's heart; j, whirlwind; k, Sweet Medicine's cave in Bear Butte with solid ground underneath and groups of sacred symbols; l, bow lance; m, crooked lance; n, cotton- wood; o, rattlesnake elk-horn scraper; p, direction of Cheyenne oath over buffalo chips; q, dogwood; r, Sun Dance center pole; s, Cheyenne medicine wheel; t, sacred tipi with pins in form of whirlwind; u, red stick for Cheyenne way; v, black stick for buffalo way; w, yellow stick for sun way; x, white stick for moon way; y, chief sticks all around tipi, four big chief sticks at top; z, badger; aa, Sutai oath; bb, buffalograss; cc, buffalo skull; dd, water; ee, buffalo tracks; ff, painted sticks used for rainbow on Sun Dance altar; gg, white sage bundle; hh, colored disk representing four directions; ii, sweetgrass; jj, Kit Fox rattle; kk, Dog Soldier rattle; ll, paint pots; mm, meat rack for war; nn, meat rack for peace; oo, sacred pipe; pp, moon and stars; qq, eagle symbol; rr, lightning symbol; ss, tribal symbol used on moccasins

9

Social Interactions

Anglo-Americans are accustomed to thinking dualistically in explaining their own behavior and the behavior of other people. We think in terms of right and wrong, good and bad, moral and immoral. Consequently it is difficult for us to understand the Cheyenne way of thinking about morality and social relationships, which is based on entirely different notions of how the world works and how human beings are motivated. In this chapter I will try to explain the traditional Cheyenne idiom and vocabulary for discussing social interactions, and how these notions are different from Anglo-American ideas. Perhaps the best place to start is to describe what a perfect world would be, from a Cheyenne perspective.

The cosmology explains, and the ceremonies reiterate, that the material world is inert and lifeless, and that all power, energy, and life come from the blessings emanating from Maheo. There is no other source. There are no devils or demons in Cheyenne tradition, seducing people and giving them evil powers, and Cheyenne cosmology has no place for witchcraft, by which evil people undertake to harm other people. Bad things happen, by Cheyenne standards, when the legitimate channels of Maheo's power are not respected, and the power and energy created by Maheo get out of control.

Legitimate power flows from Maheo to human beings through several kinds of correct channels. First, there is a descending hierarchy of spirits, *maiyun*, birds, and animals, as explained before, with superior spirits and personages giving power to inferior spirits and creatures. The power relationships among the spirits and *maiyun* are very complex and mysterious, but the observable birds and animals are said to receive their power in the same manner as human beings, through dancing, singing, eating certain herbs, and painting themselves. The sun, moon, and star symbols exhibited by various birds, for example, are emblems of their special relationships with those spirits. (In the Cheyenne language, the colors and markings of birds and animals are referred to as their "paints.") The mating dances and displays of plains birds and animals provide another method for them to obtain Maheo's blessings, and the singing of birds, the screaming of eagles, and the howling of wolves, coyotes, and other animals also constitute bird and animal songs which are being used to obtain power. For this reason, Cheyennes imitate the songs, dances, and face and body paints of birds and animals as one means of obtaining power from Maheo, either directly or through the intercession of the creatures they imitate. To be legitimate, the power obtained from birds and animals must be obtained with their permission, through an actual encounter, a dream, or a vision experience.

Tobacco provides a special means for people to obtain blessings from above through various legitimate channels. On vision quests, Cheyenne men offer a pipe to the spirits they encounter and solicit. Pipes and prayers are also offered directly to Maheo or his subordinate spirits by men participating in Pipe Ceremonies of various kinds. Pipes are also offered to birds and animals encountered casually on the plains. By all such means, power from above is brought within the domain and control of human beings.

Blessings received through ceremonies are under the control of priests, and here too the power is both received and passed along by means of pipes and tobacco. The priests offer prayers to Maheo through tobacco smoke, and receive their power either directly from Maheo or by way of the sacred mountain, the sacred arrows, or perhaps the center pole of the Sun Dance. They pass along their power to subordinate priests, pledgers, and dancers by smoking with them. At one special point in the Sun Dance, the priests communicate the blessings of Maheo to all the families by smoking family pipes in their behalf. Power is passed along to women and children by physical contact within the family, and the sharing of food and other gifts.

This is the ideal picture of the transfer of power, energy, and blessings from supernatural sources to the Cheyennes, and from one Cheyenne to another. If all goes well in this transfer of power down the hierarchical chain, then all the families are healthy, sheltered, happy, and well fed. But many things can go wrong, because this transfer is subject to human foibles which can cause energy to be lost or misdirected, causing sickness and death. The network of human relationships for transferring power is very fragile, and depends on every person behaving in a selfless and ritually perfect manner. If they did, then no one would be sick or unhappy. But as it happens, people frequently behave selfishly or misunderstand their roles and duties, and hence human existence is full of problems, danger, illness, and death.

Crossing Pipes and Ritual Malfeasance

Ideally, each transfer of power among men is symbolized by a pipe and a promise. Each pledge or promise must be clear and must not contradict any other promise. For example, when a man decides to pledge the Arrow Ceremony, he must carry a pipe to the home of his selected instructor and ask his help, smoking with him on the promise to put up the ceremony. Then they must both go to the arrow keeper and state their intentions, smoking with him in the arrow tipi, and setting the date for the ceremony. But suppose that a second potential pledger has in the meantime gone to his instructor, pledged the ceremony, set a different date, and the two men have smoked on it. Then the two pipes on which contradictory promises have been made are said to be "crossed."

Pipes can also be crossed because of the ambiguity of some promises. For example, a man might approach a Sun Dance priest and promise to put up the ceremony, meaning he will do so within the customary time limit of four years. The priest might infer, unless the promise is made explicit, that the pledger is promising to put up the ceremony in the coming year, so they are smoking on different personal interpretations of the same ambiguous verbal promise. Since the pledge or promise accompanying the Pipe Ceremony is usually not written down, there is tremendous opportunity for misunderstanding. Consequently, Cheyenne chiefs and priests go to great lengths to discuss exactly what is being promised before a pipe is smoked. If pipes become crossed, a great deal of ritual and discussion is required to straighten them out. All the participants must be present for a discussion, and everything must be smoked again, perhaps in several ceremonies to create an unambiguous system of promises, and hence an unambiguous transfer of blessings among the various participants. The previous promises can be erased in a short ceremony known as "brushing off," in which a priest uses sage wands or willow branches to brush over the bodies of the people whose pipes are crossed, saying appropriate prayers which will allow new promises to be made. In the meantime, a person can place four flickertail feathers on his outside door to deflect uncontrolled energy until matters are resolved.

Sometimes there is an insurmountable disagreement about whose pipes are crossed and who promised what in a Pipe Ceremony. In that case, a person might go ahead with the pledge or promise, taking the risk that his pipe might indeed be crossed. For example, if the pledger of a ceremony ignores the claim of another pledger and goes ahead with the ceremony, Cheyennes believe that, if his pipe is crossed, the ceremony will do him no good, and in fact, if energy is unleashed by the rituals, the power will not be under control and might kill the pledger or some member of his family, or make them ill.

Just as uncontrolled energy is unleashed by pledgers with crossed pipes, it is also unleashed by pledgers and instructors who make mistakes in the conduct of the ceremonies. Pledgers and priests who are insincere, who have bad motives or lack dedication, are said to be easily distracted from the proper conduct of ceremonies so that they make mistakes. For example, a priest might pass a pipe to the man on his left on the third try instead of the fourth, thereby putting both men in danger. Or a participant might accidentally mishandle or drop some ritual item. This, too, requires brushing off and perhaps restarting that part of the ceremony. Or a person might have a coughing fit, a headache, or cramps in his legs during a ritual. This, too, by Cheyenne standards, indicates that something is wrong.

Ritual malfeasance is often a matter of opinion. For example, I once fell off my thick cushion while seated in a tipi for a Pipe Ceremony. Everyone present laughed it off, and remarks were made about how white people didn't know how to sit on the ground. But later, when someone was angry with me for another reason, the incident was mentioned as a ritual mistake, for which I was accountable and consequently in danger. On another occasion, I noticed a man who kept rubbing his legs during a Pipe Ceremony. I thought it was his special demeanor in passing the pipe, but someone else said his legs were itching because he was not a full-blood Cheyenne and shouldn't have been in the tipi.

During rituals and ceremonies, priests, singers, and pledgers, even those women and children who carry food and water into the ceremonial lodges, are under heavy scrutiny for mistakes and mishaps. For that reason, some priests and singers are truly reluctant to undertake a ceremonial role, especially if their family has recently been the object of criticism in the community. Under these conditions, each family member knows that they will be under extra scrutiny by the members of other families, who will be quick to criticize them for perceived ritual errors.

Something also needs to be said about the pointing sticks used by Cheyenne religionists, which are misunderstood even within the Cheyenne community. Since men with religious standing are believed to possess great power, they must not point with their fingers at anyone for fear of doing them harm. To prevent this, such men carry short sticks that they use to gesture and point. Unknowledgeable people don't like to have these sticks pointed at them, thinking that they are being "witched" in some manner. But they have got it backward – the use of the stick is not intended to harm the people being pointed at, but to protect them.

Food

Just as power travels down the hierarchy of priests, pledgers, and families, food travels up. The families of newly-elected members of soldier societies must feed the families of old members. The families of sun dancers must feed the families of their dance instructors. The family of a main pledger must feed the family of the instructor. When a man is elected chief, his family must feed everybody, symbolizing the chief's position as servant of all. At the very top levels of the food hierarchy, pledgers, priests, and vision seekers offer bits of food to spiritual forces, leaving the food outside with accompanying prayers. An offering of food is part of many rituals and ceremonies.

Just as there can be crossed pipes, so can there be food which is spiritually polluted. For example, if a promise between pledger and instructor is flawed, the food given from pledger to instructor might cause illness. At the annual ceremonies, a great deal of food is shared among families, but everyone wants to know where each bit of food came from. Ordinarily, people do not eat food which came from people with crossed pipes, who have been guilty of ritual malfeasance, or who have been elected chief under questionable circumstances.

Since food and cooking are largely under the control of women, they can use this control to influence the conduct of ceremonies, and the outcome of political events as well. For example, if a man is elected chief or headsman of a soldier society, he must conduct a giveaway and feed everyone to confirm his election. To feed everyone, three or four women of his family must spend a day or two cooking and putting away traditional foods. But suppose the women of his family disapprove of him for some reason. Suppose he has been drinking or perhaps neglecting or abusing his wife or children. In that case, they might refuse to cook for him, so that his election as chief or headsman cannot be confirmed.

In the same way, a man cannot pledge the Sun Dance or Arrow Ceremony, or dance in the Sun Dance, or go on a vision quest, without the favor of a group of women who are willing to cook for him. In actual practice, women usually indicate their veto of a man's plans far in advance, often as a way of pressuring a man to behave himself. A wife, her sister, and her mother, for example, might make it clear that they will cook for a man to pledge a vision quest only under certain conditions – that he must, for example, get a job, stop drinking, stay at home, fix up the house, or whatever. On the other hand, women in their role as cooks have it within their power to greatly enhance the status of a man, by turning out a memorable meal on the occasion of his election to an office, or his pledging of a ceremony.

Theory of Disease

Cheyenne traditionalists have not one theory of disease, but several. They believe that general health and well-being depend on participation in religious activities in a proper and legitimate manner, so that blessings proceed to everyone through legitimate channels. They believe that people who do not participate, or who cross their pipes or commit ritual errors will sicken and die. A person's malfeasance, I should emphasize, extends to his family, and is not limited to the actor. The consequence of dropping a ritual pipe, for example, might be the death or illness of a niece or grandson, not necessarily the death or illness of the person dropping the pipe. These ritual mistakes cause the disruption of the transfer of power so that some people and some families, so to speak, are left to wither on the vine. A pipe smoker is the conduit of energy to his family, and so they all suffer from his mistakes.

Irreconcilable disputes often occur among religionists and their families, and it is not always clear to other families which of the disputing families has conducted themselves properly and which has not. Such disputes are usually left to the test of time: that is, it is believed that members of the family at fault will soon begin to sicken and die. If one of the main protagonists dies, then clearly he was the one at fault.

Cheyennes believe that people can become ill for reasons other than their faulty participation or lack of participation in religious events. They recognize that Europeans brought with them diseases which they had never known before and to which Cheyennes were vulnerable, such as diabetes, tuberculosis, and alcoholism. In recent years they would also add insanity and the dementia of old age to the list of diseases brought by white people. Although the Cheyennes have had medicine people and treatments for many kinds of illnesses and injuries over the centuries, they have had no traditional response to the particular diseases brought by Europeans, and so they rely on the white man's doctors for relief. It is interesting to note that Christianity, in the form of the Native American Church, is seen more as a medicine lodge than what white people would call a "church." And in fact the most frequent illness brought to the peyote tipi for treatment is alcoholism. The logic is that if the white man brought the disease, he must also have brought the means for treating it, Christian prayer.

While Cheyennes have no specific traditional response to some modern diseases, they believe nonetheless that participation in the great ceremonies can provide relief of a general kind to any sort of disease. So people sometimes pledge the ceremonies if a parent, for example, has been diagnosed with terminal cancer or some other hopeless condition. Cheyenne religionists point with pride to people whose apparently hopeless conditions have cleared up after the performance of a Sun Dance or other ceremony in their behalf. Similar claims are made for the peyote religion.

The Negative Side of Familism

The bleakest and darkest side of Cheyenne society, to my mind, is the sometimes brutal and destructive familism which prevails, especially among the large, traditional, prominent extended families. Time after time, the plans of intelligent young leaders, progressive tribal officials, and well-meaning outsiders founder on the rocks of inter-familial rivalry and jealousy. An organization is no sooner introduced among the people than the families begin to fight over who will control it, especially if there is any money at stake. Health programs, language programs, and education programs of all kinds have suffered over the years from these internecine struggles. Consistently, more energy is devoted to the inter-familial struggle than to the successful completion of the project.

Frequently, the idiom and vocabulary of the struggle consists of accusations about religious events as described above. Families try to disqualify other families from organizations or committees because the other family has misbehaved at ceremonies, as evidenced by recent illnesses or deaths in the family. Sometimes the accusations are explicit and vocal, as families actually try to drive other families out the door of the meeting place. Naively, government and other organizations continue to try to organize new projects by calling meetings to which "all are invited." In recent years, pushing and name-calling are sometimes the result.

Accusations about religious misbehavior among families are supplemented by all kinds of gossip about other kinds of misbehavior. This gossip tends to fall into certain recurrent stories which have an apocryphal style. Let's say the accusations are about a fictional person, Mr Bad Bear; the gossip might run as follows:

1   I haven't seen Mr Bad Bear for two weeks. I guess he just stays at home and drinks.
2   I saw Mr Bad Bear driving a new car. He says it's his son's car, but it's really his. He drove right by me on the road and didn't give me a ride.
3   Mr Bad Bear was supposed to go to Los Angeles for a government meeting. Instead of that he met Mrs Bad Deer in Las Vegas and they gambled with tribal money and had a good time. Mrs Bad Bear doesn't know anything about it.
4   Mr Bad Bear's son is in prison in Washington state. He says he's in the army but I know better.
5   Mr Bad Bear has a Swiss bank account for the money he got from that program. My niece saw the check going out to Switzerland.

Over the last 20 years, I have heard these same kinds of stories told about scores of different people. In most cases I knew at the time that the stories were not true. They do have a function, however, which is to maintain the boundaries of extended families. People within a boundary tend to believe the stories about members of other families, while denying and refuting the same kinds of stories told about themselves.

Traditionally, there has been a recognition within Cheyenne culture of the destructive potential of untrammelled familism, and methods have been devised over the years for dealing with it. For example, to avoid confrontations with other families, Cheyenne traditionalists usually do not go to a meeting unless they know exactly which families are going to be there and what is going to be decided. If they are not sure, they cruise around the meeting place at meeting time to see whose cars are there. The ideal Cheyenne meeting comprises families who know what the meeting is about and who are already in agreement before they get there. The purpose of the meeting, then, is to express a consensus and adopt some course of action. Traditional Cheyenne people are not comfortable in a situation where serious issues are in contention, and there are arguments. Their traditions do not include the public expression of irreconcilable ideas among equals, and the dominance of a majority over a minority.

We should note that in a traditional Cheyenne context, such as the great ceremonial camp, the work is divided by extended families, who are not required to work side by side with other extended families. That is, the family is the unit which works to gather supplies for the pledger, puts up their tents and tipis, and cooks for him. When representatives of different families are gathered together, such as the dancers, or the priests and pledger, it is always under the control of a designated leader. At this type of meeting, the atmosphere is set by the ideology and values of these leaders, which is always strictly pan-familial and tribal. They are committed to overcoming familism and endorsing tribally-shared values, and they make these values very explicit, although they do so in a low key and gentle manner. The following advice to his people, to work together and forget their familial differences, was given by Arrow Keeper Edward Red Hat in 1972:

> I am going to tell you something
> that is good,
> and it means something
> that is good to know.
> I wish that you would all think this way.
> It would be real good
> if you would listen
> to the wisdom of this
> that is good to know.
> I wish you would all be together,
> and be thankful about good things.
> We would be thinking about good things,
> but something has led us off,
> something has led our thoughts
> from the way of our Cheyenne life.
> But let it go at that,
> even though we must suffer the results of it.
> That is the way it is,
> the way our prophet taught us.
> That is the way the law was put down
> to us on this earth.
> We try to live in good thoughts,

that way we all come together.
That is what is really important to us . . .
We all belong together,
we never got this far by telling lies
about each other.
Just let it go this way,
our only way – always know the truth . . .
That is the way Maheo provided for us.

Speeches like these and the one by Teeth quoted in the first chapter are made for good reasons. For much of the year, Cheyenne people live in a constant atmosphere of bickering and hostility among the families. But at another level, most Cheyennes realize that if they are to be successful with their annual ceremonies, and if they are to be successful in running their tribal government, they must overcome familism and work together. For this reason, men like Ed Red Hat in the south or Ted Rising Sun among the Northern Cheyennes are deeply admired because they try to overcome the familism which immobilizes their collective plans. For this reason, the Cheyenne chief is defined as a person who is impossible to anger, someone who does not participate in gossip, someone who tries to keep the peace among families.

So there is a constant tension in Cheyenne society between the ideals of familism, and the ideals of chiefship. One requires an absolute devotion to family against the demands of other families. The other requires an objectivity and fairness to all families, which can undermine the solidarity of one's own family. On many occasions I have seen Cheyenne chiefs behave like chiefs over the objections of their own family. That is why the chief's road is a hard road.

Kinship and Familism

I would define a Cheyenne extended family in modern times as a group of related people who, if they do not actually live together, share resources on a regular basis. They also act together politically, in their expressed attitudes toward ceremonial issues, the election of chiefs, and tribal elections. Each extended family has one or more elders who act as leaders of the group, whose opinions are solicited on every subject.

An extended family usually has as its core a married couple and several of their adult, married children. To construct a strong extended family, additional ancestors and in-laws can be recruited to live with and support the family. The largest Cheyenne extended families are built around two parents in their 50s, some of their parents and parents' siblings, a large cohort of children, the children's spouses and children, and perhaps the siblings, nieces, and nephews of the two parents. Such a family can number 50 or 60 people.

The status of such families among other families in the traditional community is determined by the number of chiefs and priests in the family, their visibility as pledgers of ceremonies and sun dancers, and their generosity to other families. In contrast to Anglo-American families, their status does not depend on the kind of jobs held by members of the family and their income, although the adult members of a family are expected to find a job if they can and if the job does not interfere with their religious and ceremonial obligations.

The status of a family can be increased by recruiting allies along ties of kinship, and publicly recognizing these ties at ceremonies, pow-wows, and giveaways. By some route or another, nearly every Cheyenne person is related to every other Cheyenne, and so a relationship between any two people is not only probable, but is also most likely of multiple dimensions. That is, an aunt's male cousin on the father's side might also be a grandfather's nephew on the maternal side, and in fact there might be five or more known connections of this kind. The task in creating an alliance is to trace genealogies and emphasize the closest connection, especially if that connection is made through a famous chief or other historically-known person. As a result of this genealogical work, it might be announced at a giveaway that a particular family wants to honor their grandfather's nephew, who is, like them, a descendant of a prominent chief. By such means, a family can increase its size and influence.

Unlike most Anglo-American families, Cheyenne extended families strive to be inclusive, and to recruit as many people as possible to live with the family or support it in some way. Elders are especially valued as family members, and are frequently solicited to join a particular extended family where they have relatives. The presence of these elders in the home, especially if they speak Cheyenne and are knowledgeable about tribal traditions, enhances the status of the extended family. Also, if the elder receives a pension or some kind of public assistance payments, their presence adds to the available income of the whole group.

Living Arrangements

When all the Cheyennes lived in tipis, there were two kinds of extended families, polygynous and monogamous. At that time, Cheyennes did not live as long as they do now, and that fact, too, influenced the structure of the extended family in that there were more younger people and fewer older people. Women married earlier, at about 16–18 years, and men married at about 18–21. By the time they were 40, most people had grandchildren, and few people lived beyond 50. Perhaps it was the scarcity of elders in that period which made them so valuable as the custodians of tradition, an attitude which carries on to the present.

Normally, a man who intended to be polygynous would marry the eldest of a cohort of sisters, and if he was a good provider and a good husband, he then married the next youngest sister, or perhaps a cousin who was a classificatory sister, until he had married perhaps three or four women related as sister or cousin to one another. Usually, it was only men and women from large, prosperous families, with lots of horses and lots of trade goods, who married in this way. A great chief might have several polygynous sons living with him, and in addition he might have several unmarried or relatively poor men in his band, to whom he loaned horses and from whom he received food or service by way of rent on the horses. This whole group constituted a chief's "bunch" or *manhastoz*. In the winter, this group lived by itself in some secluded area, for security and to conserve grass for their horses. The living arrangements of Limpy, a prominent polygynous chief in 1880, are shown in figure 9.1, using standard genealogical symbols with a circle representing a female and a square a male; the numbers give their ages. Limpy himself, aged

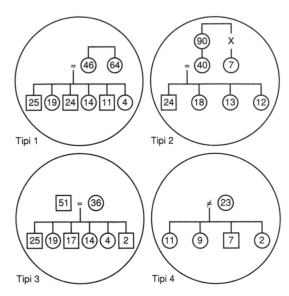

Figure 9.1   Living arrangements of the polygynous chief Limpy in 1880 (from Moore 1991b: 328)

51, lived in tipi 3 with his 36-year-old wife at the time of the 1880 census. In tipi 1 was his oldest and presumably first wife, with her older sister. Tipi 2 housed another wife, with her mother and young cousin. Tipi 4 was occupied by a young woman who described herself as an ex-wife, with some children. The children shown in the tipis were not necessarily living with their biological mothers, but were distributed among the mothers and their tipis for various practical reasons. Plate 9.1 shows the adults of another polygynous family of the same period, but without most of the children.

Monogamous families lived in smaller groups, called "camps" or *vestoz*, in which the family heads or their wives were siblings to one another. The camps in the mid 19th century comprised about 45 people; the bunches were about twice that size. At that time, about 40 percent of all Cheyennes lived in polygynous families, and about 60 percent lived in monogamous families. In the summer, the various extended families would come together under the leadership of prestigious chiefs, and would gather for the ceremonies and travel around the plains in various combinations for the entire summer.

In early reservation times, several factors conspired to under-

Plate 9.1 Scalp Cane and family (photo by Christian Barthelmess, Smithsonian Institution National Anthropological Archives)

mine the structure of these extended families, whether polygynous or monogamous. First of all, there was rampant deadly disease and a lowered birth rate, which diminished the size of the population and therefore the sizes of all the families, so that the remains of different families were forced together to form new living units. Second, missionaries and Indian agents in the reservation period used various means to outlaw and discourage polygyny, so that the large chiefs' bunches began to disappear. And last, after individual ownership of land was assigned in 1891, the Cheyennes were encouraged to split up the extended families so that each nuclear family would occupy a small house on their own land. To this end, the government withheld rations and used the military to break up the extended families.

The Cheyennes resisted the break-up of families until the 1930s, when employment was made available through New Deal programs at camps of the Civilian Conservation Corps and in small towns in Montana and Oklahoma under Works Progress Administration and other projects.[1] Many people left their extended families to join these programs, and this period was followed by World War II, which called a large number of Cheyenne men into military service. After the war, many Cheyennes formed nuclear families and moved to town.

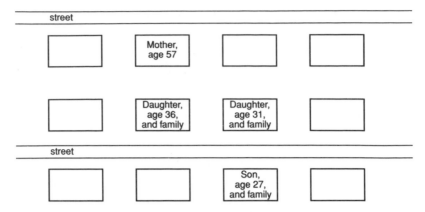

Figure 9.2   Living arrangements of a Northern Cheyenne extended family in a housing project

Since World War II, Cheyenne extended families have re-formed themselves in the towns on the reservation area, although some extended families continue to live in rural areas. Since the 1930s, the Cheyenne population has increased dramatically, so that people once again have large families, and young and middle-aged people have lots of brothers and sisters. It is around these large sibling cohorts that the modern extended families are organized. These are the groups which act together ceremonially and politically, which recruit elders to live with them, and which try to live together.

Whenever possible, even in the towns, extended families try to live in the same neighborhood, on the same street. Figure 9.2 shows the living arrangements of one prominent Northern Cheyenne extended family in a housing project in Lame Deer, Montana. The residences of a rural extended family in Oklahoma are shown in figure 9.3 (this time triangles represent males).

In sum, extended families are still the fundamental building blocks of Cheyenne society. Although they feud and fuss with one another, often to the detriment of the whole tribe, they also have developed a system for taking care of one another within the family, and creating alliances with other families to accomplish larger goals. Just as several extended families were allied together to comprise a band in aboriginal times, so do modern extended families within a community cooperate for local proj-

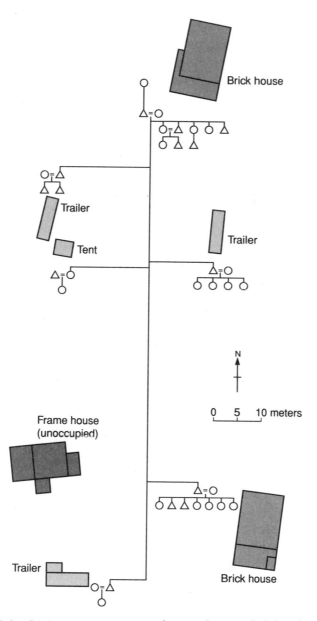

Figure 9.3   Living arrangements of a rural extended family in Okla-homa (from Moore 1987: 328)

ects, such as organizing pow-wows or supporting a community center. And on a grand scale, they still cooperate to produce their elaborate and complex annual ceremonies.

Relations with the Dominant Society

The solidarity of extended families is also the source of many misunderstandings between Cheyennes and non-Indians. For example, Cheyenne people sometimes send other members of their families – a sibling or cousin – to work in their place on a paying job when they must be absent for illness, ceremonies, or family obligations. Some employers completely reject this practice, since from their individualistic perspective, they have employed one person for a job, not a family. But other employers in Cheyenne country have become accustomed to this practice, and whoever shows up is put to work.

Giving in entirely to familism at one point, the Northern Cheyenne tribal government assigned each department of tribal operations to a different extended family. If anyone resigned from a department, they were replaced by a member of the same family. Of course this was entirely contrary to the rules regarding "nepotism" maintained by the federal government to prevent politicians from hiring their relatives, but it worked for the Cheyennes. To maintain the fiction that employees were unrelated, they were frequently employed under assumed names. To the government this looked like fraud, corruption, favoritism, and nepotism, but by Cheyenne standards this was a good traditional manner of organizing work, with each family assigned to one department, and the whole extended family held responsible for the performance of that department.

Non-Indian hospital administrators and high school principals also do not understand Cheyenne familism. When some member of an extended family is seriously ill and hospitalized, it is customary for a large portion of the family to go to the hospital to reassure the patient and tend to their needs. Consequently, for each Cheyenne patient in a bed, there are four to six people, sometimes more, in the waiting room. Hospitals designed in the Anglo-American fashion are not built for this many visitors. The expectation is that each person will have only one or two visitors at any one time, and that sometimes a patient will have no visitors at all. But the Cheyenne families literally move into the hospital, to show their concern for their family member, creating friction with the doctor, nurses, and staff.

When a Cheyenne student is in trouble at school, once again there is a big turn-out of the Cheyenne family, and frequent misunderstandings. When a principal opens the door for an interview with the family of a student, he expects to find mom, dad, or perhaps both. In the Cheyenne case, what he might find is grandmother, grandfather, and about six or eight other family members, all dressed up and ready to discuss the matter. Some principals believe that in such situations the family is trying to intimidate them, and in one case I know about, the principal quickly called in two football coaches to stand behind him and support his side, as if they were going to have a fist-fight.

To determine the general climate in which Cheyennes must live, I have made it my business over the years to ask naive questions of non-Indians within the areas of the Cheyenne Reservations in Montana and Oklahoma. I often ask someone in a store, restaurant, or gas station what tribe lives around here, or what they do at a pow-wow or ceremony, or simply what they think about Indians. I ask these questions as a tourist might, and not in the presence of Cheyennes.

Some of the responses I get are very rude and surprising, such as "I don't know what tribe they are and I don't care." When I suggested to a woman in a dry goods store that the people might be Cheyennes, she said, "I don't know the difference between Shy Annes and any other kind of Annes." Asking about the ceremonies at an ice plant, I was told, "First they eat a raw cow and then they have a sex orgy." Frequently, Cheyennes are characterized as drunk or dirty. And in fact alcoholics are clearly visible on the streets of many reservation towns. Of course, most Cheyennes are neither drunk nor dirty, but the impression lives on as a racist caricature.

The most aggressive enemies of Cheyenne culture are the fundamentalist missionaries and the Ku-Klux-Klan. The missionaries not only knock on the doors of Cheyennes constantly, preaching to them, but also show up as an organized force at the ceremonies. Especially when the ceremonies were held at the Walking Woman allotment near Watonga, Oklahoma, a group

Figure 9.4   Lou White Eagle's drawing of the cross-burning at the Cheyenne ceremonial site

of missionaries with a flatbed truck would pull up on the county road near the site and begin preaching though loudspeakers about heathen religion and devil worship. Of course their least favorite part of the ceremony was the phallic symbolism.

At the Walking Woman site, the portable rest rooms were set up next to the road, which gave the missionaries a captive audience. Early one morning in 1979, I was awakened by the loudspeakers and looked out of my tent to see a preacher on a flatbed truck remonstrating with about 40 Cheyennes, most of them children who had just got up, and were standing in two lines for the toilets. Throughout the ceremonies for two weeks, the truck returned for episodes of preaching and bible-pounding, and was met mostly with good-natured forbearance by those Cheyennes who were waiting to use the toilet.

More ominous was a cross-burning at the Walking Woman site. In 1980 the priests had just moved into the ceremonial site, where the Sun Dance arbor from the previous year was still in place. At about four in the morning, the priests were disturbed by the sound of men running from the old arbor toward the road. Looking out, they saw several cars speeding away and a cross burning near the arbor. Luther Black Bear, now known as Lou White Eagle, an arrow priest, took photographs of the cross after dawn broke, and made a drawing of the event, shown here as figure 9.4. After this incident, the ceremonies were held at other sites where there was less chance of disruption or interference.

In general, the inter-cultural situation of the Northern Cheyennes is different from that of the southerners. The northerners have managed to retain their reservation pretty much intact, and few non-Cheyennes live there. Their interactions with non-Indians occur largely at surrounding off-reservation towns such as Ashland, Hardin, and Forsyth (see map 6.3, page 150). But the Southern Cheyennes live among and around large numbers of non-Indians. In fact Indians constitute only about 6 percent of the population in the seven-county area where they live. Consequently they are in constant contact with non-Indians, and suffer more from racism and misunderstandings.

10

Early Reservation Life

The reservation history of the Cheyenne Nation can be divided generally into two periods. During the earlier period, from the end of the Indian Wars until the passage of the Indian Reorganization Act (IRA) in 1934, the Cheyennes were essentially treated like prisoners, lined up and counted periodically, living where they were ordered by the army, subsisting mostly off government rations, sent involuntarily to boarding schools, subject to imprisonment without trial, and unable to own property – they were non-citizens to whom the Bill of Rights did not legally apply.[1] After the IRA and its equivalent for Oklahoma Indians, the Oklahoma Indian Welfare Act, the Cheyennes were gradually permitted to have a larger voice in their own affairs, but they did not become citizens until 1924, and the Bill of Rights was not extended to them until 1968.[2] Even now, the officials of the Bureau of Indian Affairs can veto any action of a tribal government, or any transaction concerning privately-owned Cheyenne land which is in trust. Indian activist and attorney Geoff Standing Bear has described American Indians as "the most highly regulated and most carefully watched ethnic minority in the history of the world."

After the Battle of Summit Springs in 1869 (see plate 10.1), most of the Southern Cheyenne bands took up residence on their Oklahoma reservation, where they received rations and were watched over by Army troops at Fort Reno and Fort Supply. In these early years, the Southern Cheyennes were still armed and they undertook periodic expeditions from their assigned reservation, some authorized by the Indian agent for hunting, and some unauthorized expeditions for raiding or visiting other

*Plate 10.1   After the Battle of Summit Springs, Army surgeons dis-
membered the corpses of Cheyenne casualties and sent the remains to
the Smithsonian; in 1993 these and other remains were repatriated to
the Southern Cheyennes and Arapahoes, who laid them to rest in a
special ceremony, shown here (photo by Darrell Rice of the* Watonga
Republican*)*

tribes. The most serious outbreak occurred in 1874–5, propelled
by the imminent destruction of the southern buffalo herds by
professional hunters, who were killing thousands of buffaloes
and shipping out the dried hides using the railroads of southern
Kansas. Still dependent on buffaloes for food and for robes to
trade at the agency, the Cheyennes were alarmed by the movement of buffalo hunters south of the Arkansas into Texas and
western Oklahoma in the early 1870s. Allied with Kiowas and
Comanches who were also still dependent on the buffaloes,
Cheyenne warriors attacked the main trading post of the buffalo
hunters at Adobe Walls, Texas, in June of 1874. Repelled by the
hunters, they undertook a series of smaller raids in the
Texas–Kansas area until driven back to the reservation by hunger
in 1875.

When they returned, 31 Cheyenne men and one woman, the alleged "ringleaders" of the outbreak, were put in leg irons and sent to prison at Fort Marion, Florida, without trial or hearing. Some of them became famous as graphic artists, based on the drawings they made for visitors to Fort Marion, and some later went to school at Carlisle, Pennsylvania, from where they returned to the reservation as "models" of good behavior. Meanwhile the rest of the Cheyennes in Oklahoma suffered greatly. To prevent further outbreaks, Agent John Miles sold off their horses, collected weapons, and forced the people to live in a large camp near the fort, which became increasingly unsanitary over the next several years, and which in addition was full of whiskey traders and surrounded by horse thieves and other unscrupulous non-Cheyennes who undertook to acquire any-thing the Cheyennes had left which had any monetary value. Several hundred militant Southern Cheyennes and their families managed to escape from this situation to join the Northern Cheyennes, who were still living in freedom with the Lakota north of the Platte River, in Montana and the Dakotas.

The Northern Cheyennes maintained their freedom longer, but at great cost. After the Battle of the Little Big Horn in 1876, the various bands were gradually subdued and forced to march to Oklahoma under armed guard, although a few bands man-aged to take refuge with the Lakotas on the reservations being established for them in South Dakota, or with the Arapahoes on their Wyoming reservation. By summer of 1877, the Southern Cheyennes and most of the Northern Cheyennes were confined near the Darlington Agency in Oklahoma, across the river from Fort Reno, where the Northern Cheyennes were increasingly uncomfortable, unaccustomed to the heat of the southern plains, the disease, and lack of food.

In September of 1878, 300 Northern Cheyennes left Okla-homa in the hope of joining the other Cheyennes who had taken refuge with the Lakota. After two months spent both fighting and avoiding the troops sent out to bring them back, the Northern Cheyennes split into two groups, one led by Little Wolf and the other by Dull Knife (see plate 10.2).[3] The Dull Knife group was captured by soldiers in October, disarmed, and imprisoned in a barracks at Fort Robinson, Nebraska. After more than two months of captivity, the group still refused to return to Oklahoma, and so their food, water, and firewood

Plate 10.2   *The graves of Little Wolf and Dull Knife on the Northern Cheyenne Reservation, with prayer cloths tied to the nearby fence (photo by Ken Blackbird)*

were cut off. After three days of suffering, and now determined to escape, on a freezing night in January, 149 men, women and children broke out of the barracks and headed north on foot. During a bloody all-night attack by the soldiers who guarded them, 61 Cheyennes were killed. Of the rest, some escaped and the rest were returned to Fort Robinson, from which they were finally allowed to travel north to join their kin at the Pine Ridge Reservation. The Army gave up trying to send the northerners south, and a Northern Cheyenne Reservation was set up in eastern Montana in 1884. To occupy the reservation, the various Northern Cheyenne bands were assembled from South Dakota, from Fort Keogh in Montana, from Wyoming and Oklahoma, a total of about 1,200 people.

By 1878 it had been decided that the Southern Arapahoes, currently living with the Southern Cheyennes in Oklahoma, would remain with them instead of joining the Northern Arapahoes in Wyoming. The government had two purposes in creating this situation. First, they felt that the Arapahoes would be a calming influence on the Cheyennes, whom they regarded as hostile and militant, and it gave the government an opportunity to play off one tribe against the other. Second, this policy prevented the Arapahoes from uniting on one reservation, allowing the government to use the same divide-and-conquer strategy between the Northern Arapahoes and Shoshones, both assigned to the Wind River Reservation in Wyoming.

To administer the Plains Indians on their reservations, the government relied on the Bureau of Indian Affairs (BIA), which had been transferred from the War Department to the Department of the Interior in 1849.[4] In the War Department, the main duty of the BIA was to administer the treaties, many of which had stipulated that Indian tribes would receive annual rations in exchange for the land they had given up. Moved to the Interior Department, the duties of the BIA were broadened, so that they administered all the daily affairs of Indian people, distributing rations, conducting censuses, organizing schools and missionary efforts, and employing some Indians to work for the Bureau. But especially, the BIA took over the administration of reservation land, deciding where the Indians should live and how the land should be used.

Between 1878 and 1892, government agents, backed by the military, made strenuous efforts to break up Cheyenne political and social structure, convert the Indians to Christianity, and turn them into farmers in the Anglo-American style. Ignoring the fact that Cheyennes already knew how to farm, the government hired "farmers-in-charge" in Oklahoma and Montana to teach them how to plow, and encouraged them to grow, of all things, potatoes, which were quite inappropriate for the climate and soils of both reservations. Despite a lot of bad advice, and with the help of a Quaker missionary John Seger, the Southern Cheyennes and Arapahoes did figure out how to farm in a manner appropriate to the prairies, and by 1890 were well on the way to self-sufficiency. Instead of depending on the government for seed and technology, they borrowed seed from the nearby Caddoes and used traditional hoes to make their gardens. The Northern Cheyennes, likewise eschewing bad advice, began growing wheat and hay and raising horses and cattle for sale.

While the Cheyennes were being "taught" how to farm, they subsisted on rations supplied by the government. Usually these rations consisted of dry foods, such as flour and sugar, which could be easily transported by rail and wagon from the east. But

Plate 10.3   Southern Cheyennes butcher their beef allotment after a short chase near Cantonment, Oklahoma, about 1890 (Western History Collections, University of Oklahoma)

rations also included live cattle, leading to the colorful institution of the "beef issue." At the request of the Cheyennes, each beef was let loose on the run, and the hunters ran it down and shot it with arrows, just as they had hunted buffaloes. Then they butchered the animals in a traditional way, and distributed the meat (see plate 10.3).

Both in Montana and in Oklahoma, the BIA made a terrible mistake in policy as they tried to make Cheyennes self-sufficient. If a family worked hard in their gardens and began to produce their own food, their rations were cut off. That is, the "reward" for hard work, if you can call it that, was that you were not better off, but worse off. During this period the Northern Cheyennes were encouraged to build a dam and irrigation ditches to provide water for their fields. The ditches collapsed after a few years, and the remains of this very expensive project can still be seen between the towns of Lame Deer and Birney.

As a consequence of receiving rations which were both inadequate in quantity and of poor quality, the Cheyennes on both reservations experienced high mortalities and rates of illness from diseases such as tuberculosis, trachoma, and dysentery. As a way of excusing themselves from the charge of mismanagement on the reservations, the government helped to create the myth that Indians simply had no resistance to these diseases, and the theme developed in American culture that Indians were inevitably headed for extinction. Another theme in popular culture was that the Plains Indians in particular were simply heartbroken that they could not follow the buffaloes, and that their broken spirits led to illness and death. The real picture of reservation life in these years, however, was of hungry, malnourished Indians desperately trying to figure out how to survive in a situation where they were surrounded and harassed by their recent enemies (soldiers, ranchers, and farmers), constantly given bad advice by the government, and under cultural attack from missionaries and bureaucrats.

The attack on Cheyenne religion consisted of outlawing their annual ceremonies and assigning Christian missionaries to convert them, in accordance with policies adopted in 1872, which determined which denominations should proselytize on which reservations.[5] Despite the hostility of bureaucrats, missionaries, and soldiers, however, the ceremonies went forward under various guises invented by the priests and chiefs. At various times in the early reservation period the ceremonies were referred to as the "Homecoming Celebration," "Reservation Fair," and "Fourth of July Celebration." In these years, according to modern elders, they did in fact have a craft show or a flag-raising on the first day, perhaps a parade and some speeches, and when the white people went home, they had an Arrow Ceremony and a Sun Dance. In some years, depending on who the Indian agent was and the attitude of the current missionaries, the ceremonies were held without any need for deception. In these years several anthropologists intervened in behalf of the Cheyennes, so that they could conduct their ceremonies without interference. These anthropologists included George Dorsey, James Mooney, and George Bird Grinnell.

The first missionaries to arrive among the Southern Cheyennes were the Quakers, the primary actors in President Grant's "peace policy." Of the Quaker missionaries, only John Seger stayed the course, founding a colony of Cheyenne and Arapaho farmers on the southern part of the reservation. The Quakers began a reservation school system, beginning in 1876. The Mennonites arrived in Oklahoma in 1882 and likewise began a school as well as missionary activities. In addition to the reservation

Plate 10.4 Uniformed Cheyenne and Arapaho children at the board-ing school at Cantonment, Oklahoma, about 1900 (Smithsonian Institution National Anthropological Archives)

schools, some Cheyenne children were sent off to boarding schools, as far away as Carlisle, Pennsylvania.

The Catholics were the first denomination to arrive among the Northern Cheyennes, in 1883, and they have continued to operate the St Labre mission school in Ashland until the present. The Mennonites, after some success in getting Cheyenne converts in Oklahoma, arrived in Montana in 1899, where they operated a school for a while and still maintain a church. In addition, other Northern Cheyenne children were sent to mission schools and some to boarding schools around the country. In both Montana and Oklahoma, enrollment in boarding schools was often involuntary, and sometimes rations were withheld or threats were made by the military to force Cheyenne families to send their children away to school (plate 10.4).

The attitude of Cheyennes toward Christianity has always frustrated Christian missionaries, from the beginning until now. Cheyennes in general have never felt that religious belief should be exclusive, and while many have been ready to embrace Christianity, they have not wanted to give up their traditional beliefs or ceremonies. That is, Christianity has been perceived as merely an additional source of power from Maheo, with Jesus serving in the role of an anthropomorphic spirit. Of course the missionaries wanted the Cheyennes to embrace Christianity exclusively, and not only that, to embrace some denomination exclusively. Beginning with the Mennonites, missionaries have condemned traditional beliefs as devil worship, and have felt betrayed if Cheyennes attended church on Sunday and a peyote meeting or a traditional ceremony later in the week. But most Cheyennes maintain the attitude that if participating in one religion is good, then participating in two or three religions is even better, so that a person can collect blessings from Maheo through several sources.

The efforts of the BIA and the Army to manipulate Southern Cheyenne politics have been the subject of two books by the eminent historian Donald Berthrong, and will be the subject of yet another book by Berthrong and another by the anthropologist Loretta Fowler. Essentially the government manipulated politics by playing off the Arapahoes against the Cheyennes, favoring the Arapahoes in government policies and administration, and then encouraging Cheyenne resentment. In addition, the government took advantage of Cheyenne factionalism and familism, once again by favoring, or seeming to favor, certain groups over others. By this means the Southern Cheyenne chiefs and headsmen were kept in disarray throughout the early reservation period.

In Montana the situation was different. There were, first of all, fewer Cheyennes to deal with, and for the first several decades they were in such desperate physical condition that no manipulation was necessary. The population had dropped to about 800 by 1900. This was followed by a period of relative prosperity, when the Cheyennes began to raise and market cattle, and throughout this period the Cheyenne leadership seems to have been united compared to the Southern Cheyennes. It was the assault on Southern Cheyenne lands which caused the manipulation of Native politics to be so intensive in Oklahoma.

Cheyenne Reservation Humor

Although the Cheyenne people faced serious, even life-threatening situations in the early reservation period, they maintained a sense of humor. Although they suffered from their interactions with the BIA, they still managed to make jokes about it, creating humorous stories which survive to the present time.[6] These stories reflect their experiences with white people and explain puzzling aspects of the inter-cultural situation. They sometimes make fun of white people and their ways, and make fun of themselves in their attempts to understand and participate in Anglo-American culture. One very popular story seeks to explain why the personnel of the Bureau of Indian Affairs are apparently so lazy and indolent.

Custer and the BIA

In 1876 General Custer was the Commander of Fort Lincoln when a message came to mobilize his forces immediately for a campaign into Montana Territory. Quickly he collected the men, horses, and wagons of the Seventh Cavalry and headed for the main gate. On the way he was intercepted by an official of the BIA, running alongside and waving a thick sheaf of papers. "General Custer," he said, "you need to sign these papers before you go."

"No time, now," said the General, "the Cheyennes have broken out and are making trouble."

"But General," said the bureaucrat, "these are requisitions for rations, tools, horses, wagons, everything we need. You're the only person authorized to sign."

General Custer pulled up his horse. "I've got to get on the trail," he said. Then he paused thoughtfully. "I tell you what, take those papers back to the office and put them on my desk, and just don't do anything until I get back." And he turned his horse and rode off to the Little Big Horn.

Another story concerns the attempts of the government to get the Cheyennes to farm by plowing with horses. Here the main character is a "farmer-in-charge" hired to teach Cheyennes how to plow and harrow.

The Farmer and the Plows

It was late in the year when the plows finally arrived on the train from Washington. Immediately the Farmer notified all the Indian men to meet him at the railroad siding next morning, where he would distribute the plows.

Early next morning everyone had assembled, and they helped the Farmer unload a big wooden crate containing one of the plows. They watched him pry apart the crate, take out the parts of the plow, and assemble it. Then he brought out a harness, hitched a team to the plow, and plowed a few rows. "Well, that's all there is to it," he said. Then he unhitched the horses, took apart the plow and put it back in the crate and gave it to the Chief. The rest of the crates were distributed to the other men, and they put them on their wagons and took them home.

About a week later the Farmer decided to visit all the camps and see how the plowing was coming along. As he rode along on his horse, he was disappointed to see that very little had been accomplished. Some fields had as many as ten or fifteen rows finished, but most had hardly started plowing, and nobody had begun to plant. Towards dark he arrived at the Chief's house, and noted immediately that the Chief's plow was still in the crate. The Chief came out to greet him. "Well, Chief," the Farmer said tentatively, "how's the plowing coming along?"

"Not very well," said the Chief, "it takes a long time to farm this way. It's usually mid-morning before we get the plow out of the crate and put together, and we have to start taking it apart in the middle of the afternoon if we're going to get it back in the crate by dark. I've been working hard all day, and I only plowed five rows. I think we'd better go back to farming with a hoe."

The First Government Rations

The people were camped around the fort waiting for their rations. There was no game, and they were hungry. Finally the Agent came around in a wagon and gave each tipi a bag of rations. "This is all I have right now," he said, "there'll be more later."

One Cheyenne family opened their bag and found a box of salt, a box of pepper, a slab of bacon, some green coffee, and some lye soap. They had never seen these things before and didn't know what to do with them. Finally they decided to cook them Indian fashion, so they put a kettle of water on the fire to boil, and they poured in all the salt, pepper, and coffee, and they cut up the bacon and soap and put them in too. They watched hungrily as the salt and lye soap dissolved, and the pepper, bacon, and coffee boiled round and around. The green coffee swelled up very big, like beans. Finally the woman of the house decided the food was cooked, and she took a spoon to taste it.

"Whew," she grimaced, "this tastes awful. Maybe we didn't cook it right." She put the spoon back into the kettle. Her husband tried the stew, "Argh," he made a bad face but managed to swallow a mouthful. In a few minutes he grabbed his stomach. "I don't feel good," he said. Then Grandmother spoke up, "I think we had better call the Medicine Man and see what he thinks about all this before we eat any more."

After a few minutes the Medicine Man arrived and stirred the pot a little, watching the mess go round and round. "I'll try it," he said at last, and sat down by the fire. He took a small bowl of stew and ate several spoons full. Finally he made a horrible face, "Yech," he said, "I can't stand to eat any more," and he set it aside. Then he sat quietly while the family waited to hear what he would say.

"Well," he said finally, "it's clear to me that the white man's food is not very good, but in addition to that, I think we've solved a mystery that has been troubling me for a long time." "What mystery is that?" asked the Grandmother." "Well," said the Medicine Man, "have you noticed that the white man's hair falls out on top of his head, that he has freckles and fuzz all over his body, and that he always looks like he's mad about something? Well at last we understand why – they must eat this every day!"

The Ghost Dance Religion

A more serious response to the threat of cultural domination was the Ghost Dance religion, which swept among all the plains reservations in the 1880s.[7] The cult originated with the prophet Wovoka, a Southern Paiute living in Nevada. Beginning about 1870, various versions of his prophecy were communicated from him among the Plains Indians, with little effect at first. But many tribes, including the Cheyennes, sent delegates to Nevada to talk with Wovoka and receive his instructions.

In a letter written about 1889, Wovoka instructed the Cheyennes how to pray and take care of themselves in preparation for a cataclysm which would soon destroy the white people, raise Indian people from the dead, and restore the plains to their former condition, with plenty of buffaloes and other game. He said that the agent for this restoration would be Jesus, who had already returned from Heaven and was walking upon the earth. In response to Wovoka's instructions, hundreds of Cheyennes were soon engaged in erecting tipis and Sweat Lodges in preparation for the dance.

To participate in the dance, a Cheyenne man had to go through the Sweat Lodge and then receive a feather from a priest. The dance itself was simply a huge round dance, with all the participants, men and women, shuffling to their left in an immense circle while the special Ghost Dance songs were sung (plate 10.5). The high point of the dance was toward the end, after it was dark, when many of the participants assumed hypnotic states and fell to the ground, or sat down in trances to receive visions of dead relatives.

Different plains tribes interpreted and elaborated Wovoka's message differently concerning how the new world would be achieved. In the Cheyenne version, a new earth, a hemisphere to their way of thinking, would be built to the west of the present earth and would move east to cover and overlap the present earth, as the right hand moves to overlap the left. At the leading edge of the new earth would be a great fire, which would burn the white man and drive him into the sea. Ghost Dance practitioners would avoid the fire by their special dance feathers, and would rise over the fire to land on the new earth. They would then sleep for four days and rise to greet all their old friends, risen from the dead. Then they would live as they had before the coming of the white man.

What most concerned the white authorities about the Ghost Dance was the medicine of the Ghost Dance shirt, which was alleged to be impervious to bullets, protecting the wearer from all firearms. To the military, this kind of shirt implied that an armed uprising was being planned, an alarming prospect in view of the fact that most military installations on the plains had been cut back since the end of the Indian Wars. If all the tribes attacked the forts in a coordinated way, it was not clear to military planners what the results would be. Consequently, they

Plate 10.5 The Ghost Dance camp near Darlington, Oklahoma, in 1889: the great circle of dancers can be seen in the center of camp (Shuck Collection, Western History Collections, University of Oklahoma)

were nervous and jumpy as they communicated with each other about the Ghost Dance meetings held all across the plains in 1889–91.

In this agitated and nervous condition, Major Whitside of the Seventh Cavalry (the same unit commanded by Custer at the Little Big Horn) was asked to capture Big Foot's band of Lakota, some of whom were of Cheyenne descent, who were headed for a Ghost Dance assembly in December of 1890, and bring them to the Pine Ridge Agency. When confronted by the soldiers, Big Foot and his band of about 340 people, including 106 warriors, consented to go back with them. When they stopped for the night, the Big Foot band was told to camp in a small depression, where they were surrounded by 470 armed troops and four Hotchkiss machine guns. In the morning, when the troops tried to disarm the Indians, a fight broke out and the machine guns were unleashed on the village of tipis, killing 300 Indians, mostly women and children, and 60 soldiers. Most of the soldiers were apparently killed by the Hotchkiss guns, since the guns could not fire into the village except through the circle of guards. This was the Massacre at Wounded Knee.

When word of the massacre reached the Cheyennes, it effectively ended the Ghost Dance, for two reasons. First of all, it was apparent that the highly-touted ghost dance shirts, which were supposed to deflect bullets, had not worked at Wounded Knee. Second, the massacre reinforced the credibility of those Cheyennes who had said all along that practicing the dance would only give the soldiers an excuse to kill them. And so most Cheyennes abandoned the cult, although incorporating some elements of the dance into their major ceremonies. And ironically, some Cheyennes were attracted to the Christian churches because of their participation in the Ghost Dance and their continuing belief in the second coming of Jesus.

Allotment in Severalty

The episode which contributed most to destroying Cheyenne culture and society in the late 19th century, more than the Sand Creek Massacre, more than anything done by General Custer, was allotment in severalty.[8] As outlined in the Dawes Act, passed by Congress in 1888, allotment in severalty was a plan for distributing small portions of land, allotments, to each individual Indian, and selling the rest of the reservation, the "surplus" land, to white people. For the Southern Cheyennes and Arapahoes, the "surplus" land amounted to six sevenths of the reservation, about three million acres. Allotment in severalty was backed in the US Congress by an odd alliance of interests. On the one hand, the land interests and real estate speculators were anxious to put the land under the gavel for their own profit, while the congressional progressives deluded themselves that if individual Indians only had some land of their own, they would quickly come to resemble white people – farming with plows, learning English, building houses, abandoning their extended families for nuclear families, and becoming Christians.

But whatever their motives, there was a barrier to implementing the desires of Congress among the Southern Cheyennes. According to the Treaty of 1867, solemnly signed by both sides, Cheyenne and Arapaho reservation land could not be alienated for any purpose unless three fourths of the males over 18 years of age consented. With over half of the Cheyennes caught up in the Ghost Dance religion in 1890, the chances that any sizeable number would cooperate with the government and sign away their land was very slim. So the Jerome Commission was organized to overcome the "irrational resistance" of the Cheyennes to losing their land. The commission consisted of David Jerome, Alfred Wilson, and Warren Sayre, and they were authorized by Congress to collect signatures of Indians consenting to the allotment of land.

Arriving in Oklahoma in July of 1890, the Jerome Commission undertook a few book-keeping tasks to make their job easier, regarding the number and kinds of signatures which were necessary. First of all, over the objections of both groups, they considered the Cheyennes and Arapahoes as a single tribe, so that to allot the Cheyennes they only needed signatures of three fourths of the combined tribes, not just the Cheyennes. Since the Arapahoes had already been given half the jobs on the reservation (although there were twice as many Cheyennes as Arapahoes), it was felt that the Arapahoes would sign more willingly than the Cheyennes to maintain their privileged position. Second, the Jerome Commission asked the Indian agent, Charles Ashley, to "certify" the total number of males over 18 at a lower figure than appeared on the official 1888 Census, which counted 827 people in that category. Obligingly, Ashley certified that there was only a total of 618 men over 18 in both tribes. This meant that the commission only had to secure 464 signatures instead of 620.

In late October the arm-twisting began. First the Indians who worked for the agency and Army were told to sign the agreement or lose their jobs. Then certain mixed-blood interpreters were given bribe money sent from land speculators in the east, and this money was paid to others who would sign. These people, as admitted later by the commission, signed not once but several times, using their different Indian names. The names of women and children around the agency were entered, without any indication that these were not men over 18 years. But even after a month of such coercion and bribery, the commission still had only 146 authentic signatures, mostly people who worked for the government.

So an additional bit of chicanery was employed by members of the commission, who assigned themselves phoney "powers of attorney" for Indian men who would not or could not sign. This included all the students away at boarding schools, as well as all the men gathered in the Ghost Dance campgrounds in the western part of the reservation, where the commission was afraid to go. Still short by a few names, the commission members themselves, perhaps in a giddy or jovial mood, entered the names "Oscar Wild," "Chester A. Arthur," and "Jay Gould." Then they wrote a gloating, self-congratulatory letter to the President of the United States that their mission had been a huge success, and that they had made three million acres of land available for "white settlement" at a cost of only $250,000 cash, which comes to less than ten cents per acre. In exchange for the three million acres, each Cheyenne received 75 silver dollars.

A few years later, after the "surplus" reservation land had been sold to whites and occupied by them, the frauds perpetrated by the Jerome Commission were exposed. But in the infamous Lone Wolf decision of 1903, the Supreme Court ruled that even if the land had been obtained fraudulently, since Congress had ratified the arrangement, it could not be undone. Meantime, in the rush of land-hungry settlers, mostly "boomers" from Kansas, Cheyenne horse herds were stolen, people displaced, and worst of all, the crops which had finally been brought to fruition by Cheyenne farmers were trampled underfoot by the invaders or eaten by their stock. In a report to Washington, the Indian agent said that 1891 would have been the first year in which the Cheyennes had become self-sufficient in food, had it not been for allotment in severalty and the machinations of the Jerome Commission.

Because the Northern Cheyenne Reservation in Montana was not so desirable from the standpoint of local farmers and ranchers, and because the density of Indians was higher, the Northern Cheyennes managed to avoid allotment in severalty until the period 1926–32. In the meantime, they had become very successful cattle ranchers, beginning with a herd of 1,000 cows and 40 bulls in 1903. The Northern Cheyenne men found it easy to become cowboys, since they already had long experience on horseback, and by 1912 the herd had grown to 12,000

Plate 10.6   Winter feeding of cattle on the Northern Cheyenne Reservation (photo by Ken Blackbird)

head, and the stock was being regularly shipped to Chicago where it was sold for good prices (see plate 10.6). The Cheyennes were becoming prosperous, and then the government stepped in.

Urged on by local cattle ranchers who were being undersold in the cattle markets, government officials decided that the Cheyennes were guilty of overgrazing and other mismanagement of the herds, and so they took over the cattle operations in 1914. After a series of disastrous mistakes in management, including leaving the cattle out on the ridges in the middle of winter, the herd had dwindled to about 4,000. In 1924 the government sold off the rest of the herd and opened the reservation to grazing by white lessees, who only had to pay ten cents per acre, half as much as on surrounding grassland. Once again ground into poverty, the Northern Cheyennes agreed to accept allotment in severalty.

Supposedly, the land allotted to individual Cheyennes would belong to them in perpetuity, and be inalienable and tax-free permanently. The land was "in trust," its status guaranteed by the federal government. But by 1902 all Southern Cheyenne surplus land had been sold, and the value of the land in trust had risen to $12 an acre, 1,200 percent of the price the Cheyennes had received for it 11 years earlier. There was enormous pressure to make the remaining trust land available to whites, and so the Dead Indian Act was passed. By this act, the land of original allottees could be sold when they died, with the legal heirs receiving the proceeds. To encourage heirs to sell their land, local whites offered generous credit to them, to be paid off when they sold their land. In addition, by using all kinds of nefarious methods, explained by Berthrong in his book, Southern Cheyennes were prevented from pursuing their own careers as farmers and ranchers. Consequently, by 1910 over 80 percent of the allotted land had been sold, and most of the rest was leased by local whites through the BIA land office, with the Cheyennes receiving annual checks of "grass money."

By 1925, both the Northern and Southern Cheyennes, despite their best efforts, had been forced by the collusion of local interests and the BIA into a situation of perpetual, grinding poverty. In this regard, as Berthrong has explained, it is important to note that the private operators – ranchers and bankers – and the government agents were frequently the same people, as many local whites went through the revolving door between private business and federal employment. Among the worst was Agent John Miles, who enriched himself with cattle intended for the Cheyennes and money paid by grass lessees to begin his own profitable cattle operation after allotment in severalty. More numerous, however, were the many ranchers who negotiated "sweetheart deals" with the BIA, gaining access to Cheyenne land for less than half of what they would have paid on the free market, either in leases or by outright sale of reservation land.

11

Late Reservation Life

By 1930 it had become apparent to government planners that Plains Indians were not becoming extinct, that in fact their population had begun to increase, and that plans had to be made to organize the reservations on some permanent basis. By this time, allotment in severalty, the Dead Indian Act, and other legislation designed to transfer Indian land to whites had run their course, and Plains Indians had very little land remaining to them, mostly not of agricultural quality. Also, political forces friendly to Indians had become influential in Congress, largely because of the conditions of Indian health and education exposed by the Meriam Report of 1928. Then, too, the New Deal was brewing with the election of Roosevelt in 1932, making some kind of "new deal" for Indian people nearly a certainty.

The new deal for Indians was in the form of the Wheeler–Howard Act, better known as the Indian Reorganization Act (IRA), passed in 1934, followed soon after by the supplemental Oklahoma Indian Welfare Act in 1936. These acts called a halt to the sale of Indian trust land and, more than that, provided money to buy back land for landless Indians. In addition, the acts contained guarantees of religious freedom for Indians, allowed them to set up their own reservation governments, and made credit available from a federal revolving fund for tribal investments. The architect of the acts, and the man who would administer them, was John Collier, a reformer for Indian causes who was appointed head of the BIA in 1934 (see Philp 1977).

After a half-century of neglect, abuse, chicanery, and deception, the Cheyennes in 1936 frankly did not believe that the government had any intentions other than to continue to defraud them as it had in the past. Like many Indian tribes, they simply ignored the legislation, thinking it was some new trick to get their land. It required a trip by John Collier himself to visit the Cheyennes before they would consent to be organized by the provisions of the act. And so, in 1936 the Northern Cheyennes organized a tribal government, and in 1937 the Southern Cheyennes and Southern Arapahoes (known collectively as the "C and As") did likewise.

The IRA allowed some latitude in tribal organization, and the Northern and Southern Cheyennes ended up with tribal governments which were and are somewhat different. The northerners formed a "tribal council" to which representatives were elected from districts. The southerners were forced to organize a government with the Arapahoes in which each group had equal representation of 14 members on a "business committee," even though there were more Cheyennes than Arapahoes in the population. In Oklahoma, Cheyennes and Arapahoes vote separately for their representatives.

The Northern Cheyennes then moved quickly to use federal money to buy back "surplus" reservation land which had been sold beginning in 1932. In 1937 only half the reservation had been alienated and by 1990, after over 50 years of small purchases, the tribe had bought back nearly the entire reservation (see Waist 1977; Campbell 1994). In Oklahoma the situation was different. Reservation land had been sold much earlier, and white people had attained so much political power in the local, state, and federal governments that it proved impossible to get much back. However, the C and A government has managed to buy back several hundred acres of land and put it in trust in the name of the two affiliated tribes.

Friction between Cheyennes and Arapahoes has continued to characterize events in the Oklahoma tribal government, with regular name-calling at the business committee meetings and even occasional hair-pulling and fist-fights. The wiser leaders among both groups periodically call for the separation of the two tribes, a prospect that becomes less likely each year with continued intermarriage between the two, and an increasing number of persons with ancestry in both tribes. Also, there is continual friction between the officially-elected business committee and the Cheyenne traditionalists. These constitute the opposing political poles of reservation politics. Often the traditionalists, led by the chiefs and ceremonial priests, are able to effectively veto the actions of the committee, simply by instructing their kinfolk not to cooperate.

Another issue between officials of the tribal government and the rest of the people is the high salaries paid to those Indian people who work either for the tribal government or the BIA. Although the salaries are modest by government standards, by reservation standards a salary of $30,000 a year is a fortune, about three times the income of an average family. Consequently there is a lot of jealousy and criticism of tribal and government employees who seem to be living better than everyone else.

The creation of the tribal governments did not mean that the BIA went out of business. To the contrary, it received greater funding after the IRA was passed than before. But the general intention of Congress was to gradually transfer money and responsibility for services to the tribal governments, and allow the BIA to wither away. In fact this has not happened. In addition to continuing many of its traditional functions in administering land and overseeing the implementation of legislation concerning Indian people, the BIA has also adopted an oversight function for the tribal governments, actually giving it more to do. For the Cheyennes in particular, we find two tribal governments in parallel with two local BIA field offices, and in fact duplicating many functions. Some of these functions have been centralized, however, to the BIA office in Anadarko for the Southern Cheyennes and to the Billings office in Montana. This has caused the BIA field offices on the reservations to become gradually smaller in the last half-century, although the BIA has become larger and more centralized.

Government-Funded Projects

Despite all kinds of political problems, both the Northern and Southern Cheyennes, working through their tribal governments, have managed to put together an impressive list of tribal projects, beginning with the New Deal and continuing through Lyndon Johnson's War on Poverty, up to modern bingo and other gaming. All of these projects have employed significant numbers of Cheyennes, and most have brought much-needed social services to the resident population. In many cases, the programs began under BIA management and then were transferred to the tribal governments. The more important and interesting programs and projects are listed below.

The Johnson-O'Malley Act

Under this act, passed in 1934, public schools receive per capita money for their Indian students. With additional money provided by other legislation in 1972 and 1978, Cheyenne children have been gradually integrated into the public school system in Oklahoma, where there are no longer any reservation schools run exclusively for the Cheyenne and Arapaho children. This is not necessarily a good thing, however, since there are continual struggles to include Cheyenne history and culture in the public school curriculum. In the late 1960s, frustrated Cheyenne parents started their own Freedom School in Hammon, Oklahoma, using their own resources. The school lasted about four years.

In Montana, where the vast majority of students on the reservation are Cheyennes, schools have been maintained for kindergarten, elementary, and middle-school students since 1936 (plate 11.1). There are now six schools on the reservation. High-school students, however, must be bussed to attend school at Hardin, Colstrip, or the St Labre High School in Ashland. At Hardin and Colstrip, but not at St Labre, there is a continual struggle to include information on the Cheyennes in the high-school curriculum (see plate 11.2)

With federal assistance, the Northern Cheyennes have organized their own institution of higher learning. Dull Knife Memorial College was chartered in 1975 and offers several academic and vocational degree tracks, a library (see plate 11.3), and placement services.

Plate 11.1 *A class in Cheyenne language on the Northern Cheyenne Reservation (photo by Ken Blackbird)*

Health care

From the beginning of reservation life, the federal government has had legal responsibility for the health of Indian people, because of various treaties, agreements, and legislation passed by Congress. During the early reservation period, the BIA did not take these responsibilities very seriously, and provided inadequate and often inappropriate health care to the Cheyennes in Montana and Oklahoma. The few doctors who were present complained that there was very little they could do because of the rampant malnutrition and unsanitary living conditions.

In 1955, however, the Indian Health Service (IHS) was transferred out of the BIA and conditions began to improve. At present, the IHS maintains a health center in Lame Deer, Montana, and a hospital in Clinton, Oklahoma. In addition, two

Plate 11.2 The Busby school in Montana with family houses in the foreground (photo by Ken Blackbird)

Plate 11.3 The library at Dull Knife Memorial College (photo by Ken Blackbird)

clinics are maintained on the Oklahoma Reservation in Concho and Watonga. Enrolled Cheyennes can receive treatment at these facilities free of charge. The treatment however, although free, is often inconvenient and tied up in bureaucracy to the extent that Indian people use it only as a last resort. To obtain some kinds of treatment or medication, for example, Oklahoma Cheyennes must travel to other clinics or hospitals around the state, perhaps hundreds of miles away. Any Cheyenne with money or health insurance, then, prefers to use private doctors. Consequently, this has caused a progressive disuse of IHS facilities in the last two decades. Ironically, in a special report issued in 1990, the IHS concluded erroneously from its statistics that the progressive disuse of IHS facilities meant that Indian health was improving.

Two particular diseases which have hit the Cheyennes harder than the general population are alcoholism and diabetes. Both are difficult diseases to treat because they apparently have both a genetic and a behavioral component. Disentangling these and finding proper treatments has been a very difficult problem for health researchers and IHS physicians and nurses. For alcoholism, the most effective treatment has proved to be encouragement to attend the Native American Church, in a program designed by health researcher and adopted Cheyenne Bernard Albaugh.

Housing

Another legal obligation imposed on the BIA by Congress was to maintain Indian people in proper housing, but as with health care, the money supplied to the BIA was not adequate to meet its obligations. During the early reservation period in Oklahoma, therefore, Cheyennes continued to live in tipis. After allotment in severalty, some houses were built of logs and sawn timber on the remaining allotments, but tipis and tents remained the major form of housing (plate 11.4). Typically, a log house on the Oklahoma Reservation in the late 1930s would be surrounded by several tents and tipis, plus one or more brush arbors for cooking and summer sleeping. In winter, the whole extended family moved into the house. This was the typical housing arrangement for most Southern Cheyennes until money was made available under the IRA to build houses

Plate 11.4   A standard rough-lumber Cheyenne house in Oklahoma in 1900 (Campbell Collection, Western History Collections, University of Oklahoma)

Much of the area of the Northern Cheyenne Reservation is forested, and soon after their reservation was established, a sawmill was built where the people could get lumber for building free of charge. In this period a large number of small log houses were built, which were necessary for the cold winters of Montana. These houses, with their small wood stoves, contributed to the rampant trachoma and tuberculosis infections on the reservation in the early period.

The events of the New Deal and World War II caused many Cheyennes to live in better housing. For example, a large number of Cheyennes participated in projects organized by the Civilian Conservation Corps (CCC) and the Works Projects Administration (WPA). The CCC camps often maintained large dormitories for workers, while the WPA, based in small towns on and around the reservations, often rented regular houses and hotels for its workers. In addition, many Cheyennes lived in standard housing while they worked in war industries in Dallas, Tulsa, Seattle, and Los Angeles. When Cheyennes returned to the reservations after the war, then, many of them with money in their pockets, they undertook to build or buy larger wood houses, both in the rural areas and, increasingly, in town. In Montana, housing continued to be constructed of local logs and lumber, but in Oklahoma many Cheyennes built medium-sized frame houses identical to those of surrounding white people. One Southern Cheyenne community, however, in Hammon, Oklahoma, did not move from tents and tipis until they received payment from a treaty claim in 1968, enabling them to move to town from the area they called West Camp. They may have been the last of the "tipi Indians" anywhere in the United States or Canada.

Beginning in the 1960s, the BIA and tribal governments have organized various kinds of "self-help" programs to create Indian housing. Usually the program requires that a house will be built to one of several standard plans, often for small, frame houses, some of them brick-faced, with a contractor providing the materials and supervision, and the family who will live in the house providing most of the labor (plates 11.2 and 11.5). The house is not free, however. Government funds are used to pay the contractor, and the family must make monthly mortgage payments to the government. Under these kinds of programs, 939 houses have been built in Montana, and 830 for the Southern Cheyennes and Arapahoes in Oklahoma. In fact, most Cheyennes on the reservations now live in this kind of house.

The quality of housing provided by the self-help programs has been a continual source of friction among Cheyennes and with the federal government. Because many of the houses were built in rural areas, they had bathrooms but no sewage system or running water. Consequently many families had to augment their new brick home with an outhouse. In addition, there have been regular accusations that contractors substituted low-quality materials for standard materials, increasing their profits but causing the houses to deteriorate prematurely.

The Economic Opportunity Act (the War on Poverty)

Assisted by the Association on American Indian Affairs and other sympathetic non-profit organizations, the Northern and Southern Cheyennes immediately applied for and began to receive, about 1965, the full panoply of social action and

Plate 11.5 Two self-help houses near Canton, Oklahoma (photo by author)

community service programs, including Head Start, Legal Aid Services, Community Health Program, Job Corps, Neighborhood Youth Corps, and Upward Bound. Later projects were added as they were funded by Congress, including the Community Action Program and New Careers. Originally channeled through the BIA, such programs are now received directly by the tribal governments. Another improvement in administration was achieved when the money was received in the form of block grants, giving the tribal governments more flexibility in planning and shifting money from one program to another.

The armed forces have also provided significant employment for Cheyennes. In part because of their warrior tradition, young Cheyenne men have often been attracted to a military life, especially in the US Army and the Marine Corps. The second generation of leadership in the tribal governments, following World War II, were often veterans of military service, who had learned about government organization, paperwork, and bureaucracy during their stint in the Army. With the advent of the all-volunteer force in recent years, many Cheyennes have been motivated to finish high school by their desire to enter the Army. At present, many young Cheyenne women as well as men enter the armed forces every year. Many Cheyennes have become career soldiers, retiring to the reservation with a small pension after 20 or 30 years.

The Private Sector

Although government jobs have supplied a core of permanent employment for Cheyenne people, wage work in the private sector has often been of equal or greater importance, although it has been unstable. For Southern Cheyennes, it was easy to find daily wage work in western Oklahoma when wheat farming began to boom about 1915, and regular seasonal employment was available from then until about 1970, when the various operations of the wheat harvest became almost totally mechanized and were accomplished largely by out-of-state combine crews, who annually sweep the Great Plains from Texas to Alberta from May to August. Ironically, during the period of intensive agricultural wage work in Oklahoma, many Cheyenne men worked on land that had formerly belonged to an ancestor, and in some cases on land which they partially owned as heirs of the original allottee. Even now, an unofficial agreement to employ heirs as wage workers is part of many leasing agreements for pasture or farm land (see Littlefield & Knack 1996).

In Montana, wage work on farms and ranches was more difficult to find because the people were more distant from the intensive agricultural areas, and there was no paved road through the reservation until 1954. In recent decades, however, significant employment on or near the reservation has been provided not only by ranchers and hay farmers, but also by the Montana Power Company, Betchel Power Company, Western Energy Company, and Marin Financial Corporation. In western Oklahoma, there has been very little employment for anyone – Indian, white, or black – since the 1960s. Consequently, young Cheyennes have moved to the cities of Tulsa, Oklahoma City, Dallas, Chicago, and Los Angeles to find work.

Over the years, a significant number of Cheyenne women have found employment making moccasins and other beadwork for the tourist trade. In Oklahoma, the market for these products began with the sleek passenger trains of the Santa Fe Railroad after World War I, which made stops at El Reno and Clinton, where there were souvenir shops at the train stations. In addition, US Highway 66 (the fabled "Route 66" of song and story) passes through the reservation, and there were craft shops along the road as it became a popular motoring route after World War II. With the building of the interstate highway system, these craft shops have shifted away from Highway 66 to Interstate 40, where about $200,000 in Cheyenne craftwork is sold every year. In Montana, the Northern Cheyennes operate their own craft shop on the reservation.

For nearly all their wage work, the Cheyennes have been paid less than the minimum wages established by federal law in the last 40 years. When working on farms and ranches, Cheyenne men are paid by the day. At present, they receive about $20 or $30 a day, which is about half the minimum wage. The prices paid to Cheyenne moccasin makers reflect an hourly wage of only about a dollar an hour. But Cheyenne people are forced to work for these low wages because they have no other options, unless they travel away from their families to Oklahoma City or Dallas. But to do so takes them away from the free health clinics, subsidized housing, and other benefits which many families desperately need. Consequently many Cheyennes, despite their poverty, feel that they must stay in place on the reservation.

Leasing and Energy

"Grass leases," which result from the leasing to non-Indians of pasture and farm land held in trust, has gone on since early reservation days. Presently, the BIA in Oklahoma administers leases on about 50,000 acres of Cheyenne and Arapaho land, which produce nearly a million dollars a year in income. The book-keeping on these leases is very complicated. After four or five generations, some parcels have as many as 200 owners, or "heirs," each of whom must receive part of the lease money. In some cases, a Cheyenne might receive a check for as little as $2, as a share of the grass lease. Someone who is the sole owner of an original allotment, however, might receive as much as $3,000.

Ironically, it is heirship which has protected Southern Cheyenne trust land from being sold. Any sale of land requires the signature of all the owners, who might be hard to find. With much land protected by this means from immediate sale, the tribal government has created long-term plans for buying all such trust land and keeping it under tribal control.

In Oklahoma, some Cheyennes also own rights to oil and natural gas, either on land they own outright, or for which they do not own the "surface rights" but only the sub-surface mineral rights. Here, again, Cheyennes are not trusted to run their own affairs, and the lease payments are administered by the BIA. In the case of oil and gas, the payments vary wildly from year to year, depending on the petroleum market, and depending on whether oil has been struck on a particular parcel of land. During one oil boom year, 1980, about $2 million were paid to Cheyennes in the form of drilling fees, production shares, and "adjustments" due to changes in prices. The amount paid to individuals varied, however, from a few hundred dollars to tens of thousands.

One of the most dramatic situations in recent Cheyenne history concerns the rights to mine sub-surface coal on the Northern Cheyenne Reservation. When coal resources were first fully assessed in 1972, it turned out that a seam of soft coal underlay nearly the whole reservation, an estimated total of 5.2 billion tons.[1] This coal was close enough to the surface to be strip-mined, a process by which the surface soil is removed and the coal extracted by enormous shovels and draglines. After evaluating the alternatives, the tribal council in 1980 signed a lease agreement with Atlantic Richfield Co. which promised an immediate "bonus" of $6 million to be paid to the tribal membership. Some individual owners of trust land, however, concerned about the effects of strip-mining and deterioration of air quality, and wanting to negotiate their own leases, went to court to prevent implementation of the tribal lease.

The drama of the situation was that if the lease were approved, about 5,000 impoverished Cheyenne people would receive immediate relief in the form of the bonus, continued payments for coal that was removed, and employment. But the price they would pay was the destruction of nearly the entire reservation area, and the pollution of the air. The two alternatives were poignantly expressed by my friend Ted Rising Sun, who has opposed any development of the coal resources: "I would rather be poor in my own country, with my own people, with our own way of life than be rich in a torn-up land where I am outnumbered ten to one by strangers" (quoted in Ambler 1900: 90).

After a long, emotional, and hard-fought battle, the Northern Cheyennes decided to remain poor rather than submit to the destruction of their land. They did arrange, however, to modify their standards of air quality in exchange for preference in employment on some off-reservation mining operations, which has improved the economy and standard of living to some extent.

Because they are near to some populous cities, the Southern Cheyennes have been able to profit from bingo and smoke shops, catering to people driving in or being bussed in from Oklahoma City, Lubbock, Amarillo, or Dallas. The various gambling operations of the Southern Cheyennes and Arapahoes presently gross about $6 million, and the smoke shops, where tax-free tobacco products are sold, produce another million dollars a year. Because of their distance from large cities, the Northern Cheyennes have not been able to profit from such activities.

Treaty Claims

In seizing Cheyenne lands in the 19th century, the federal government frequently acted hastily and illegally. This resulted in a large number of law suits and potential law suits which were called to the attention of the federal government after the passage of the IRA. Seeking to minimize the damage from the law suits, the federal government in 1944 set up the Indian Claims Commission (ICC), which was empowered to hear all claims resulting from broken treaties, mismanagement, or in fact any claim at all (see Sutton 1985).

By this time, Indian people had become convinced of the sincerity of the New Deal and the IRA, and the immediate response of the Cheyennes to the founding of the ICC was very hopeful. Many felt that finally they would get some justice for all the land taken from them, which had been guaranteed by treaty. And, in fact, acting on a claim initiated by the Northern Cheyennes in 1948, the tribal government in Montana was awarded over $4 million in 1963 for "all legal claims against the government." Although the amount of money was not nearly the current value of the land lost, many Northern Cheyennes seemed satisfied with the settlement, and the Southern Cheyennes waited hopefully for the settlement of their own much larger claim. They were going to be disappointed.

Although the calculations of the amount of the claim were very complicated, it essentially involved establishing the value of the land and resources taken illegally *at the time of the treaty*. This included land, gold, timber, etc., and amounted to a fair sum, over $20 million. But from that total, the government then subtracted "offsets," consisting of all the expenses of running the Indian agencies since they were organized, every plank and nail, every blanket and tool, every bean and potato, even the salaries of the Indian agents. The trick is that these disbursements were figured *at the inflated prices of later years, when the purchases were made*. For the Northern Cheyennes, these offsets were a manageable amount, since the reservation had been established later and the population was smaller. But for the Southern Cheyennes and Arapahoes, the book-keeping was devastating. After months of work, the government figured that the Cheyennes and Arapahoes *owed the government* about $2 million. Finding this result "unconscionable," the Indian Claims Commission set the amount of the claim arbitrarily at about $2,000 per person, an amount distributed in 1968 which, according to the government, liquidated all Cheyenne tribal claims against the United States of America.

Another on-going claim of the Northern Cheyennes has been for the Black Hills of South Dakota, which they claim to have owned before the Lakotas, and which they claim to have occupied continually until driven off the Black Hills by the US Army in 1877. Of course the Lakotas in the last several decades have been pursuing a highly visible claim to the Black Hills, coordinated with political demonstrations of various kinds. Until 1980 the Lakotas had always opposed the claims of the Cheyennes, feeling that it interfered with their own claims. In that year, however, the federal government offered a small settlement to the Lakotas, $17.1 million, for the entirety of the Black Hills, which Lakota traditionalists feared the tribal governments might accept. To confound the claim, the Lakotas urged the Cheyennes to file suit for the Black Hills, and the Northern Cheyennes hired me to do the historical research.

After conducting some archival research and sending my student Gregory Campbell to Montana to conduct interviews with elders, a report was sent to the Northern Cheyenne tribal council and to the Lakota traditionalists which contributed to the impasse which still exists concerning payment of the money. The Lakota traditionalists remain firm in asserting that they don't want the money – they want the Black Hills back.

Exempted from the ICC payments to the Southern Cheyennes in 1968 was compensation for the Sand Creek Massacre, which was promised and never paid. From the language of the treaty of 1865, it was concluded by the ICC that this compensation could not be paid to the tribe collectively, but had to be paid to the individuals attacked, or their descendants. Payments for Sand Creek, then, were explicitly excluded from the ICC decision, so that the claim is still alive.

The difficulty in determining claimants for Sand Creek is that, after so many years of intermarriage among the Cheyenne families and with non-Cheyennes, there are about ten thousand claimants spread all over the country. Nonetheless, working with Cheyenne volunteers, my students and I managed to create a list of qualified claimants, which in turn attracted the attention of a major law firm which agreed to pursue the claim for a share of the settlement.

After many people representing different families had worked in harmony on the research for years, the possibility of actually succeeding with the claim unfortunately inflamed their familistic tendencies. Within two years of acquiring lawyers, there were six different Sand Creek descendants' associations, each run by a particular family and each claiming to be the one and only authentic organization to pursue the claim. This situation tended to demoralize the attorneys, who weren't clear about who they were supposed to deal with, and so the claim is still in confusion, with groups of descendants appearing and disappearing every few months.

Civil Rights

Two landmark pieces of civil rights legislation pertaining to the Cheyennes and other Indians were the extension of citizenship to Indians in 1924, and the establishment of their constitutional rights in 1968.[2] In neither case, however, did this legislation automatically remove all illegal and unconstitutional restrictions on Indians. The total burden of illegal policies and restrictions has had to be removed one piece at a time, each piece requiring a law suit. For example, grass and oil lessees still cannot seize control of their own property; it is still administered for them by the land office of the Bureau of Indian Affairs. To prove that they are Indians, people still have to submit to an investigation of the BIA, after which they receive a "Certificate of Degree of Indian Blood," which they must carry around to gain entry to Indian facilities. Indian activists complain that if white people don't have to prove that they're white, why do Indians have to prove that they're Indians? In the Cheyenne case, however, tribal citizenship is now established by tribal enrollment offices, rather than the BIA.

Another civil rights problem concerns the special status of reservation and trust land. While the reservation status of the Northern Cheyenne area has never been in doubt, a myth was generated during allotment in severalty in Oklahoma that all the reservations had been "dissolved." This was only an administrative myth perpetrated by BIA officials, however, since there is no legislation which contains any provision for undoing reservation status. In fact, each piece of legislation drafted in Washington was careful to explicitly preserve reservation status. None the less, the Oklahoma Cheyennes have had to go to court several times to establish the "reservation" status of each parcel of land which the tribe owns or has acquired.

Tied to the issue of reservation land has been the status of trust land, land owned by tribes or by individual allottees and their descendants. The status of trust land has been at issue not only in Montana, where all the trust land is on the reservation, but also in Oklahoma, where most of the trust land, in the form of the remaining allotments, is scattered over a seven-county area. The thorniest problem of trust status is that, since the trust

land is federal, police from state and local governments have no
authority over it. That is, if a crime is committed on trust land,
even a murder, only federal marshals have authority. After years
of confusion about how to deal with law-breakers under these
conditions, a system has been worked out in Oklahoma so that
Indian police, with offices at the tribal complex, have reciprocal
police powers with local police. Not only are local police sworn
in as federal marshals, but Indian police are sworn in as deputy
sheriffs. Still at issue, however, is the question of how much
authority Indian police have over non-Indians on trust and
reservation land, a complex issue presently under litigation all
around the country. For one thing, Northern Cheyenne tribal
police would like to know if they can issue tickets to non-Indians
speeding across the reservation, especially since Montana no
longer has a definite speed limit.

Because of their special legal status, and because of their
geographical location, Cheyenne people live in a situation where
economic laws of supply and demand are severely distorted.
Consequently, the income of Cheyenne families is not only low,
but erratic and unreliable. For most families, income is cobbled
together from wage work, lease money, social services, and
sometimes from tribal jobs that come and go with the political
winds. In recent years, the average per capita income for
Cheyennes both in Montana and in Oklahoma has ranged from
$2,000 to $3,000. This means that a large extended family of
eight to ten people (counted by the government as two to four
nuclear families) has to subsist on a combined family income of
about $25,000 (less than $10,000 per nuclear family), which
puts most Cheyenne families under the poverty line established
by the federal government. To feed themselves, more than 40
percent of Cheyenne families rely on food stamps and government "commodity" foods. Over half of Cheyenne adults who
want to work cannot find work on the reservation.

Only a small portion of family income arrives regularly.
Pensions and welfare checks arrive monthly or bi-weekly. But
grass money is paid once a year, in January or February, and
payments for oil and gas leases arrive at odd times, depending
on drilling schedules, when payments are received from oil
companies to the government, and the book-keeping procedures
of the Bureau of Indian Affairs. Some families complain that
they receive no royalties at all for several years, and then

thousands of dollars all at once. They are unable to borrow money from local banks because of their low income, and very few Cheyennes have bank accounts. When checks arrive, they cash them at local stores where they do business.

Keeping a Perspective

All of this recitation of economic statistics, programs and legislation, law suits and bureaucrats, does little to communicate to non-Indians the nature of the interaction between modern Cheyennes and the local agents and institutions of the dominant society. For the Southern Cheyennes, more than the Northern Cheyennes, each day contains puzzling and confusing episodes in which both whites and Cheyennes are trying to figure each other out – client and social worker, BIA employee and Cheyenne elder, local police and Cheyenne youth. Although they live with and among thousands of white people, Southern Cheyennes march to a different drummer; they hear a different voice advising them how to conduct their daily affairs. When they interact with whites, they maintain a totally different mindset, different motivations, different goals. Not surprisingly, this theme has become a subject of Cheyenne humor.

The following story is recent in origin, and was told by Roy Bull Coming from an actual event that occurred in the mid 1970s. Roy was not only a chief and priest of the Cheyennes, but also one of the most entertaining story-tellers in the Cheyenne Nation. Although he is gone now, his stories have been preserved in the archives of the Oklahoma Historical Society. This was his favorite. Like a Marx Brothers comedy, it describes a building complexity of misunderstandings and bizarre situations between whites and Indians, which are finally resolved when everyone is carried off in custody. To understand the story properly, the reader must know that since aboriginal times Cheyenne people have marked dead animals which they killed or which belonged to them by tying a piece of clothing or some other personal item to the dead animal. This is true even in modern times in Oklahoma, on those occasions when local ranchers donate injured cows to Cheyenne families. That is, if an animal is injured to the point that it is not marketable, the rancher will call some Cheyenne friends to come and get the animal, butcher it, and distribute the meat among themselves. When they come to get the animal, the family will tie a scarf or handkerchief to the foot or horn, to establish a claim. Another way to claim an animal, traditionally, is to count coup on it, to sit on it, or to sit nearby, touching the animal.

The Wreck of the Cattle Truck

Early one Sunday morning in the fall, a few years ago, a big cattle truck from a local ranch, with thirty cattle aboard headed for market in Oklahoma City, missed the curve north of Seiling, Oklahoma, ran off the road, rolled over, and broke apart. It created a tumultuous sight, with the broken wooden trailer, a dazed driver sitting on the shoulder of the road, and with dead and injured cattle lying on the ground and running or limping around on the shoulder of the road, between the highway and a barbed wire fence.

As it happened, three carloads of Cheyenne people from Seiling, all dressed up to attend church in a nearby town, came down the road right after the accident. The men were dressed in "Indian Western" style with cowboy hats, neck scarves, jeans, jackets, belts with big buckles, and cowboy boots. The women wore long dresses, shawls, and lots of beadwork and turquoise jewelry. They were all dressed up.

When they saw the wreck, they stopped their cars and got out to help the driver. It turned out the driver was a local rancher they knew, so they made him comfortable and sent one of the cars to call for an ambulance. When the driver came to his senses, he realized what the situation was, and he kindly told the Cheyennes to help themselves to the dead and injured cattle, since they couldn't be taken to market anyway. So another of the Cheyennes went to town to call all their relatives to come out and help them butcher and haul the cattle. In the meantime, the Cheyennes who were at the wreck site went around among the dead cattle placing their scarves, hats, shawls, belts, and jewelry on the cattle to claim them for their families. They put scarves on the horns, they put hats and hatbands on the heads, and belts around the necks of the cattle. Running out of these items, some men put their boots on the feet of the cows.

Pretty soon the relatives started arriving from town with their cars and pickups, and the ambulance arrived to take the driver to the hospital. About the same time the Sheriff and two deputies drove up, to determine the extent of the injuries at the site. They didn't know what to make of the scene in front of them. They saw a bunch of dead cows decorated with jewelry, scarves, hats and clothing, and they saw some Indian men chasing injured cows around and trying to kill them with axes, hammers, and tire tools. Their pants were falling down because they didn't have any belts. Some had no shoes and others had been kicked and hurt by the injured cows. There was blood everywhere. One man was splattering blood all around by hitting the cows with a big stick, counting coup. They saw Indian women sitting on dead cows, spattered with blood, and over by the fence they saw a man who was laid out on the ground, covered with blood, stretched out between two dead cows. They decided they had a catastrophe on their hands and called out the ambulances from all the surrounding towns.

Soon the ambulances began to arrive and the first man they singled out for attention was the one stretched out between two cows. He seemed conscious but he wouldn't get up. Every time they grabbed him, he flopped back on the ground and stretched out to touch the two cows. Finally he got angry and yelled, "Leave me alone! That's my beef." The ambulance attendants grabbed him again and tried to put him on the stretcher. He resisted. The Sheriff had overheard the conversation from a distance and walked up to help. "Has somebody got a beef?" he asked. "Yeah," the Cheyenne man yelled angrily." The attendants released him. "What's your beef?" asked the Sheriff. "The two little brown ones," said the man, and walked over and flopped back on the ground between the two cows.

Meantime some of the Cheyennes had decided that the Sheriff was trying to prevent them from taking the cows, so instead of butchering the cows on the spot, they frantically began pushing dead cattle into the backs of pickups and even into the seats of cars. Two young heifers were shoved into the back seat of an old Chevrolet sedan. At the same time, the ambulance attendants, from the seven or more ambulances which had arrived from surrounding towns, were looking all around for injured people. Whenever they saw a woman spattered with blood and sitting on a cow, they asked if they were injured. The Indian women, not wanting to appear rude, always said yes and climbed into the ambulance.

Two ambulance attendants walked up to the Chevrolet sedan and looked in the back seat for more victims of the disaster. One said to the other, "You better look for yourself; you're not going to believe it." The other attendant looked inside to see two dead heifers sitting in the seat, one with a hat on and the other with a turquoise belt for a necklace.

About that time one of the injured cows became conscious, jumped up, and started running. Two young Indian men grabbed it around the neck and it began dragging them along the shoulder of the highway. Seeing this, one of the deputies was afraid the cow would injure someone, so he pulled his gun and ran up alongside the cow, shooting it in the heart. The cow dropped, pinning one of the Indian men, who began yelling in Cheyenne. The other man thought the deputy had shot his friend, so he got scared and took off across the highway, running in front of a passing car full of people, which had to go into the ditch to avoid him, bumping everybody's heads and throwing them around in the car. Fortunately for them, there were plenty of ambulances around.

By this time the Sheriff had had enough, so he stood up on the side of the cattle trailer and fired his gun in the air three times. "Everybody listen up," he yelled. "Be quiet and listen. I want you to know that everybody here is either going to the hospital or going with me." When he said that, one of the Indian women who had a cow in her pickup peeled off and headed for home. A deputy jumped in the police car and gave chase, sirens and lights blazing. The driver of the Chevrolet sedan with the two heifers took advantage of the situation and peeled off in the other direction. He was later arrested driving down the main street of Watonga with the two dressed-up heifers in the back seat, but the local police couldn't figure out what to charge him with.

After the vehicles had peeled out, the Sheriff fired his gun in the air again. "All right, I want everybody to form two lines. If you're going to the hospital, line up on my left. Everybody else line up on my right."

And so they lined up as they were told, and the people who went to the hospital had to take their clothes off and were checked all over, and the people who went with the Sheriff were taken to jail and fingerprinted. The people who went home with the beef had plenty to eat, but it took nearly two weeks to get everybody out of jail, and get everything straightened out. After that incident, the families who stopped to claim the cows that day were known as the "Beef Band."

12

Modern Times

To cope with the uncertainties of income described in the last chapter, in which a family might have thousands of dollars in cash one week, and nothing at all for several months, the Cheyenne people have developed a system for the redistribution of resources which takes the highs and lows out of their monthly income. The public manifestation of this system is the "giveaway," a lavish distribution of gifts to perhaps hundreds of people at a time (Moore 1993). The giveaways, however, are only the public and symbolic aspect of a much more intensive system by which food and money are redistributed among families throughout the year.

Although the members of a Cheyenne extended family share among themselves automatically and casually, normally there are several times each year when money or food, or both, run out. At these times, families must call on other families for support. Generally, the family in need makes its request to a family in the same community that has just received one of the modest bonanzas generated by oil and gas leases, land sales, or from the personal income of someone just returned from working in a city or the armed forces.

The request is made quietly and seriously, with a family member visiting the home of another family and explaining the problem. Perhaps food is all gone, or heating oil has been used up, or someone needs to go to the clinic or hospital, or someone needs a ride to the city where employment has been promised. The family being solicited helps as best it can; no request is refused absolutely. Even when families are feuding or angry with one another, a request for assistance is always answered in some manner.

It is the giveaway which enables a family which was in need to say "thank you" in a public manner to the families which have helped them during the year. They do this by calling out the members of these families and giving them beautiful, traditional gifts, usually blankets and shawls. In the same way, they will receive shawls, blankets and other gifts from families they have helped during the year, when they have had food or money to spare. The structure of gift-giving at ceremonial giveaways, then, represents the pattern of real assistance provided in a reciprocal manner among allied or related families, or families in the same community. Although the gifts circulated at giveaways are seldom sold or even used, they have value as symbols, indicating patterns of mutual support among Cheyenne families. The giveaway, as a public event, is connected with a whole spectrum of social, ceremonial activity which includes the local giveaway, the local pow-wow, and even the huge spectacles that are organized mostly for the benefit of thousands of spectators.

The Simple Giveaway and Pow-Wow

Giveaways are required in Cheyenne culture to recognize many different kinds of events – election as chief or tribal official, a funeral, an anniversary, graduation from high school or college, election to a soldier society, or receiving a name, just to mention the most common events. In each case, the recipients of a gift symbolize the legitimacy of the honor, or otherwise demonstrate their solidarity with the giver, simply by attending the giveaway and accepting the gift. Usually, the giveaway is preceded by a "feed," a dinner provided by the sponsors to all who come. There is a great deal of latitude about when a giveaway can be held to recognize a significant event. Usually a family waits until they have some cash on hand, have accumulated the necessary gifts, and can buy the food necessary for the dinner. Most often, a giveaway is held within a year of the event being recognized.

The sponsors of the giveaway are usually the extended family of the honoree, who might be assisted by other extended families to which they are related, or other members of the same soldier society, Chiefs' Society, or church. The sponsors must provide dinner and gifts, usually a blanket for each adult man and a shawl for each woman. At funerals, guests usually receive only a blanket or shawl, but gifts distributed at other kinds of give-aways might include pots and pans, beadwork, sets of dishes, even furniture, horses, and cars. During the height of the oil boom in 1980 a Cheyenne woman, embarrassed by the size of her royalty checks, gave away several pickup trucks to her old friends.

In warm weather, a giveaway is usually held outside. If dinner is served before the distribution of gifts, there is a prayer and then people pass by tables where their plates are served with traditional foods, such as boiled meat, corn soup, and fry bread. Each person in attendance is supposed to bring their own plate, bowl, and silverware to eat with, and a folding chair to sit in. The families in attendance arrange their chairs in the yard in a huge semi-circle, facing the porch, brush arbor, or canvas fly where the sponsors will stand to distribute the gifts. All the chairs and some of the dishes of the participants bear the names of the families they belong to. Some of the chair paintings are quite elaborate, incorporating birds, eagle feathers, or American flags into a name spelled with ornate, stylized lettering. The trend in recent years is for the sponsor to provide paper plates and plastic silverware, so that people don't have to bring their own.

After the meal is finished and cleaned up, the sponsoring family and the honoree, often accompanied by a master of ceremonies, stand in front, facing the crowd. Two aspects of the giveaway which follows are often puzzling to white people. First is the fact that the person being honored receives nothing. He or she is honored when their family or other sponsors distribute gifts to everyone else. This is in contrast to the dominant society's notion of honoring someone, where it is the honoree who receives a trophy, certificate, gold watch, or plaque bearing their name.

Another puzzle to white people, when they attend a giveaway, is that they receive expensive gifts, even if they don't know the honoree. But this is in the tradition of Cheyenne hospitality toward strangers. Guests don't pay for food and they receive elaborate gifts. Sometimes passing tourists who stumble into a giveaway in a public place embarrass everyone by asking, "What's the catch?" There is no catch. They have simply been the object of Cheyenne hospitality.

To receive gifts, people respond when their name is called and walk forward to receive a shawl from a woman sponsor, if the recipient is a woman, or a blanket from a male sponsor to a male recipient. The recipient then has the honor of shaking hands with the sponsors, the honoree, and perhaps with the master of ceremonies. When everyone has received a gift, the simple giveaway ends with another prayer.

In cold weather giveaways are held indoors, in "community houses" built for such purposes, in the facilities of a non-Indian local service organization such as the Elks Club or American Legion, in a school gymnasium, in a National Guard armory, or increasingly in "multi-purpose centers" built in the last decade with federal and tribal money.

Giveaways which are part of more festive occasions, such as graduations as opposed to funerals, often incorporate Cheyenne singers and their pow-wow drum, which is positioned in the center of the arena or open area, and they invite costumed pow-wow dancers to perform around the drum. Figure 12.1 shows how an indoor pow-wow is arranged. The addition of a drum makes the event, more properly, a pow-wow (plate 12.1). One or more giveaways can be incorporated into the pow-wow, usually one after dinner, and another after the gourd dancers are finished. Typically, at a small local pow-wow, there might be eight to ten gourd dancers and the same number of war, straight, or fancy dancers (plate 12.2). In addition, everyone in attendance is invited to join in round dances and other social dances, which don't require any special paraphernalia except perhaps a shawl for a woman. The pow-wow might be co-sponsored by a combination of several extended families, a Gourd Dance group, and perhaps a military society, each of which might honor one of their members with a giveaway. The typical order of events might be:

Opening prayer
Dinner
Giveaway
Gourd dancing
Giveaway
Social dancing

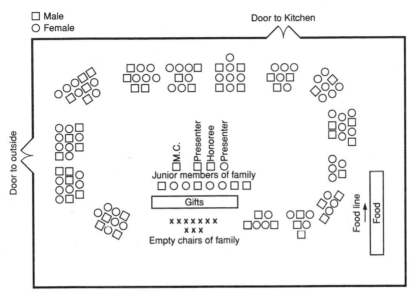

Figure 12.1   Arrangement of an indoor pow-wow (from Moore 1993: 246)

Giveaway
Costumed dancing
Closing prayer

Another way of honoring a person, besides a giveaway, is to sponsor a "special" during a pow-wow. For a special, the singers are asked to sing an appropriate song, and the honoree puts on a shawl or blanket and lines up with sponsors as the first row of a group of dancers. When the song begins, the family and supporters of the honoree travel slowly clockwise around the drum while other people in attendance place money in a hat carried in front and then join the procession. The honoree does not keep the money, of course, but usually gives it to the singers, to an elder, or to some costumed princess or uniformed soldier in attendance at the pow-wow.

While there is usually no publicity for a simple giveaway, except word of mouth, pow-wows are often advertised by flyers and in local and tribal newspapers, listing the names of the sponsors. If the pow-wow is being used as a fund raiser, door prizes and auction prizes are announced in advance. A typical flyer is shown in plate 12.3. Special language is used in the flyers

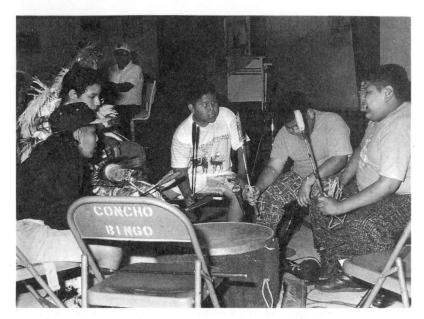

Plate 12.1   A group of young aspiring singers, the Polar Bears, make their appearance at a local pow-wow (photo by Darrell Rice of the Watonga Republican)

to indicate what kind of pow-wow it will be, and who will participate. BYODC means "bring your own dishes and chairs." To attract a wide participation, members of large extended families beyond the sponsoring family are selected for special roles as pow-wow dancers. HMD is the "head man dancer" and HLD is the "head lady dancer." They are supposed to dress up and be the first to dance for each song. Otherwise, no one will get up to dance, since Cheyenne values and etiquette dictate that no one should want to be first.

As larger and larger pow-wows are organized, the special roles and offices can become very elaborate, and can include any or all of the following:

MC   Master of Ceremonies – announces all events and keeps the program moving.
AD   Arena Director – makes sure that all participants get into and out of the arena on time.
HD   Head Drummer – the leader of the singers, responsible for making sure that enough singers show up, and that a drum is ready for use.

Plate 12.2   Fancy war dancers perform at a local pow-wow (photo by Darrell Rice of the Watonga Republican)

HGD   Head Gourd Dancer – ensures participation of one or more Gourd Dance groups.

HSD   Head Straight Dancer – leads those dancers who dress in conservative tribal regalia.

HLBD   Head Lady Buck-skin Dancer – leads women who dance in traditional fringed buck-skin dresses.

HWD   Head War Dancer – leads war dancers who perform with knives, axes, and coup sticks.

HLCD   Head Lady Cloth Dancer – leads women who dance in cloth rather than buck-skin dresses, carrying a shawl.

HFD   Head Fancy Dancer – usually a young man who solicits other fancy dancers to attend from surrounding areas.

HNLD   Head Northern Lady Dancer – leads young women who dance in a Northern Cheyenne style, twirling around with very active steps.

WB   Water Boy – makes sure that singers and dancers have water to drink.

While pow-wows of all sizes occur during the year in Montana and Oklahoma, there are some qualitative differences between

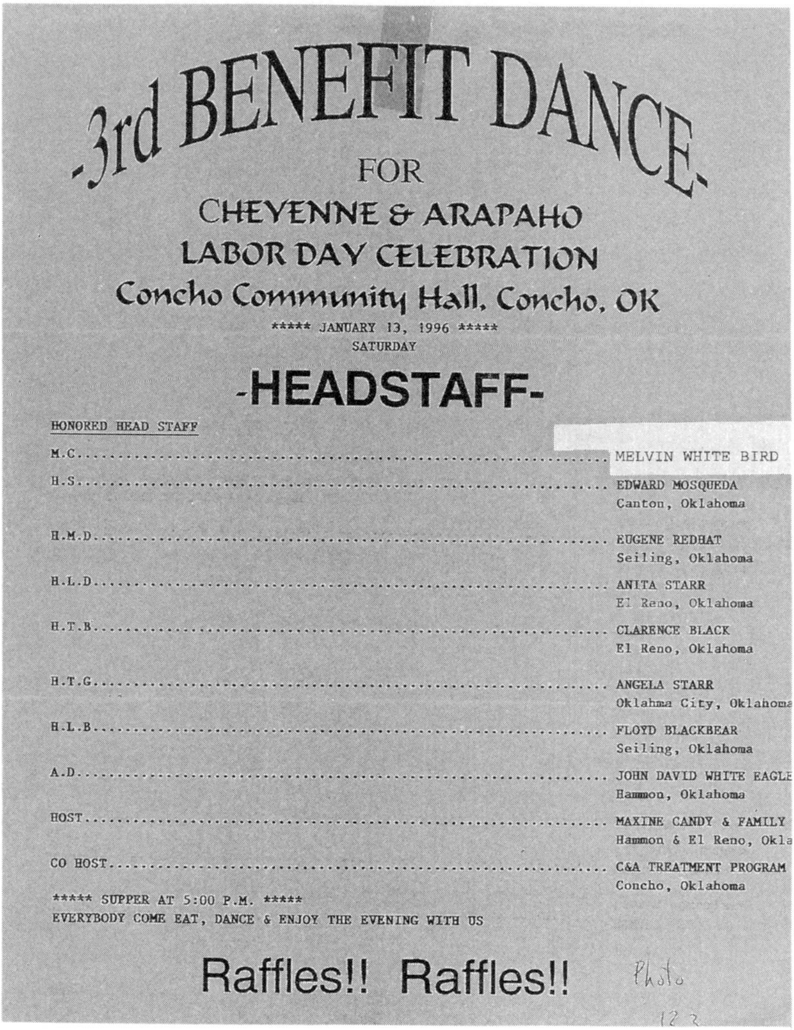

Plate 12.3   A flyer advertising a recent Southern Cheyenne pow-wow

those pow-wows which are community affairs, mostly for residents of the community and their friends, and the pow-wows which are truly commercial.[1] The differences are that the commercial pow-wows charge admission, don't serve dinner, and offer substantial prize money to costumed dancers. To offer prize money, pow-wow organizers will solicit sponsors such as local businesses, a college or university, or a tribal government.

The biggest current pow-wow is the Red Earth Pow-Wow, held each summer in Oklahoma City, which regularly features ten or more drums in the arena at the same time, and hundreds of competitive dancers who perform over several days for prize money in the thousands of dollars. In these days, it is possible for the very best dancers and singers to support themselves and their families entirely on earnings from "the pow-wow circuit" which comprises reservations and major cities all across the plains. As one celebrated Cheyenne fancy dancer put it to me, "It beats working."

The program for these huge commercial pow-wows can be very long and elaborate. It includes at least the following elements:

Gourd dancing all afternoon of opening day
A procession of all the dancers to officially open the pow-wow
An invocation
Raising the flag and flag song
Round dances and other social dances
Straight dancers
Cloth dancers
War dancers
Buck-skin dancers
Fancy dancers
Northern lady dancers
Other dancers
Closing ceremony and prayer

At the larger pow-wows, giveaways and specials are discouraged, and they are non-existent at the big commercial pow-wows. While a giveaway may be the high point of a local pow-wow, the dancing is the attraction at the big pow-wows. The dancers have to pay entry fees, and everyone has to pay admission.

But still, all things considered, and especially in terms of attendance, the small pow-wows are much more important than the commercial pow-wows. First of all, there are more of them. Each year in Oklahoma, for example, there are only six large commercial pow-wows, while there are over 500 local pow-wows advertised in newspapers, on the radio, and by flyers. Estimated attendance at local pow-wows is about 100,000 people per year, although many participants attend a score or more different pow-wows. Attendance at commercial pow-wows is about the same, but largely consists of tourists and other white people. Of all the local pow-wows performed in Oklahoma each year, about half are organized by Cheyennes and Arapahoes.

The social agendas for the two types of pow-wow are quite different. At the local pow-wows, one celebrates familism, family alliances and friendships, community and tribal values. Most people at a local Cheyenne pow-wow know all the other people. The commercial pow-wows, although they comprise many of the same people, participating as singers and dancers, are pan-tribal, impersonal, and pecuniary. It is interesting that a group of Cheyenne dancers might dance at a local pow-wow one week, in honor of a community elder, for which they receive free dinner and no money, and then dance the next week at a commercial pow-wow for which they must pay an entry fee, wear a number for identification to strangers, and compete for money (plate 12.4). It is a tribute to Cheyenne flexibility and their adaptation to a foreign culture that they can successfully participate in pow-wows which exhibit such entirely different values, and exist in such entirely different surroundings.

Everyday Life

If one only knew about Cheyennes from attending pow-wows or seeing movies about them, one might not know what to expect when visiting them at home. In their daily life, Cheyenne people do not wear pow-wow clothes, and do not spend most of their time talking about their history and ceremonies. They also have a practical, domestic existence, just like everybody else. Having visited scores of Cheyenne families in Montana and Oklahoma, on hundreds of occasions, let me try to describe, as best I can, what it looks like and what it feels like for an Anglo-American to visit a traditional, rural, reservation family of Cheyennes in modern times. Let us suppose that you have met a Cheyenne adult while working together on some useful project. Since you expressed an interest in Cheyenne culture, you are invited home.

Rural Cheyennes frequently live off the beaten path and most don't have telephones. To visit Joe Antelope, the former arrow

Plate 12.4 Numbered lady cloth dancers at the Blue Sky Pow-Wow south of Geary, Oklahoma, in 1992 (photo by Darrell Rice of the Watonga Republican)

keeper, for example, you had to drive through two pasture gates and wind around a forested riverbank to find his house. The roads to Cheyenne houses are frequently unpaved and ungravelled, neglected by county officials because Cheyennes don't pay taxes, or so the officials say. The residence area, when you find it, most often includes one or more self-help houses, with perhaps an older frame house nearby. In addition, there might be tipis or tents in use, especially in the summer, and perhaps a trailer or two, as shown in figure 9.3 (page 26). There will be a flock of kids playing around in the common area in front of the houses, and one kid, as soon as they see you, will no doubt run to tell an adult that a visitor has arrived.

In rural areas, it is polite to sit in the car for a while after arrival, so that your hosts can get dressed, put things away, or otherwise get ready for a visit. And then, typically, the man of the house will come and greet you, while the children gather around. He will be followed by other adults, and will introduce each one. From each you will get a Cheyenne handshake, a soft folded hand that shakes just once. After an initial smiled greeting, everyone will be careful not to stare at you, only glancing occasionally at you while you are talking.

During the day, if it's warm, you will sit outside, but the chairs will not be arranged in a circle or facing one another, since that would invite rude stares, but rather side by side or eccentrically, so that no one is embarrassed. A young woman brings coffee from the kitchen. The conversation is light-hearted, and jokes are made about the condition of the road, or the distance from town, or getting lost. The guest admires the scenery, and the family talks about how long they have lived there, and who the original allottee might have been. After talking a while, some of the women will go to the kitchen and you hear pots and pans clanking, and soon wonderful aromas are floating out the kitchen windows.

In a corner of the yard, several young men are working on a car. Cheyennes spend a lot of time working on cars, and there are usually three or four cars in the yard, and only one or two in working condition. Some cars have bedding in them, where people have been sleeping. Young men come and go during the afternoon, borrowing car parts and tools, trying to get a car in shape before someone has to go to work, or go to the clinic.

Sticking up behind a house you can see the tips of a set of tipi poles, and in the carport you see tents, tipis, and other camping equipment used during big summer pow-wows and the annual ceremonies. You might also see in the garage or carport some of the sacred paraphernalia from a recent Sun Dance – a fire spoon, a bunch of sage, or a willow crown, kept in the open to bless the family as they go about their daily business.

Various paths lead into the nearby woods. Some of them have buffalo or cow skulls next to them, to show that one shouldn't go down these paths because they lead to medicine bundles or other sacred objects kept in the woods. Other paths lead to gardens, a toilet area, or a swimming hole.

When at their leisure, Cheyenne people like to share clippings from newspapers and magazines which reflect and reinforce their own notions of the way the world is, and what the world is becoming. A clipping might be passed which reports that a sheep rancher in Wyoming, hunting eagles from a helicopter, was killed when an eagle dived into the rotor blades, causing the helicopter to crash. People read the clipping and comment "Ah-ho" for their brother the eagle. Another clipping reports that a cougar has been seen in western Oklahoma, the first in many years. The people are glad and say they hope they see one. I pass around my photo of a buffalo encountered unexpectantly on a country road, and people wonder which cave it came from. Reports of pollution, nuclear radiation leaks, and new diseases are passed around, supporting Cheyenne prophecy that white people will someday kill themselves with their own selfishness, waste, and technology.

Dinner is called and you discover that the men and guests eat first, served and surrounded by the women of the family, who eat next, while the children eat last. The food is the best in the house, whether it's venison or baloney. The tastiest meal I ever ate in a Cheyenne house was buffalo hump with garden vegetables; the simplest was boiled macaroni with nothing on it. But in both cases, it was the best they had to offer.

There are cultural juxtapositions in Cheyenne life which seem strange to outsiders. In one room several members of the family are planning their participation in the Sun Dance. In the next room children are watching *The Flintstones* on television. In the driveway, children are trying to rollerblade, overseen by a buffalo skull peering from the garage. There is a picture of Jesus on the wall, in a frame with a beaded felt border. On a table is a bouquet in a vase, but the bouquet is not flowers, it is the colorful feathers of eagles, hawks, and macaws.

If you are spending the night, you are first offered sole occupancy of the best bed. But you decline, saying you don't like to sleep by yourself. Two young children say they'll sleep with you. So you go to bed with two children, and you wake up with five. The bed is full of knees and elbows. People get up and down all night. Someone awakes and has a smoke and disturbs someone else, who awakes and has a smoke. A relative arrives about 2 a.m. from a distant city; they couldn't get a ride until late.

People get up slowly, and when everyone is up, the women make a big breakfast. All the adults from all the houses come to eat. They plan their day, who's going to work, who's going to the tribal office, social service office, or clinic, who's staying home with the children. One woman says she has some cheese and baloney and apples, and will make lunch for everyone.

People disperse for the day, collecting together again for the evening meal.

Gossip and Trauma

After you have known a family for a while, they will begin to gossip about other families, gently at first, and you come to understand which families are friendly and supportive of one another, and which are not. Hearing and participating in the gossip almost makes you a member of the family, and makes it difficult to get to know other families. The guest is under pressure to accept the perspective of the hosts, and to disbelieve what others are saying about the host family. In my case, I always refuse to gossip and in fact often interject kind and positive remarks about the people being criticized. Consequently I am not intimate with any family, but generally tolerated by all the families.

At any one time, there is usually at least one big traumatic issue under constant discussion. Usually the issue is with the tribal government or the BIA – the royalty checks didn't come, some policy has been changed, or some tribal official stole some money, the school is being closed or a source of income has dried up. Official Indian affairs are such that one never lacks traumas which have to be resolved; there always seems to be a bureaucrat somewhere who is making a policy which will have a dramatic effect on the daily life of Cheyenne people. Lest the reader think I exaggerate, let me narrate here just one trauma which appeared out of nowhere in 1985.

Beginning in 1975, self-help or mutual-help houses were built on the Oklahoma reservation on trust land owned by the tribe or by individuals. The houses were built to standard designs, some larger than others, and were appraised at between $10,000 and $16,000 upon completion between 1975 and 1982. They carried mortgages of $50–100 per month and were administered by a Housing Authority (HA) created jointly by the BIA, the federal agency called HUD (Housing and Urban Development), and the tribal government.[2]

The first houses built were constructed by a company that

promptly went out of business, leaving the occupants complaining about walls that collapsed into the yard, doors that fell off the hinges, and plumbing and heating that didn't work. In protest, some Cheyenne and Arapaho families stopped paying their mortgages. In retaliation, the HA refused to inspect the houses it had built, and refused to repair them. In 1981 the oil boom ended, and was followed by an economic depression in western Oklahoma, so that Cheyenne and Arapaho unemployment rose to above 80 percent and many families were desperate. Additional mortgagees stopped making their payments, having money only for food, medicine, and heating oil.

By 1985 a situation had developed where several hundred families were in arrears, and HUD was threatening to cut off any further housing money until something was done about the delinquent payments. The HA, without opposition from the tribal government, decided to make an example of the families most in default. A list was made of 106 houses from which the residents would be evicted. Nearly all these houses were in rural areas and, not coincidentally, most were occupied by the traditional faction which consistently opposed the tribal government.

One difficulty in evicting the families was that the houses sat on trust land owned by the family, and so other families could not be moved into the houses. The solution to this problem, as developed by local HA and BIA officials, was a plan for jacking up the houses and moving them off trust land, at a projected cost of $20,000 each. The HA hoped that part of the cost of moving the houses could be recovered by selling them. The first targets for eviction were the families of the arrow keeper and certain traditional chiefs and priests who had been vocal in their criticism of the HA.

On May 2, 1985, four cars of federal marshals, a moving van, a tractor, and several trucks full of workers arrived at the site of the first house to be seized, the house of the arrow keeper. After an angry confrontation with the occupants, their furniture was moved outside, the brick facing of the house was torn away, and the house was jacked up and put on wheels to be towed away. Several of the Indian marshals, finally realizing what they were supposed to do, refused to do it. Some were weeping and some sided with the occupants and were later fired. Plate 12.5 shows one of the houses after it was moved to a nearby town and offered for sale.

Plate 12.5   A self-help house from which the residents were evicted and the house moved to a nearby town where it was offered for sale (photo by author)

The occupants were ejected from about 20 houses in the first month of evictions. Only a few were sold. One evicted owner bought his own house back for $500 after a few months, and put it back on his lot, now mortgage-free. While only about $200,000 would have paid off the mortgages for the 106 houses, nearly a million dollars was budgeted for eviction, house moving, and administrative costs, resulting in homelessness for about 500 people. Another odd result of the episode was that some families, applying for housing through a different family member over the next several years, came to occupy new houses with new mortgages.

I include this narrative not only to expose the peculiar logic employed by those who administer Indians, but also to show the kind of situation that Cheyennes and other Indian people must deal with constantly. Any adult reservation Indian can tell you three or four other such episodes of government mismanagement comparable to this one. Dealing with these situations is exhausting for Indian people, and actually prevents them from dealing with the dominant society in a reasonable way. There is a constant stress to being a Cheyenne. Although they try to laugh about it, the stress takes a toll. Cheyenne people say that being an Indian in America is like being in the Army, or being in prison.

As a consequence of their victimization by federal laws and policies, Cheyennes become experts in the rules and regulations which affect them. During the housing crisis narrated above, for example, hundreds of Cheyennes became familiar with the array of federal laws and regulations regarding public housing. When the coal controversy hit the Northern Cheyennes, scores of ordinary Cheyenne people became experts in energy assessment and pollution standards. When the Concho School was closed in Oklahoma, Cheyenne and Arapaho parents learned a lot about education policy, and the relationship between state and federal funding for public schools, although they could not save their school. Almost any adult Cheyenne can discuss intelligently the content of various treaties signed with the federal government, or the provisions of the Dawes Act. To function effectively as an adult, a Cheyenne must gain a layperson's knowledge of about five or six areas of federal law and policy – housing, education, leasing, treaties, welfare requirements, health policies – each about as complicated as personal income tax. In an extended family, it falls to the "unemployed" adults to tend to all these bureaucratic affairs. In most families, these are the busiest members of the family, and the hardest working.

Among Cheyennes, there are constant complaints about the tribal government, the BIA, and the federal government. But Cheyennes, like other Indian people, find themselves in an odd situation with respect to the federal government. The same agencies which regularly harass them, oppress them, and order them about, are the very agencies which constitute their lifeline from the dominant society. Only through these agencies can Indian people hope to obtain even a modicum of the resources promised in treaties and federal law. And over the years they have become familiar with and learned to manipulate these agencies as best they can. Stuck in a bad relationship, the Cheyennes, like other Indian people, prefer to stay in the relationship rather than being cast adrift to fend for themselves in a dominant Anglo-American society they find to be often racist, selfish, and hostile.

Daily Reminders

I want to end this book on a lighter note, with some interesting and colorful beliefs collected for me, just for fun, by a Northern Cheyenne family.[3] We were talking one day about how difficult it is for a Cheyenne person to maintain a traditional perspective on life, being constantly buffeted by the agents and agencies of the dominant society. One woman mentioned that each time she obeyed one of the little rules of living taught to her by her elders, it made her feel more like an Indian, more like a Cheyenne. Some of the rules for living she wrote down for me over the next several weeks are as follows:

1   Do not lulu (make a ululation) unless a soldier is returning.
2   Do not bury your family with feathers; feathers belong in the sky.
3   When a little child looks between his legs, he is looking for his unborn sibling. That means his mother is pregnant.
4   Don't sweep out the house after dark; you might mistakenly sweep out a spirit belonging to someone in the house.
5   Pick up a crying baby. If they think they're not wanted, they might die and return to the spirit world.
6   Don't walk through little dust devils; they are lost spirits.
7   Don't wear the clothing of anyone from outside the family; you might lose your own personality and become like them.
8   Do not imitate crippled people, or the imitation will become permanent.
9   Don't cry unless you mean it, or you will be given something real to cry about.
10   If your right ear rings you will get good news; if your left ear rings it will be bad news.
11   When calling your children, always use their Cheyenne names, to make sure that all their spirits are assembled.
12   Don't sit outside after dark; a spirit might twist your mouth.
13   Treat dogs with kindness, for in the past they often sounded the alarm and saved the Cheyenne people.

And most importantly,

14   Don't joke with your sisters and brothers.
15   Let the men do the talking.
16   Obey your grandparents.

17 Bad luck:
 Your tipi blows over
 Disturbing the home of a bird or animal
 Hearing an owl
 A bird flying into your house
18 Good luck:
 A white horse grazing who looks at you
 A falling star on a dark night
 An eagle flying alongside as you drive your car

Notes

Chapter 1   Cheyenne Origins

1 Thanks to my colleague M. J. Hardman for providing these examples.

Chapter 2   Cheyenne Migrations

1 Personal communication, Patricia Albers, University of Utah.
2 Grinnell 1962: vol. 1, 1–46; Wood 1971: 51–68; Riggs 1893: 194.
3 My thanks to David Breker of the US Department of Agriculture in Lisbon, ND, for providing this information.

Chapter 3   Pastoral Nomadism

1 Laubin & Laubin 1957; Nabokov & Easton 1989; Faegre 1979; Campbell 1915; Fagin 1988.
2 My special thanks to Catherine Bull Coming, a qualified and experienced Cheyenne tipi maker, for providing me with this information.
3 Roe 1955; Ryden 1970; Denhardt 1975; Ewers 1955; Moore 1987: 127–75.
4 Tracking down this tradition among the Mescalero Apaches in 1982, I discovered that the medicines used for horses by the Apaches were the same as those used by the Cheyennes, but that the Apaches do not customarily put such items into a discrete "bundle" with sacred restrictions, as the Cheyennes do.
5 See Estes et al. 1982; Hitchcock 1950; Leithead 1971.

6 My thanks to Dwain Johnson of the University of Florida Animal Science Department for information about jerky.
7 See Kindscher 1987; Gilmore 1977; Hart 1976.

Chapter 4   Trade and Politics

1 See the other articles in the same book as Schlesier 1994.
2 Prof. Albers, of course, is not responsible for any damage I have done to her elegant model in trying to extrapolate and elaborate from it.

Chapter 5   Cheyenne Warfare

1 See pp. 124–6 for an explanation of 'counting coup'.
2 See Grinnell 1915; 1907, Marquis 1931; Stands in Timber & Liberty 1967; Hyde 1968; Berthrong 1963.
3 See Petersen (1964) for a comprehensive account of the histories of the Cheyenne soldier societies. See Mishkin (1940) and Secoy (1953) for an overview of plains military societies.
4 This narrative is edited slightly from Interview T–152, Doris Duke Oral History Collection, Western History Collections, University of Oklahoma, Norman, OK.
5 Leckie 1963; Hoig 1993; Finerty 1961; Utley 1984.

Chapter 6   Bands and Tribal Structure

1 For an overview of American Indian population trends, see Thornton (1987).
2 This evidence is discussed at length in Moore (1987).
3 Three interesting narratives of Cheyenne life from a woman's perspective are provided in Michelson (1932), Marriott (1977), and Sooktis (1976).
4 See Moore (1984) for a full discussion of personal names.

Chapter 7   Literature and Values

1 These versions are based on the narratives contained in Randolph (1937).
2 The Veho stories are taken from Tall Bull & Weist (1971).
3 This story is edited and abridged from Grinnell (1908).

4 For a full discussion of military society costumes, see Petersen (1964).

Chapter 8   Cosmology and Ceremonies

1 This was a comment by Eugene Black Bear, Jr., to a group of assembled priests in 1979.
2 See pages 232–4 for a description of the peyote religion.
3 Karl Schlesier has provided an excellent discussion of *maiyun* in Schlesier (1987): 3–18.
4 In addition to Powell (1969), another early and partial description of the Arrow Ceremony appears in Dorsey (1905).
5 For a general description of the peyote religion, see La Barre (1959); a Cheyenne Peyote Ceremony is described in Goggin (1938).

Chapter 9   Social Interactions

1 New Deal projects among Indian people were reported in the government periodical *Indians at Work*.

Chapter 10   Early Reservation Life

1 The classic source for the Southern Cheyennes in this period is Berthrong (1976). A source emphasizing the Northern Cheyenne experience is Svingen (1993).
2 The important documents of Indian policy are collected in Prucha (1990).
3 A fictionalized account of the flight of the Northern Cheyennes is *Cheyenne Autumn* by Mari Sandoz (1953), which was made into a motion picture directed by John Ford.
4 A thorough history of the BIA is provided in Schmeckebier (1927); a more humorous version of Indian administration and access to other published sources is contained in Feraca (1990).
5 See Bowden (1981) for an overview of Christian missionary activity among Native Americans.
6 These particular versions were told to me by Henry Tall Bull.
7 For a complete account of the Ghost Dance, see Mooney (1965).
8 For the Dawes Act and its aftermath, see Otis (1973) and Carlson (1981).

Chapter 11   Late Reservation Life

1 See Ambler (1990) for a discussion of Indian energy resources in general, with Cheyenne coal as a featured illustration.
2 For an excellent general discussion of government policies and Native American civil rights, see Barsh & Henderson (1980) and Hoxie (1984).

Chapter 12   Modern Times

1 My thanks to Robert Fields and Ray Satepauhoodle for sharing with me their vast knowledge of the pow-wow scene in Indian country.
2 This narrative is compiled from my own field notes and those of several of my students who were living with Cheyenne families when these events transpired, especially Carole West, who interviewed many of the affected families, the officials pursuing the evictions, and officers of the tribal government, and attended the public hearings. To her credit, Ms West did her best to find competent legal counsel for the people being evicted, to no avail.
3 For collecting these traditions, my thanks to Aurelia Littlebird and her family.

References

Adjutant General's Office 1979 *Chronological List of Actions, Etc., with Indians from January 15, 1837 to January, 1891.* The Old Army Press.

Albers, Patricia C. 1993 "Symbiosis, Merger and War: Contrasting Forms of Intertribal Relationship Among Historic Plains Indians." In John H. Moore (ed.), *The Political Economy of North American Indians*, Norman, OK: University of Oklahoma Press, 94–132.

Ambler, Marjane 1990 *Breaking the Iron Bonds: Indian Control of Energy Development.* Lawrence, KS: University Press of Kansas.

Aubin, George F. 1975 *A Proto-Algonquian Dictionary.* National Museum of Man, Mercury Series, Canadian Ethnology Service Paper no. 29. Ottawa: National Museums of Canada.

Aufderheide, Arthur C., Elden Johnson and Odin Langsjoen 1994 *Health, Demography, and Archaeology of Mille Lacs Native American Mortuary Populations.* Plains Anthropologist Memoir 28, vol. 39, no. 149.

Barsh, Russell and James Y. Henderson 1980 *The Road: Indian Tribes and Political Liberty.* Berkeley, CA: University of California Press.

Berthrong, Donald J. 1963 *The Southern Cheyennes.* Norman, OK: University of Oklahoma Press.

—— 1976 *The Cheyenne and Arapaho Ordeal.* Norman, OK: University of Oklahoma Press.

Bloomfield, Leonard 1975 *Menomini Lexicon.* Charles F. Hockett, ed. Milwaukee Public Museum Publications in Anthropology and History no. 3. Milwaukee: Milwaukee Public Museum.

Bowden, Henry W. 1981 *American Indians and Christian Missions.* Chicago: University of Chicago Press.

Brose, David S. 1978 "Late Prehistory of the Upper Great Lakes Area." In Bruce C. Trigger (ed.), *North-east*, vol. 15 of William C. Sturtevant (gen. ed.), *Handbook of North American Indians*, Washington, DC: Smithsonian Institution, 569–82.

Campbell, Gregory R. 1994 "Cheyenne." In *Native America in the Twentieth Century: An Encylopedia*, New York: Garland Publishing Co., 100–3.

Campbell, Stanley 1915 "The Cheyenne Tipi." *American Anthropologist* 17: 685–94.

Carlson, Leonard A. 1981 *Indians, Bureaucrats, and Land*. Westport, CT: Greenwood Press.

Carver, Jonathan 1956 *Travels Through the Interior Parts of North America, in the Years 1766, 1767, and 1768*. Minneapolis, MN: Ross and Haines.

Chalfant, William Y. 1989 *Cheyennes and Horse Soldiers*. Norman, OK: University of Oklahoma Press.

Chittenden, Hiram M. 1902 *The American Fur Trade of the Far West*, 3 vols. New York: Harper.

Chittenden, Hiram M. 1935 *The American Fur Trade of the Far West*. New York: Press of the Pioneers.

Coe, Michael, Dean Snow and Elizabeth Benson 1986 *Atlas of Ancient America*. Oxford: Facts on File/Equinox.

Conn, Richard G. 1961 "Cheyenne Style Beadwork." *American Indian Hobbyist* 7, 2: 47–62.

Cooke, Phillip 1862 *Cavalry Tactics*. Philadelphia: J. B. Lippincott and Co.

Denhardt, Robert M. 1975 *The Horse of the Americas*, Norman, OK: University of Oklahoma Press.

Department of Indian Territory 1863 *Single Rank Formations and Skirmish Drill for Mounted Rifles*. Reprinted by Oklahoma Historical Society (1994), Oklahoma City, OK: Oklahoma Historical Society.

Dorsey, George A. 1905 *The Cheyenne, I. Ceremonial Organization*. Field Columbian Museum Publication 99, Anthropological Series, vol. IX, no. 1. Chicago: Field Columbian Museum.

Estes, James, Ronald Tyrl and Jere Brunken (eds) 1982 *Grasses and Grassland*. Norman, OK: University of Oklahoma Press.

Ewers, John C. 1955 *The Horse in Blackfoot Indian Culture*. Bureau of American Ethnology Bulletin 159. Washington, DC: Government Printing Office.

Faegre, Torvald 1979 *Tents: Architecture of the Nomads*. Garden City, NY: Doubleday.

Fagin, Nancy L. 1988 "The James Mooney Collection of Cheyenne Tipi Models at Field Museum of Natural History." *Plains Anthropologist* 33, 120: 261–78.

Fay, George E. (ed.) 1977 *Treaties Between the Tribes of the Great*

Plains and the United States of America: Cheyenne and Arapaho, 1825–1900. Greeley, CO: Museum of Anthropology, University of Northern Colorado.

Feraca, Stephen E. 1990 *Why Don't They Give Them Guns?* Lanham, MD: University Press of America.

Finerty, John F. 1961 *War-Path and Bivouac.* Norman, OK: University of Oklahoma Press.

Fitting, James E. 1978 "Regional Cultural Development, 300 B.C. to A.D. 1000." In Bruce C. Trigger (ed.), *North-east*, vol. 15 of William C. Sturtevant (gen. ed.), *Handbook of North American Indians*, Washington, DC: Smithsonian Institution,44–57.

Frazer, Robert W. 1972 *Forts of the West.* Norman, OK: University of Oklahoma Press.

Frison, George C. 1991 *Prehistoric Hunters of the High Plains.* San Diego, CA: Academic Press.

Garrard, Lewis H. 1955 *Wah-To-Yah and the Taos Trail.* Norman, OK: University of Oklahoma Press.

Gilmore, Melvin R. 1977 *Uses of Plants by the Indians of the Missouri River Region.* Reprinted from the Thirty-Third Annual Report of the Bureau of American Ethnology (1919). Lincoln, NE: University of Nebraska Press.

Glenmore, Josephine Stands In Timber, and Wayne Leman 1984 *Cheyenne Topical Dictionary.* Busby, MT: Cheyenne Translation Project.

Goddard, Ives 1967 *Notes on the Genetic Classification of the Algonquian Languages.* Bulletin 214. Ottawa: National Museums of Canada.

Goddard, Ives 1979 "Comparative Algonquian." In Lyle Campbell and Marianne Mithun (eds), *The Languages of Native America*, Austin, TX: University of Texas Press, 70–132.

Goggin, John M. 1938 "A Note on Cheyenne Peyote." *New Mexico Anthropologist* 111, 2: 26–30.

Gregg, Josiah 1962 (1844) *Commerce of the Prairies*, 2 vols. Philadelphia: J. B. Lippincott Company.

Gregg, Josiah 1968 (1844) *Commerce of the Prairies*, 2 vols. New York: Citadel.

Grinnell, George B. 1907 "Some Early Cheyenne Tales." *Journal of American Folklore* 20, 78: 169–94.

—— 1908 "Some Early Cheyenne Tales. II." *Journal of American Folklore* 21, 82: 269–320.

—— 1915 *The Fighting Cheyennes.* Norman, OK: University of Oklahoma Press.

—— 1918 "Early Cheyenne Villages." *American Anthropologist* 20, 4: 359–80.

—— 1962 (1923) *The Cheyenne Indians*, 2 vols. New York: Cooper Square.

Hart, Jeff 1976 *Montana – Native Plants and Early Peoples*. Helena, MT: The Montana Historical Society.

Hennepin, Louis (Lewis) 1698 *A New Discovery of a Vast Country in America, With a Continuation*. London: M. Bentley, J. Tonson, H. Bonwick, T. Goodwin, S. Manship.

—— 1938 *Description of Louisiana*. Minneapolis, MN: University of Minnesota Press.

Hickerson, Harold 1962 *The South-western Chippewa*. American Anthropological Association Memoir 92, vol. 64, no. 3, part 2.

Hitchcock, A. L. 1950 *Manual of the Grasses of the United States*. Department of Agriculture Miscellaneous Publication no. 200. Washington, DC: Government Printing Office.

Hoig, Stan 1993 *Tribal Wars of the Southern Plains*. Norman, OK: University of Oklahoma Press.

Holder, Preston 1970 *The Hoe and the Horse on the Plains*. Lincoln, NE: University of Nebraska Press.

Hoxie, Frederick E. 1984 *A Final Promise: The Campaign to Assimilate the Indians, 1880–1920*. Lincoln, NE: University of Nebraska Press.

Hrdlička, Aleš 1927"Catalogue of Human Crania in the United States National Museum Collections: The Algonkian and Related Iroquois; Siouan, Caddoan, Salish and Sahaptin, Shoshonean, and California Indians." *Proceedings of the United States National Museum 69*: 1–127. Washington, DC: US National Museum.

Hyde, George E. 1959 *Indians of the High Plains*. Norman, OK: University of Oklahoma Press.

—— 1968 *Life of George Bent*. Norman, OK: University of Oklahoma Press.

Jablow, Joseph 1951 *The Cheyenne in Plains Indian Trade Relations 1795–1840*. Monographs of the American Anthropological Association no. XIX. Locust Valley, NY: J. J. Augustin.

Kenner, Charles L. 1969 *A History of New Mexican–Plains Indian Relations*. Norman, OK: University of Oklahoma Press.

Kindscher, Kelly 1987 *Edible Wild Plants of the Prairie*. Lawrence, KS: University Press of Kansas.

Kraenzel, Carl F. 1955 *The Great Plains in Transition*. Norman, OK: University of Oklahoma Press.

La Barre, Weston 1959 *The Peyote Cult*. New York: Schocken Books.

Language Research Department 1976 *English–Cheyenne Student Dictionary*. Lame Deer, MT: Northern Cheyenne Title VII ESEA Bilingual Education Program.

Laubin, Reginald 1980 *Native American Archery*. Norman, OK: University of Oklahoma Press.

Laubin, Reginald and Gladys Laubin 1957 *The Indian Tipi*. New York: Ballantine.

Lavender, David 1954 *Bent's Fort*. Garden City, NY: Doubleday.

Leckie, William H. 1963 *The Military Conquest of the Southern Plains*. Norman, OK: University of Oklahoma Press.

Leithead, Horace L., Lewis Yarlett and Thomas Shiflet 1971 *100 Native Forage Grasses in 11 Southern States*. Agriculture Handbook no. 389, Soil Conservation Service. Washington, DC: US Department of Agriculture.

Leman, Wayne (ed.) 1987 *Naevahoo'ohtseme We Are Going Back Home*. Memoir 4, Algonquian and Iroquoian Linguistics. Winnipeg: Algonquian and Iroquoian Linguistics.

Littlefield, Alice and Martha Knack (eds) 1996 *Native Americans and Wage Labor*. Norman, OK: University of Oklahoma Press.

Marquis, Thomas B. 1931 *Wooden Leg, A Warrior Who Fought Custer*. Lincoln, NE: University of Nebraska Press.

Marriott, Alice L. 1977 *Dance Around the Sun: The Life of Mary Little Bear Inkanish, Cheyenne*. New York: Crowell.

Michelson, Truman 1932 *The Narrative of a Southern Cheyenne Woman*. Smithsonian Miscellaneous Collections vol. 87, no. 5: 1–13. Washington, DC: Smithsonian Institution.

Mishkin, Bernard 1992 (1940) *Rank and Warfare Among the Plains Indians*. Lincoln, NE: University of Nebraska Press.

Mooney, James 1903 Manuscript 2213. Washington, DC: Smithsonian Institution Anthropological Archives

— 1907 *The Cheyenne Indians*. Memoir 1. Washington, DC: American Anthropological Association.

— 1965 *The Ghost Dance Religion and the Sioux Outbreak of 1890*. Chicago: University of Chicago Press (orig. part 2 of 14th Annual Report of the Bureau of American Ethnology, 1892–93, Government Printing Office, Washington, DC).

— n.d. Sketchbook no. 2. Washington, DC: Smithsonian Institution Anthropological Archives.

Moore, John H. 1981 *The Cheyennes in Moxtavhohona*. Lame Deer, MT: Northern Cheyenne Tribe, Inc.

— 1984 "Cheyenne Names and Cosmology." *American Ethnologist* 11, 2: 291–312.

— 1987 *The Cheyenne Nation*. Lincoln, NE: University of Nebraska Press.

— 1988 "The Dialects of Cheyenne Kinship: Variability and Change." *Ethnology* 27, 3: 253–69.

— 1991a "Kinship and Division of Labor in Cheyenne Society." In Alice Littlefield and Hill Gates (eds), *Marxist Approaches in Econ-*

omic Anthropology, Lanham, MD: University Press of America, 135–58.

—— 1991b "The Developmental Cycle of Cheyenne Polygyny." *American Indian Quarterly* 15, 3: 311–28.

—— 1993 "How Giveaways and Pow-Wows Redistribute the Means of Subsistence." In John H. Moore (ed.), *The Political Economy of North American Indians*, Norman, OK: University of Oklahoma Press, 240–69.

Mourant, A. E. 1954 *The Distribution of the Human Blood Groups*. Oxford: Blackwell.

Nabokov, Peter and Robert Easton 1989 *Native American Architecture*. New York and Oxford: Oxford University Press.

Nagy, Imre n.d. *Indiánok*. Budapest: Múzsak Közművelódési Kiaoó.

Nagy, Imre 1994 "A Typology of Cheyenne Shield Designs." *Plains Anthropologist* 39, 147: 5–37.

Neumann, Georg K. 1952 "Archeology and Race in the American Indian." *Yearbook of Physical Anthropology* 8: 213–55.

Ossenberg, Nancie S. 1974 "Origins and Relationships of Woodland Peoples: The Evidence of Cranial Morphology." In Elden Johnson (ed.), *Aspects of Upper Great Lakes Anthropology*, Minnesota Prehistoric Archeology Series 11, St Paul, MN: Minnesota Historical Society, 15–39.

Otis, D. S. 1973 *The Dawes Act and the Allotment of Indian Lands*. Norman, OK: University Of Oklahoma Press.

Parkman, Francis 1903 *The Oregon Trail*. Boston: Little Brown and Co.

Petersen, Karen D. 1964 "Cheyenne Soldier Societies." *Plains Anthropologist* 9: 146–72.

Petter, Rodolphe 1915 *English–Cheyenne Dictionary*. Kettle Falls, WA: Mennonite Mission.

—— 1952 *Cheyenne Grammar*. Newton, KS: Mennonite Publication Office.

Phillips, Paul C. 1961 *The Fur Trade*, 2 vols. Norman, OK: University of Oklahoma Press.

Philp, Kenneth R. 1977 *John Collier's Crusade for Indian Reform, 1920–1954*. Tucson, AZ: University of Arizona Press.

Pilling, James C. 1891 *Bibliography of the Algonquian Languages*. Bureau of Ethnology Bulletin 13. Washington, DC: Government Printing Office.

Powell, Peter J. 1969 *Sweet Medicine*, 2 vols. Norman, OK: University of Oklahoma Press.

—— 1981 *People of the Sacred Mountain*, 2 vols. San Francisco, CA: Harper and Row.

Prucha, Francis Paul 1990 *Documents of United States Indian Policy*. Lincoln, NE: University of Nebraska Press.

Randolph, Richard W. 1937 *Sweet Medicine*. Caldwell, ID: Caxton Printers.

Riggs, Stephen R. 1893 *Dakota Grammar, Texts and Ethnography*. Contributions to North American Ethnology, vol. 9, Dept. of the Interior, US Geographical and Geological Survey of the Rocky Mountain Region. Washington, DC: Government Printing Office.

Roe, Frank Gilbert 1955 *The Indian and the Horse*. Norman, OK: University of Oklahoma Press.

Ryden, Hope 1970 *America's Last Wild Horses*. New York: E. P. Dutton.

Sandoz, Mari 1953 *Cheyenne Autumn*. New York: Hastings House.

Schlesier, Karl H. 1987 *The Wolves of Heaven*. Norman, OK: University of Oklahoma Press.

—— 1994 "Commentary: A History of Ethnic Groups in the Great Plains AD 150–1550." In Schlesier (ed.), *Plains Indians, AD 500–1500*, Norman, OK: University of Oklahoma Press, 308–81.

Schmeckebier, Laurence F. 1927 *The Office of Indian Affairs: Its History, Activities and Organization*. Baltimore, MD: Johns Hopkins Press.

Secoy, Frank R. 1953 *Changing Military Patterns on the Great Plains*. Monographs of the American Ethnological Society, no. XXI. Locust Valley, NY: J. J. Augustin.

Siebert, Frank T., Jr. 1967 "The Original Home of the Proto-Algonquian People." *Contributions to Anthropology, Linguistics I (Algonquian)*, National Museum of Canada Bulletin no. 214, Anthropological Series no. 78, pp. 13–59. Ottawa: National Museum of Canada.

Sooktis, Rubie 1976 *The Cheyenne Journey*. Ashland, MT: Religion Research Center.

Stands in Timber, John and Margot Liberty 1967 *Cheyenne Memories*. New Haven, CT: Yale University Press.

Storm, Hyemeyohsts 1972 *Seven Arrows*. New York: Harper and Row.

Strong, William D. 1940 "From History to Prehistory in the Northern Great Plains." *Essays in the Historical Anthropology of North America in Honor of John R. Swanton*. Smithsonian Miscellaneous Collections no. 100, pp. 353–94, Washington, DC: Smithsonian Institution.

Sutton, Imre (ed.) 1985 *Irredeemable America: the Indians' Estate and Land Claims*. Albuquerque, NM: University of New Mexico Press.

Svingen, Orlan J. 1993 *The Northern Cheyenne Indian Reservation*. Niwot, CO: University Press of Colorado.

Tall Bull, Henry and Tom Weist 1971 *Ve'ho*. Billings, MT: Montana Reading Publications.

Tanner, Helen Hornbeck 1987 *Atlas of Great Lakes Indian History*. Norman, OK: University of Oklahoma Press.

Thornton, Russell 1987 *American Indian Holocaust and Survival: A Population History Since 1492*. Norman, OK: University of Oklahoma Press.

Trimble, Michael K. 1986 *An Ethnohistorical Interpretation of the Spread of Smallpox in the Northern Plains Utilizing Concepts of Disease Ecology*. Reprinted in Anthropology vol. 33. Lincoln, NE: J. & L. Reprint Co.

Tuck, James A. 1978 "Regional Cultural Development, 3000 to 300 BC." In Bruce Trigger (ed.), *North-east*, vol. 15 of William C. Sturtevant (gen. ed.), *Handbook of North American Indians*, Washington, DC: Smithsonian Institution, 28–43.

Ubelaker, Douglas H. 1992 "The Sources and Methodology for Mooney's Estimates of North American Indian Populations." In William M. Denevan (ed.), *The Native Population of the Americas in 1492*, Madison, WI: University of Wisconsin Press, 243–88.

Uhlenbeck, C. C. and R. H. Van Gulik 1930 *An English–Blackfoot Vocabulary*. Amsterdam: Verhandelingen der Koninklijke Akademie van Wetenschappen te Amsterdam. Nieuwe Reeks, 29, 4.

Utley, Robert M. 1984 *The Indian Frontier of the American West, 1846–1890*. Albuquerque, NM: University of New Mexico Press.

Wallentine, Douglas 1988 *Making Indian Bows and Arrows ... the Old Way*. Liberty, UT: Eagle's View Publishing Co.

Webb, Walter Prescott 1931 *The Great Plains*. New York: Grosset and Dunlap.

Wedel, Waldo R. 1961 *Prehistoric Man on the Great Plains*. Norman, OK: University of Oklahoma Press.

Weist, Tom 1977 *A History of the Cheyenne People*. Billings, MT: Montana Council for Indian Education.

Will, George F. 1914 *Proceedings of the Mississippi Valley Historical Association for the Year 1913–1914*, vol. 7, pp. 67–78.

Wilson, Gilbert L. 1917 *Agriculture of the Hidatsa Indians*. Studies in the Social Sciences no. 9, Bulletin of the University of Minnesota, Minneapolis, MN.

Wood, W. Raymond 1971 *Biesterfeldt: A Post-Contact Coalescent Site on the Northern Plains*. Smithsonian Contributions to Anthropology no. 15. Washington, DC: Smithsonian Institution Press.

Wood, W. Raymond and Margot Liberty 1980 *Anthropology on the Great Plains*. Lincoln, NE: University of Nebraska Press.

Wright, James V. 1981 "Prehistory of the Canadian Shield." In June Helm (ed.), *Sub-Arctic*, vol. 6 of William C. Sturtevant (gen. ed.), *Handbook of North American Indians*, Washington, DC: Smithsonian Institution, 86–96.

Index